18—

12—

EDITH SITWELL
Fire of the Mind

EDITH SITWELL
Fire of the Mind

An Anthology by
Elizabeth Salter & Allanah Harper

FOREWORD BY SACHEVERELL SITWELL

THE VANGUARD PRESS, INC. • NEW YORK

ﾚ᠀ᒿᖇ

*Published by Vanguard Press, Inc.,
424 Madison Avenue, New York, N. Y. 10017.
Published simultaneously in Canada by
Beatty & Church Co., Toronto, Ontario.*

*Library of Congress Catalogue Number: 81-40798
ISBN: 0-8149-0809-8*

Manufactured in the United States of America.

There is a certain heat in the breast, which attends
the perception of a primary truth, which is the shining
of the spiritual sun down into the shaft of the mine.

Ralph Waldo Emerson

. . . the great sins and fires break out of me like the
terrible leaves from the bough in the violent spring.
I am a walking fire, I am all leaves—

Edith Sitwell

. . . never till Time is done
Will the fire of the heart and the fire of the mind be one.

Edith Sitwell

ACKNOWLEDGEMENTS

First and most importantly our acknowledgement goes to Michael Goodwin whose help has been unstinted throughout. This book gains a dimension because of it.

Acknowledgement is also due to Michael Stapleton for research undertaken on our behalf and to Mrs Kloegman who typed the manuscript. We should like to thank the following for letters quoted: Humphrey Searle, Benjamin Britten, James Purdy, Alberto de Lacerda, John Lehmann, Stephen Spender, Pamela Hansford Johnson, C. P. Snow, Veronica Gilliat and Tom Driberg. Permission to reprint material in this anthology has been kindly given by Jack Lindsay for his essay on *The Shadow of Cain*, by David Higham Associates for Osbert Sitwell's *The Scarlet Tree*, by Ann Cubitt for Constance Sitwell's *Bright Morning*, by Condé Nast Publications for 'Some Observations' © Vogue Magazine and by Oxford University Press for *A Bibliography of Edith, Osbert and Sacheverell Sitwell* (second edition, 1971) by Richard Fifoot.

Our most sincere thanks go to Francis Sitwell, literary executor of the estate of Dame Edith Sitwell, whose co-operation made this anthology possible and who gave permission to reprint Edith Sitwell's prose and poetry. A final grateful acknowledgement is made to Sir Sacheverell Sitwell, whose support has been a great encouragement and who has most kindly written a foreword to the anthology.

E.S.
A.H.

CONTENTS

FOREWORD

I was ten years younger than my sister, and my earliest memories of her date from when she was already thirteen or fourteen. Just then my affections were wholly taken up by my mother and my brother. But soon, only too soon, he went to school and was away from home for some nine months of the year, and it was probably during his long and sad absences that I became conscious of having a sister. Already—and this I can vouch for—she was thinking of nothing but poetry which she copied out incessantly, and in the absence of other audience read aloud to me. Her only friend was a first cousin, who always remained her friend, and during childhood I cannot think of any other. The portrait of her in Sargent's family group is just as I remember her at this time. She was aquiline of feature, tall and thin and rather solemn. She had not yet developed her powers of mimicry, of comic invention, and her inimitable and fascinating humour.

Perhaps these only appeared when she got away from home to live in London in the summer of 1914 just before the war began. She would then be twenty-seven. Her childhood and youth had been far from happy, I know that, and do not like to dwell on it; but it is equally certain that her imagination and feeling for drama did nothing to mitigate its ills and pains. Neither can I find it in my heart to blame my father and mother for not understanding their silent and awkward daughter who was so different from what either, or both of them just for once in combination together, would have wished her to be. But we have to consider that like a famous conjurer and/or magician of the present day, she had some of his powers of twisting and distorting things and even facts to suit her purpose and her personality as that was taking shape. At about sixteen years old, myself, how well I remember her happiness at leaving home, being

9

able to go to concerts (her other main interest!) and make friends of her own. She had escaped that summer of 1914; and it would be true to say that her talents, as though long repressed, which was the truth, burst suddenly and astonishingly into flower. Almost at once she became someone exceptional and unique, both physically and in the poems she was writing at the time, forming together a character and a personality there will never be again.

Her effortless, pure talent for invention and poetic achievement are manifest in *Bucolic Comedies* (1923) and *Rustic Elegies* (of 1927). Loving and admiring her as I do, I can see her so clearly as she was at the height of her talents and even before her fame. Being her brother, I like to think of her as a young woman with the touch of genius on her, and not as an old woman loaded with honours and become infirm and ill. A young woman out to alter and affect the world of letters, armed with a wit and humour all her own, if a shade belligerent and never, to be sure, disdaining or refusing battle.

It is one of the most difficult and sad of tasks to write of a much loved sister. But having lived as a child and a young man in her flowering shade I know I owe everything I have to her who was my master, and am proud to think myself her pupil, only hoping she would still accept me. I would stress that her one and unique interest was poetry, which meant more than all the world beside. This was all that mattered, and indeed little else had any importance for her. Let me emphasize also, that she was in the fullest sense of the term, self-educated. She had never been to school, and probably both her physical and literary conformity owed much to this.

It is difficult to exaggerate the effect of her reading poetry to one as a child. This is a wonderful memory, and a very precious and personal possession. Also, her affection was most touching, which she extended to my wife too from the moment they met, and which never faltered or felt the cold but was always as warm as in its beginning. But of course in thinking of her one must go back to her poetry, from which indeed any memory of her is inseparable. What a sure 'hand' and instinct she had for poetry! Her unerring senses led her, I think, nearly always straight to the target and when the sybil spoke it was almost ever wisdom. This, I know, is the voice of someone from the same poetic stable, but none the less I believe that in the end it will prove to be the truth. For one day, and it may come sooner than later, the poetry of an age sorts itself out; the dross will be separated and fall away. The too laboured of effect, the gritty and sabulous in sound, the embittered and acerbic of spirit, for there are present practitioners in all these minor arts, will have outlived their fame. And then it could be that the subject of this anthology will be revealed for what she has been all the time, a criterion and touchstone of poetry. She will have outlived the obscurity which always in England hides and befogs those lately fallen into the pit of death, and will emerge again in embrightened and renewed fame.

SACHEVERELL SITWELL
October 1975

INTRODUCTION

Since it is not my intention to intrude upon a selection which is designed to be self-explanatory, my comments are intended as guidelines only, and are based on my experience as secretary to Edith Sitwell during the last eight years of her life.

In his obituary notice, Stephen Spender wrote that: 'Edith Sitwell's personality and poetry form a single impression.' The intention of this anthology is to present the personality through the work of a unique being. It is arranged chronologically and the ideas which dominated her life unfold as the themes often commented on by critics of her work. The sensitivity of childhood, allied to early suffering, became the rage against a society in which creatures are slaughtered for the pleasure of man; in which 'the cannibal rich' grow fat on the flesh of the poor. The growing awareness of pattern, 'fern and feather [mirrored by] the frost on the window pane, the snow-flake mirrored in the rock crystal's six-rayed eternity', grew into a mature recognition of 'the immense design of the world'. Conscious-ness of the transitory nature of all things living developed into an obsession with the permanence of death.

Throughout her work is a gaiety of the spirit. It gives a sharp edge to her wit and reveals itself in the joy of battle, which remained with her to the end. To 'sharpen her claws' against the 'wooden heads' of her opponents was an outlet necessary to the high spirits which no prophetic despair could altogether subdue.

By the time I met her she was sixty-nine, created a Dame of the British Empire and awarded honorary doctorates of literature by four British universities. She was born Edith Louisa Sitwell on

7 September 1887, the eldest child and only daughter of Sir George and Lady Ida Sitwell, her birthplace Wood End, in Scarborough.

She was proud of her ancestry, especially of the self-made business-man who, she claimed, had walked barefoot from Leeds to London. He built up a fortune and became father of the 'wicked' Lady Conyingham, favourite of King George IV and instrumental in putting an end to flogging in women's prisons. She was proud, too, of her descendance from the Red Rose Plantaganets and so, col-laterally, from 'the young girl with the lion-coloured hair and the great golden haunting eyes'. In the shape of mouth and hands and the bone structure of the face, her likeness to the Tudor Queen Elizabeth I was uncanny.

Misunderstood by both her parents, she remembered her childhood as a saga of misery and delight. This was recorded in her first long poem, *Sleeping Beauty*, and in *Colonel Fantock*, named after her younger brother's tutor. Since they are in essence autobiographical, these are our first choice, though by no means her first poems. By the time she wrote them the experiments had begun. 'Finding the language of one sense insufficient', she used the language of another and by this means attempted 'to pierce down to the essence of things seen'.

Her written memories date from the house at Wood End, which she described as 'dark and forgotten and a little precious, like an unopened seventeenth-century first edition in a library.'

'The whole existence in that dark house has the curious sweet musty smell and the remoteness of such a book; the great trees outside are motionless and dark and unliving as a library lined with dusty and uncared-for meanings, and the sunrays lying upon the floor smile as dimly as the chapel's smiling cherubim. Here we cease living and the house is filled with other and darker existences; we put on their lives and go clothed in them.'

It may be surprising to find Edith Sitwell's prose given equal place with her poetry. Nor is this only because we consider it to be another facet of her genius. Very often her prose is father to her poetry. The passage quoted above is a paragraph from a series of articles which she wrote in 1922 for *The New Age*. It is a first draft of the opening stanza of *Sleeping Beauty*. We have selected some of these articles as introductions because they were, in fact, Edith Sitwell's own introduction to the poems of her childhood, *Colonel Fantock* and *Sleeping Beauty*.

As a passionate advocate of texture, Edith Sitwell's studies in technique were her attempts to match sound with sense. Her theories became a target for attack, as did her use of images, repeated symphonically throughout her poetry. She achieved a poetry akin to music. Its beauty, therefore, is greatly enhanced by being read aloud.

Allanah Harper and I have a suggestion to make:
Read her work aloud and it will be obvious why so much of it has been set to music by the composers of our day.

ELIZABETH SALTER

1887–1900

This story shall be as honest as I can allow it to be, but there is no such thing as truth, there are only points of view; and I have no nature and no character—only personality and gusts of cold air in the midst of the blackest loneliness. I had, however, roots, and I will tell some stories of these roots of mine because they are significant; some because they give the life of a time that can never come again—the reign of an aristocracy, 'bêtes d'une elegance fabuleuse', that has faded like the ladies on an ancient Flemish tapestry; some because they show why I am, above all things, a spiritual adventurer, never a spiritual *parvenu*.

Readers and Writers, July 1922

Colonel Fantock

Thus spoke the lady underneath the trees:
I was a member of a family
Whose legend was of hunting—(all the rare
And unattainable brightness of the air)—
A race whose fabled skill in falconry
Was used on the small songbirds and a winged
And blinded Destiny . . . I think that only
Winged ones know the highest eyrie is so lonely.
There in a land, austere and elegant,
The castle seemed an arabesque in music;
We moved in an hallucination born
Of silence, which like music gave us lotus
To eat, perfuming lips and our long eyelids
As we trailed over the sad summer grass,
Or sat beneath a smooth and mournful tree.

And Time passed, suavely, imperceptibly.

But Dagobert and Peregrine and I
Were children then; we walked like shy gazelles
Among the music of the thin flower-bells.
And life still held some promise,—never ask
Of what,—but life seemed less a stranger, then,
Than ever after in this cold existence.
I always was a little outside life—
And so the things we touch could comfort me;
I loved the shy dreams we could hear and see—
For I was like one dead, like a small ghost,
A little cold air wandering and lost.

All day within the straw-roofed arabesque
Of the towered castle and the sleepy gardens wandered
We; those delicate paladins the waves
Told us fantastic legends that we pondered.

19

And the soft leaves were breasted like a dove,
Crooning old mournful tales of untrue love.

When night came, sounding like the growth of trees,
My great-grandmother bent to say good-night,
And the enchanted moonlight seemed transformed
Into the silvery tinkling of an old
And gentle music-box that played a tune
Of Circean enchantments and far seas;
Her voice was lulling like the splash of these.
When she had given me her good-night kiss,
There, in her lengthened shadow, I saw this
Old military goat with mayfly whiskers—
Poor harmless creature, blown by the cold wind,
Boasting of unseen unreal victories
To a harsh unbelieving world unkind:
For all the battles that this warrior fought
Were with cold poverty and helpless age—
His spoils were shelters from the winter's rage.
And so for ever through his braggart voice,
Through all that martial trumpet's sound, his soul
Wept with a little sound so pitiful,
Knowing that he is outside life for ever
With no one that will warm or comfort him . . .
He is not even dead, but Death's buffoon
On a bare stage, a shrunken pantaloon.
His military banner never fell,
Nor his account of victories, the stories
Of old apocryphal misfortunes, glories
Which comforted his heart in later life
When he was the Napoleon of the schoolroom
And all the victories he gained were over
Little boys who would not learn to spell.

All day within the sweet and ancient gardens
He had my childish self for audience—
Whose body flat and strange, whose pale straight hair
Made me appear as though I had been drowned—
(We all have the remote air of a legend)—
And Dagobert my brother, whose large strength,

Great body and grave beauty still reflect
The Angevin dead kings from whom we spring;
And sweet as the young tender winds that stir
In thickets when the earliest flower-bells sing
Upon the boughs was his just character;
And Peregrine the youngest with a naïve
Shy grace like a faun's, whose slant eyes seemed
The warm green light beneath eternal boughs.
His hair was like the fronds of feathers, life
In him was changing ever, springing fresh
As the dark songs of birds . . . the furry warmth
And purring sound of fires was in his voice
Which never failed to warm and comfort me.

And there were haunted summers in Troy Park
When all the stillness budded into leaves;
We listened, like Ophelia drowned in blonde
And fluid hair, beneath stag-antlered trees;
Then, in the ancient park the country-pleasant
Shadows fell as brown as any pheasant,
And Colonel Fantock seemed like one of these.
Sometimes for comfort in the castle kitchen
He drowsed, where with a sweet and velvet lip
The snapdragons within the fire
Of their red summer never tire.
And Colonel Fantock liked our company;·
For us he wandered over each old lie,
Changing the flowering hawthorn, full of bees,
Into the silver helm of Hercules,
For us defended Troy from the top stair
Outside the nursery, when the calm full moon
Was like the sound within the growth of trees.

But then came one cruel day in deepest June,
When pink flowers seemed a sweet Mozartian tune,
And Colonel Fantock pondered o'er a book.
A gay voice like a honeysuckle nook—
So sweet—said, 'It is Colonel Fantock's age
Which makes him babble.' . . . Blown by winter's rage
The poor old man then knew his creeping fate,

The darkening shadow that would take his sight
And hearing; and he thought of his saved pence
Which scarce would rent a grave . . . That youthful voice
Was a dark bell which ever clanged 'Too late'—
A creeping shadow that would steal from him
Even the little boys who would not spell—
His only prisoners . . . On that June day
Cold Death had taken his first citadel.

By the flat-pearled shore of winter, in a land elegant and austere as
her body, my great grandmother, the Duchess of Troy, is driving
with a little girl, my mother. The trees have a noble and austere
beauty like that of crucifixes; the thin dark-papered leaves are sounding drearily, and the mulberries upon the trees are dark as tunes upon
a musical-box. The peruked waves curl fantastically: sometimes
sheep, as periwigged as King William and Queen Mary, run aimlessly through the fields, and my great grandmother, the Duchess of
Troy, looks at them rainily. She is very old . . . she has slipped away
again into the past; she is drowned beneath a deep still lake of sleep.
Every day she gives that little girl a present, bribing her. 'Take me,'
she would say, 'for a strange new drive!' Every day they leave the
castle of Troy by the same gateway, drive by the empty, fantastically
curling waves—there is only one drive, and only one view, but she
does not know it, for everything would be strange and fresh, if only
she could see it through the somnambulism of age.

Readers and Writers, July 1922

At Easter when red lacquer buds sound far slow
Quarter-tones for the old dead Mikado,

Through avenues of lime trees, where the wind
Sounds like a chapeau chinois, shrill, unkind—

The Dowager Queen, a curling Korin wave
That flows for ever past a coral cave,

With Dido, Queen of Carthage, slowly drives
(Her griffin dog that has a thousand lives)

Upon the flat-pearled and fantastic shore
Where curled and turbaned waves sigh, 'Never more.'

And she is sunk beneath a clear still lake
Of sleep—so frail with age she cannot wake . . .

A strange horizon and a soundless sea
Must separate wise age from you and me—

They watch life's movements ripening like fruit
And sigh, knowing the gnarled and twisted root.

Oh, people building castles on the sand,
And taking one another by the hand,

What do you find within each other's eyes?—
What wisdom unknown of the lonely wise?—

The promise of what spring, the certainty
Of what eternal life to come—what lie?

Only the sound of Time's small muffled drum,
The sound of footsteps that will never come.

The Sleeping Beauty, Canto 6

When I first remember my grandmother, she was a fantastic, wave-like Chinoiserie, a Laideronette, Princesse des Pagodes. Beaked like a harpy, she had queer-roofed, Byzantine eyes, and these characteristics I have inherited from her . . .

My grandmother had married a vastly rich man and lived in luxury like a gilded and irascible wasp in a fine ripe nectarine. Their country house was of quilted red satin, and they were surrounded by country gentlemen rooted in the mould like their own kind red strawberries. Here, every night towards the end of her life, in a large chamber where the shadows seemed dark and velvety leaves, the ceremony took place of unwigging my grandmother and embalming her for the night.

Readers and Writers, July 1922

23

'Who is this now who comes?' Dark words reply and swoon
Through all the high cold arbours of the moon:

'The slighted Laidronette, the unbidden fay,
Princess of the Pagodas . . . Shades, make way.'

The sedan-chair that hides her shade is mellow
As the trees' great fruit-jewels glittering yellow,

And round it the old turbaned ladies flock
Like apes that try to pluck an apricock.

The little fawning airs are trembling wan;
And silver as fair Leda's love, the swan,

The moonlight seems; the apricocks have turned to amber,
Cold as from the bright nymph Thetis' chamber,

And far away, the fountains sigh forlorn
As waving rustling sheaves of silver corn.

The wicked fay descended, mopping, mowing
In her wide-hooped petticoat, her water-flowing

Brightly-perfumed silks . . . 'Ah, ha, I see
You have remembered all the fays but me!'

(She whipped her panthers, golden as the shade
Of afternoon in some deep forest glade.)

'I am very cross because I am old
And my tales are told
And my flames jewel-cold.

I will make your bright birds scream,
I will darken your jewelled dream,
I will spoil your thickest cream.

I will turn the cream sour,
I will darken the bower,
I will look through the darkest shadows and lour—

And sleep as dark as the shade of a tree
Shall cover you . . . Don't answer me!
For if the Princess prick her finger
Upon a spindle, then she shall be lost

As a child wandering in a glade of thorn,
With sleep like roses blowing soft, forlorn,
Upon each bough. This, madam, is the cost
Of your dark rudeness. But I will not linger.'

And with a dark dream's pomp and panoply,
She swept out with her train; the soft sounds die
Of plumaged revelry bright as her train
Of courtiers; and all was night again.

Then through the deepest shades went Laidronette,
Princess of the Pagodas; in a pet
She left the domes, like rich and turbaned fruits
In the great gardens, and she left the lutes;

Back to her palace in her great sedan
She floats; worlds turn to snow before her fan.
She sweeps through the dark woods to her vast palace
Where now, at last, she can unleash her malice.

There in her room, an amber orange burned
On the Hesperides' dark trees and spurned
By that gold-peruked conqueror the Sun
(An Alexander whence plumed rivers run,

Fearing his fierceness), Ethiopian shapes
The heat had kissed, with lips like burning grapes,
Unwigged her for the night, while her apes beg
That she will leave uncurtained that Roc's egg,

Her head, a mount of diamonds bald and big
In the ostrich feathers that compose her wig.
Her dwarfs as round as oranges of amber
Among the tall trees of the shadow clamber,

And in Night's deep domain she monstrous lies
With every little wicked dream that flies
And crawls; with old Bacchantes black with wine,
Whose very hair has changed into a vine,

And ancient satyrs whose wry wig of roses
Nothing but little rotting shames discloses;

They lie where shadows, cold as the night breeze,
Seem cast by rocks, and never by kind trees.

The Sleeping Beauty, Canto I

My grandmother insisted on the pursuit of health, that *magie bourgeoise*. In this quest, much of my childhood was spent at the seaside. I can dimly remember my walks—I was five years old—with my queer companions by the side of the flat, black-lacquer sea, beneath the thick, swan-bosomed sky of winter. At home, in the nursery, my new-born brother was lying in front of a fire whose thin feathery spires seemed like summer grasses. The Kings and Queens on the nursery walls were nothing but bright-coloured fish in the moat of Troy Castle; the frost-flowers upon the window-panes ripened into strawberries, raspberries and glassy-pale gooseberries . . . (alas, one could never pluck them; they would chill our fingers like the touch of fate). But I, being older than he, was made to face reality as exemplified by the goose-soft snow (in which one could sink only too deeply), and the impenetrable sea and sky. My aunts, the ladies A., trailed beside me, tall as pagodas filled with an aching emptiness; their curls, like bells of the blackest coral, seemed jangling faintly beneath their 1895 sailor hats. They wore white veils and looked unhappy. Sometimes there were sideshows to be seen upon the sand—a Punch and Judy show, bright-coloured as the shrill winter sun; but even as a small child I was made unhappy and terrified by the unconscious cruelty of these puppets' fate . . . pulled backwards and forwards, to love, to annihilation, to murder, by the mechanical actions of that ragged hunger, the showman.

Readers and Writers, July 1922

Bells of Grey Crystal

Bells of grey crystal
Break on each bough—
The swans' breath will mist all
The cold airs now.
Like tall pagodas

Two people go,
Trail their long codas
Of talk through the snow.
Lonely are these
And lonely am I . . .
The clouds, grey Chinese geese
Sleek through the sky.

Now from the countrysides where people know
That Destiny is wingless and bemired,
With feathers dirty as a hen's, too tired
To fly—where old pig-snouted Darkness grovels
For life's mired rags among the broken hovels—
The country bumpkins come, with faces round
And pink as summer fruits, with hair as gold,
Sharp-pointed, as the summer sun (that old
Bucolic mime, whose laughing pantomime
Is rearing pink fruits from the sharp white rime).
They come from little rooms, each a poor booth
(Seen through the summer leaves, all smiling smooth).
There, for all beauty, is the badly painted
Ancestral portrait of their grey-beard God;
In that poor clownish booth it is so cold
The small airs prick like grass, a wooden sword.

They pass along the country roads as thick
With walls and gardens as a childish heaven,
Where all the flowers seem a pink fleshly heart
And mirage-dews sigh, 'We will never part.'

And there are young Princesses at each inn,
And poor young people poverty makes wise,
With eyes like maps of the wide summer heaven;
And on the country roads there is a shrine,
As blue and sparkling as the sea-god's wine,
For country gods and goddesses of gardens,
Where every fruit and flower to old songs hardens:
Pomona, tinsel-pink as that bright pear,

The moon—she seems a poor bucolic clown
With dry and gilded foliage for her hair,—
Where shadows cast a shallow melancholy,
An owl-soft shadow falling over folly.
The pink schoolgirlish fruits hang in bright sheaves
Between the rounded and the negroid leaves . . .
And we remember nursery afternoons
When the small music-box of the sweet snow
Gave half-forgotten tunes, and our nurse told
Us tales that fell with the same tinkling notes . . .
'Once on a time,' she said, 'and long ago.'
Her voice was sweet as the bright-sparkling rime,
The fruits are cold as that sweet music's time—
Yet all those fruits like the bright snow will fade.

The country bumpkins travel to the Fair,
For Night and Day, and Hell and Heaven, seem
Only a clown's booth seen in some bad dream,
Wherefrom we watch the movements of our life
Growing and ripening like summer fruits
And dwindling into dust, a mirage lie:
Hell is no vastness, it has naught to keep
But little rotting souls and a small sleep.
It has the same bright-coloured clarity we knew
In nursery afternoons so long ago,
Bright as our childish dreams; but we are old,
This is a different world; the snow lies cold
Upon our heart, though midsummer is here . . .

The Sleeping Beauty, Canto 16

The mauve summer rain
Is falling again—
It soaks through the eaves
And the ladies' sleeves—
It soaks through the leaves

That like silver fish fall
In the fountains, recall

So pretended not to hear—
Sweeping for it on the stair.

The little golden lights like Chinese ladies peep
Through the old queen's curtains, then like sleep

Their gentle footsteps fade again and fail,
And once again the world is ghostly pale.

In the queen's powder-closet, Mrs Troy
Teases the flames to wake them and annoy . . .

So pale are those thin ghostly flames that yet
They seem like the old notes of a spinet

That sometimes sounds a courante or gavotte
By Mozart or Scarlatti—sometimes not—

While the pale silken ribbons of the rain,
Knotted, are fluttering down the window-pane.

But suddenly the flames turn green and red
As unripe fruit; their shrilling fills her head

With noises like a painted puppet-show;
And in that music, shrieking high and low,

Dead is the pointed flames' small minuet—
And from the shrilling fire leaps Laidronette.

The ghostly apparition that appeared
Wagged from her chin a cockatrice's beard;

She crouches like a flame, the adder-sting
Of her sharp tongue is ready; hear her sing:

  'The candle flames bob
  Like strawberries low,
  Bobcherry, bobcherry,
  See them go
  In the hands of the queen's maids
  Under the trees

Of the shadow, flickering in the breeze,
Crept a starved and a humble air
From the hovels, grunting with low pig-snout—
Starved thin, creeping
Everywhere, weeping,
It blew the queen's strawberry candle-flames out.

The maids in long chequered gowns,
Hunting for these,
Find but the shadows'
Flickering trees.'

The humble ghosts like poppet maids
Walk tiptoe in the shadow glades.

Their mouths seem small red strawberries;
Their naïve naiad-titterings freeze

The airs in the long corridors
Where they must hark at hopeless doors.

And Mrs Troy rose up like a thin shriek
Or pointed flame . . . 'Oh, my poor head is weak!

Oh dear,
Oh dear,
Whatever shall I do?
In the flames' shrill rout
Laidronette slipped through.
I forget the Latin
For my prayer!
My quilted satin
Is beyond repair!
I must tell the queen
But I dare not be seen!
Oh dear, oh dear,
I tremble with fear,
Like a nectarine bough
When the sun shines through.

How harmless has been my poor life—
Yet when a young girl I had strife!
Out, alas! how I remember

That dawn, when to light the ember,
I must steal and I must creep
In the kitchen half asleep.
Noises from the sharp green wood
Burnt and bit my satyr blood,
And my cockscomb hair raised ire
In parrot-whistlers in the fire!

Now the ember as it dozes
Seems lattices of bunchèd roses,
Fuchsias and fat strawberries,
Dahlias, cherries, and one sees
Through those lattices' gold wire
The parrot-whistlers in the fire,
Pecking cherries every one.
"Polly, put the kettle on,"
Scream they; "scratch poor pretty Polly"
(Kettles hissing at their folly!).
From the wood they spring and scream,
Scald the milk, upset the cream . . .
Oh, the feathers jewel-bright!
Alas, my life was never light.'

The shrill flames nodded, beckoned, then lay dead;
Her wig awry, cross Poll Troy nods her head.

The long dark corridors seem shadow-groves
Wherein a little courtier air still roves . . .

Pale rose-leaves, wet and scented, seems the rain,
Whose bright drops cease, as soft as sleep again.

Her gown seems like a pale and tuneful rose.

.   .   .   .

Hours passed; the soft melodious moonlight grows . . .
A murmurous sound of far-off Circean seas
And old enchantments and the growth of trees.

.   .   .   .

Across the silver grass the powdered ghosts
Are wandering in dim and scattered hosts

Among the woods and fields, and they forget
Everything but that their love's hand yet
Is touching theirs; the ribbons of the moon are blue
And pink; those ghosts pick bunches from the dew

Of ghostly flowers, all poignant with spring rain,
Smelling of youth that will not come again.

The Sleeping Beauty, Canto 22

One was transported from this delicate austerity of existence by my other grandmother. She came of an honourable but commonplace family, and was like an alien being—a warmer and more clay-bound life, waxen-pale with age, with all the strangeness of a Leonardo drawing, or of a smile seen through deep water, she had a suicidal longing for triviality; she longed to live in a carven cloud like a Swiss chalet; to pop out of it mechanically, cuckoo-clock-wise, at certain hours, and to jump back again with equal regularity. But she lived mainly in a large glass—her conservatory (the largest I have ever seen)—preserved from the winds of heaven by this impenetrable but invisible substance, and surrounded by wet flower-spikes like ascending peals of pink and azure bells . . . these, however, muted by respect. I liked the hot smell of her furs, the warm, South of France feeling about her, and her faded hair that was like dry, powdery mimosa. I drove with her sometimes in an open victoria, always on some errand of mercy; and on those occasions the sea was always thick and homely like her 1880 home-made blue china, and the January sunshine had the delicate fragrance of the early white hyacinths.

Readers and Writers, July 1922

In the great gardens, after bright spring rain,
We find sweet innocence come once again,
White periwinkles, little pensionnaires
With muslin gowns and shy and candid airs,

That under saint-blue skies, with gold stars sown,
Hide their sweet innocence by spring winds blown,

From zephyr libertines that like Richelieu
And d'Orsay their gold-spangled kisses blew;

And lilies of the valley whose buds blond and tight
Seem curls of little school-children that light
The priests' procession, when on some saint's day
Along the country paths they make their way;

Forget-me-nots, whose eyes of childish blue,
Gold-starred like heaven, speak of love still true;
And all the flowers that we call 'dear heart',
Who say their prayers like children, then depart

Into the dark. Amid the dew's bright beams
The summer airs, like Weber waltzes, fall
Round the first rose who, flushed with her youth, seems
Like a young Princess dressed for her first ball:

Who knows what beauty ripens from dark mould
After the sad wind and the winter's cold?—
But a small wind sighed, colder than the rose
Blooming in desolation, 'No one knows.'

The Sleeping Beauty, Canto 8

The childhood of a poet is in nearly all cases a strange weaving together of the ecstasy that the poet knows and the helpless misery that is known by a child who is lost in the unfamiliar streets of a slum. He is in a foreign place, and the faces around him are dark and strange. Even if they try to speak to him kindly, their language is one that is unknown to him. He must suffer within his heart the mad tempests of love for the world of sight, sense, and sound, and the mad tempests of rage against the cruelty and blindness that is in the world. But he must suffer these dumbly, for among the tall strangers there is nothing but noise and buffeting. The children are terrifying to him; their eyes are on a level with his own, but they are like the blind and beautiful eyes of statues—they see nothing. He loves them and longs to be loved in return, but he knows that they, too, see him as a statue throwing some long strange shadow, or as a little foreigner dressed in mourning for someone they have never known, or playing an unknown game he has learned in far-off gardens.

Alexander Pope

When we come to that dark house,
Never sound of wave shall rouse
The bird that sings within the blood
Of those who sleep in that deep wood:
For in that house the shadows now
Seem cast by some dark unknown bough.
The gardener plays his old bagpipe
To make the melons' gold seeds ripe;
The music swoons with a sad sound—
'Keep, my lad, to the good safe ground!
For once, long since, there was a felon
With guineas gold as the seeds of a melon,
And he would sail for a far strand
To seek a waking, clearer land—
A land whose name is only heard
In the strange singing of a bird.
The sea was sharper than green grass,
The sailors would not let him pass,
For the sea was wroth and rose at him
Like the turreted walls of Jerusalem,
Or like the towers and gables seen
Within a deep-boughed garden green.
And the sailors bound and threw him down
Among those wrathful towers to drown.
And oh, far best,' the gardener said,
'Like fruits to lie in your kind bed—
To sleep as snug as in the grave
In your kind bed, and shun the wave,
Nor ever sigh for a strange land
And songs no heart can understand.'

The Sleeping Beauty, Canto 1

My father was born out of his century. His life ranged from the date eleven hundred to the end of the life of Queen Anne, and therefore he was never inwardly dull, as there were several centuries in which he could browse. But he suffered from the disabilities of the period, being obliged to watch bear-baiting, serfdom, tortures, etc. When he lived in that double life-time, he had much of the character of a bird on a bough, with a bird's strange detachment. He did not like modernity because it disrupted that inner spiritual life—it jerked his neck, like that of somebody being hanged. I think it was for that reason that he spent so much of his time lying down.

From an unpublished notebook

Sir Henry[1] was exceedingly active physically, and he had adopted his custom of pacing the passages, he said, by cultivating such a habit one ceased to trouble or even to notice if the days were wet and cold, or torrid and weighted by the heat, if the days were drawing out or drawing in. It was true that an awareness of the weather was useful as a basis for conversation, but Sir Henry did not care for conversation, and, as well, if you paid no attention to the fact, it ceased to exist. Only the sound of footsteps, and the care for his health, these remained, binding him to reality. On the other hand, he did not believe in taking risks, and though an agnostic by profession,[2] he said his prayers every night, on the chance of this proving to be a good investment. When pacing the passages, he walked very slowly, occupying as much time as possible in order that the house should seem even larger than it was—for he liked to feel that it was very large. Occasionally, about once or twice a day, he would pause outside a door, if he could hear voices speaking in the room beyond— not because he wanted to eavesdrop or to spy, since there was nothing he could hear, now, that would interest him, but because he was enabled in this way to touch, for a moment, the world in which others moved, thought, acted, without being obliged to become a part of it, and this made him feel real to himself, real in his isolation, in the separation of his identity from the world that he could yet touch at

[1] 'Sir Henry, of course, was my father.'—Edith Sitwell to Elizabeth Salter
[2] 'Though certainly an agnostic, Sir George Sitwell was too honest minded to be both agnostic and say his prayers.'—Sacheverell Sitwell

will. He would, too, spread various objects belonging to himself all over the house, in the many rooms—his hat in one room, his stick in another, his spectacle case in a third, because when he came face to face, once more, in the course of his wanderings, with these records of his own personality, he was reminded of himself, which was pleasant, and because it enabled him to stake his claim on every room in the house as sole inhabitant. Should another person enter one of the rooms in question, Sir Henry would follow him there, and, conveying suddenly the impression of great age, would make it clear by his manner that he had intended to rest there, and had hoped that he would not be disturbed; then, having by this means routed the intruder and put him to flight, he would continue his walk.

When he was not pacing up and down the passages, Sir Henry spent much of his time walking up and down in front of the house, and when he did this, he would succeed in appearing like a procession of one person—he being the head, the beginning and the end. You were conscious of the State Umbrella.

I Live Under A Black Sun

En Famille

In the early springtime, after their tea,
Through the young fields of the springing Bohea,
Jemima, Jocasta, Dinah, and Deb
Walked with their father Sir Joshua Jebb—
An admiral red, whose only notion
(A butterfly poised on a pigtailed ocean)
Is of the peruked sea whose swell
Breaks on the flowerless rocks of Hell.
Under the thin trees, Deb and Dinah,
Jemima, Jocasta walked, and finer
Their black hair seemed (flat-sleek to see)
Than the young leaves of the springing Bohea;
Their cheeks were like nutmeg-flowers when swells
The rain into foolish silver bells.
They said, 'If the door you would only slam,
Or if, Papa, you would once say "Damn"—
Instead of merely roaring "Avast"

Or boldly invoking the nautical Blast—
We should now stand in the street of Hell
Watching siesta shutters that fell
With a noise like amber softly sliding;
Our moon-like glances through these gliding
Would see at her table preened and set
Myrrhina sitting at her toilette
With eyelids closed as soft as the breeze
That flows from gold flowers on the incense-trees.'

. . . .

The Admiral said, 'You could never call—
I assure you it would not do at all!
She gets down from table without saying "Please,"
Forgets her prayers and to cross her T's,
In short, her scandalous reputation
Has shocked the whole of the Hellish nation;
And every turbaned Chinoiserie,
With whom we should sip our black Bohea,
Would stretch out her simian fingers thin
To scratch you, my dears, like a mandoline;
For Hell is just as properly proper
As Greenwich, or as Bath, or Joppa!'

Mandoline

Down in Hell's gilded street
Snow dances fleet and sweet,
Bright as a parakeet,

Or Punchinello,
All glistening yellow,
As fruit-jewels mellow,

Glittering white and black
As the swan's glassy back
On the Styx' soundless track,

Sharp as bird's painted bill,
Pecking fruit, sweet and shrill,
On a dark window-sill.

See the glass house as smooth
As a wide puppet-booth . . .
Snow strikes it like a sooth

Melon-shaped mandoline
With the sharp tang and sheen
Of flames that cry, 'Unclean!'

Dinah with scarlet ruche,
Gay-plumaged Fanfreluche,
Watch shrill as Scaramouche

In the huge house of glass
Old shadows bent, alas!
On ebon sticks now pass—

Lean on a shadow boy,
Creep like a broken toy—
Wooden and painted joy.

Trains sweep the empty floors—
Pelongs and pallampores,
Bulchauls and sallampores,

Soundless as any breeze
(Amber and orangeries)
From isles in Indian seas.

Black spangled veils falling
(The cold is appalling),
They wave fans, hear calling

The adder-flames shrieking slow,
Stinging bright fruitlike snow,
Down in the street below;

While an ape, with black spangled veil,
Plum'd head-dress, face dust-pale,
Scratch'd with a fingernail

Sounds from a mandoline,
Tuneless and sharp as sin:
Shutters whose tang and sheen,

Shrieking all down the scale,
Seem like the flames that fail
Under that onyx nail,

Light as snow dancing fleet,
Bright as a parakeet,
Down in Hell's empty street.

My mother was a young woman of great beauty—Italianate in character. She bore a strong resemblance to one of the drawings by Michelangelo in the Uffizi Gallery—a drawing of a young woman of an extraordinary summer-like beauty, facing an old woman—herself, grown old, but bearing still traces of that 'high midsummer pomp', that majestic beauty. At the same time, my mother bore a likeness to this great line describing the Furies:

'The barren daughters of the fruitful night.'

Nothing was born in her head, which was barren; but my brothers and I were born of her fruitful night.

When young, she was very gay, was very generous, and lavished on others everything that belonged to her. She had a childlike quality.

In later years, after she had fallen among thieves, her appearance still retained vestiges of that summer beauty, but as though a black veil had been thrown over it. Her hair was still dark as though it had lain under the shadow of a Fury's wing. She was still lavish, still wildly hospitable.

When at Montegufoni, she came to life and found gaiety in arranging those enormous luncheon and dinner parties, to which she and my father succeeded, inevitably, in inviting deadly enemies to meet each other. But at Renishaw, deprived of those hours of hectic hospitality, Time was for her but an empty round between the night and night, a repetition of sad nothingness, like the beat that sounded within her dress of dust; for her, the moments dropped like sad and meaningless tears.

Somehow she must cross the desert of her days, and that was all she knew.

To her, all greatness was reduced to the smallness, the uselessness of a grain of sand; those grains, the little things of life, without sense, without sap, were piled above her until she lay buried beneath them.

'I live from day to day,' she would reply in answer to enquiries as to her mode of life. She might have added, 'and for the small distractions of the hour.'

Her rages were the only reality in her life.

Taken Care Of, pp. 20–21

'I was fortunate in being [my mother's] favourite child, and in thus obtaining much of the love of which my sister was deprived. And though I saw the sufferings of this young creature, it was difficult for me to realise the extent of them; for I was privileged to a degree that she was penalised. Edith still remained in the schoolroom, and so was seldom as yet allowed to come down to see me. Her personality was too strong, her mind too imaginative, her heart too easily touched, to make her a comfortable companion for the conventional. Besides, my mother saw in her a living embodiment of some past unhappiness of her own . . .

'My sister's hours and days were most fully taken up by her dedication to these attractions of long ago; to them she was obliged to add the prevalent rites of the gymnasium, the antics which would, she was told, be as useful to her as the obsolete dances, lancers and the rest, which she was learning. ("Nothin' a young man likes so much as a girl who's good at the parallel bars.") To this curriculum was also added, in the name of health and beauty, a good deal of plain physical torture, invented by my father in consultation with a children's surgeon . . . Alas, my sister's nose was still not of the shape for which my father had bargained, so the reign of iron and manacles began. The harm inflicted both on her nervous system and her physique proved to be costly though fortunately not irreparable; a few years later it took many months to break down by electric treatment the adhesions that had formed as a consequence of the use of these instruments.'[1]

The Scarlet Tree by Osbert Sitwell

[1] It should be noted that this account does not agree with Sacheverell Sitwell's recollections of his sister's childhood.—Ed.

My friend, the baby owl . . . had to snore in order to attract the attention of mice.

Throughout my life I have been so unfortunate as to attract mice (of the human species) without the effort of snoring.

By the time I was eleven years old, I had been taught that Nature, far from abhorring a Vacuum, positively adores it.

At about that time I was subjected, in the schoolroom, to a devoted, loving peering inquisitive interfering stultifying middle class suffocation, on the chance that I would become 'just like everybody else'.

Taken Care Of

Edith Sitwell did not become 'just like everybody else' and her governesses had to admit defeat. She fought for her individuality, but her attitude towards them was compassionate. Through these gentlewomen whose poverty forced them to tutor the daughters of the establishment, the child Edith Sitwell became aware of the cruelty of the system in which she was brought up.

Let us think for a little of those people whose lives are not living, but a little reading by candlelight of some uncared-for and un-opened book, and then, the cold and unutterable darkness. When I am an old woman I shall write a book about these poor and unloved creatures whose existences have been passed on the surface of other people's lives.

Readers and Writers, August 1922

Yet there are those who do not feel the cold;
And Mademoiselle Richarde was thus,—both old
And sharp, content to be the cold wind's butt;
A tiny spider in a gilded nut
She lived and rattled in the emptiness
Of other people's splendours; her rich dress
Had muffled her old loneliness of heart.
This was her life; to live another's part,
To come and go unheard, a ghost unseen
Among the courtly mirrors glacial green,

Placed just beyond her reach for fear that she
Forget her loneliness, her image see
Grown concrete, not a ghost by cold airs blown.
So each reflection blooms there but her own.
She sits at other people's tables, raises
Her hands at other people's joys and praises
Their cold amusements, drawing down the blinds
Over her face for other's griefs—the winds
Her sole friends now, grown grey and grim as she,
They have forgotten how to hear or see.
And her opinions are not her own,
But meaningless half words by cold airs blown
Through keyholes . . . words that were not meant for her.
'Madame la Duchesse said, "The spring winds stir!" '
(Madame la Duchesse, old and gold japanned,
Whirled like a typhoon over the grey land
In her wide carriage, while a dead wind grieves
Among those seeking ghosts, the small grey leaves.)
So now, like Echo, she is soundless fleet
Save for the little talk she can repeat—
Small whispers listened for at courtly doors.
She swims across the river-dark vast floors
To fires that seem like rococo gilt carving
Nor ever knows her shrunken heart is starving . . .

Mademoiselle Richarde

When she was younger, among the shallow mirrors of the Second Empire, she had been chief embalmer to a flock of swan-like women, whose destiny was the highest society. These she embalmed, one after another, in the schoolroom, until they were perfected in their glacial chill. They swam with an infinite grace and remoteness upon the river-dark vastness of their floors; and nothing was ever changed, from their curls, falling like the fountains singing their cold forlorn madrigals, to the harp-like music of their lives, and their cheeks like pale and tuneful roses. 'Tears', said Mademoiselle Blanchatte, 'only make eyes the brighter'; and she warmed her withered hands at their fires of rococo gilt carving. 'Young ladies', said Mademoiselle

Blanchatte, 'should never leave the gardens, if unaccompanied'; and she looked approvingly at the chloratic roses.

Readers and Writers, 1922

Early Spring

The wooden châlets of the cloud
Hang down their dull blunt ropes to shroud

Red crystal bells upon each bough
(Fruit-buds that whimper). No winds slough

Our faces, furred with cold like red
Furred buds of satyr springs, long dead!

The cold wind creaking in my blood
Seems part of it, as grain of wood;

Among the coarse goat-locks of snow
Mamzelle still drags me, to and fro;

Her feet make marks like centaur hoofs
In hairy snow; her cold reproofs

Die, and her strange eyes look oblique
As the slant crystal buds that creak.

If she could think me distant, she
In the snow's goat-locks certainly

Would try to milk those teats, the buds,
Of their warm sticky milk—the cuds

Of strange long-past fruit-hairy springs—
The beginnings of first earthy things.

The Lady with the Sewing-Machine

Across the fields as green as spinach,
Cropped as close as Time to Greenwich,

Stands a high house; if at all,
Spring comes like a paisley shawl—

Patternings meticulous
And youthfully ridiculous.

In each room the yellow sun
Shakes like a canary, run

On run, roulade, and watery trill—
Yellow, meaningless, and shrill.

Face as white as any clock's,
Cased in parsley-dark curled locks,

All day long you sit and sew,
Stitch life down for fear it grow,

Stitch life down for fear we guess
At the hidden ugliness.

Dusty voice that throbs with heat,
Hoping with its steel-thin beat

To put stitches in my mind,
Make it tidy, make it kind;

You shall not! I'll keep it free
Though you turn earth sky and sea

To a patchwork quilt to keep
Your mind snug and warm in sleep.

A Penny Fare to Babylon

'A penny fare to Babylon,
A penny for each thought!'
'Oh, ma'am, no, ma'am,
Can't be bought!
The Sun gives pots of money,
The Moon, her bread and honey,
When humming like a clover field
I go up to town.

Whitened by the Moon's flour,
All the birds I own,
Lest they be baked into a pie,
Are flown, dear, flown.
Though you whistle in the corridors
That dance into my brain—
Oh, ma'am, no, ma'am,
They will not come again.'

The mind of the child resembles that of the artist inasmuch as nothing appears to it as finite; infinity alone exists. To these, perhaps the only conscious living creatures, the roundness of an apple is a portrait of the world, with its bright flashing summer colours, and the kingfisher quivering in its beauty upon a green bough, has the same lovely plumes as the sun. The house and the man who lives in it are equally imbued with life; and the one is not more favoured in this particular than the other; for to the child every human being seems to be a house, too, in which the queerest people live—hiding behind strange doors and occasionally peering at us through darkened windows . . .

To a child, logic does not exist, therefore circumstances cannot be the logical outcome of certain acts, but appear to be extraneous and marvellous growths . . . much as if a flower could be born without springing from dark roots in our common earth. To these strange beings, half seraph and half animal, the simplest things are a matter for wonder, and are stared at with eyes as fresh as a flower's eyes, completely unjaded by civilization. Heredity has not yet become a habit with them. For with the birth of each child, this ancient world is born anew; and it is only by schooling and dull parental habit that the world can be taught again to leap into its conventional middle-age. In childhood, time is abolished as a dimension, and distance is like some lovely wild creature, a half-human faun, friendly for all its shyness, that lives in the dark woods today, but is always ready to come at your call. This being the case, anything may happen at any moment, and the child may meet beings whom wise age knows to have been dead and dust for a thousand years.

In after years, when the bright visions of childhood have grown dim in the brains of most of us, the artist still retains the curious sensitiveness to impressions and mental atmosphere, the intense yet fantastic seriousness, which is the basis of the child's mind . . . Life still appears to him as a matter of sharp outlines, bright flashing colours, and strange meetings . . . The child's perception has become creative instead of being merely assimilative and inceptive; and the artist, on his part, has lost all the self-consciousness of childhood, and is taking us into his confidence. Those honey-hives that are the cells of memory have been rifled for us.

From the introduction to
Children's Tales From The Russian Ballet

Where reynard-haired Malinn
Walks by rock and cave,
The Sun, a Chinese mandarin,
Came dripping from the wave.

'Your hair seems like the sunrise
O'er Persia and Cathay—
A rose-red music strange and dim
As th'embalmèd smile of seraphim.'

He said to her by the white wave
In the water-pallid day
(A forest of white coral boughs
Seemed the delicate sea-spray);

'In envy of your brighter hair—
Since, Madam, we must quarrel—
I've changed the cold flower-lovely spray
To branches of white coral;

And when, white muslin Madam, you
Coquette with the bright wind,
I shall be but thin rose-dust;
He will be cold, unkind.'

The flowers that bud like rain and dream
On thin boughs water-clear,
Fade away like a lovely music
Nobody will hear,

And Aeolus and Boreas
Brood among those boughs,
Like hermits haunting the dark caves
None but the wise man knows.

But Malinn's reynard-coloured hair,
Amid the world grown sere
Still seemed the Javanese sunrise
Whose wandering music will surprise
Into cold bird-chattering cries
The Emperor of China
Lying on his bier.

The Sleeping Beauty, Canto 13

Life was so still, so clear, that to wake
Under a kingfisher's limpid lake
In the lovely afternoon of a dream
Would not remote or stranger seem.
Everything seemed so clear for a while—
The turn of a head or a deep-seen smile;
Then a smile seen through wide leaves or deep water,
That beauty seemed to the King's daughter;
For a flying shadow passed, then gone
Was the gleam, and the Princess was alone.

How sweet seemed the flowers of spring again—
As pink as Susan and Polly and Jane,
Like country maids so sweet and shy
Who bloom and love and wonder not why:
Now when summer comes it seems the door
To the graves that lie under the trivial floor,
And the gardens hard to touch and shining,
Where no mirage dew lies whining.
And the sweet flowers seem for a fading while
Dear as our first love's youthful smile—
Till they bruise and wound the heart and sense
With their lost and terrible innocence.

The Sleeping Beauty, Canto 9

49

When we were young, how beautiful life seemed!—
The boundless bright horizons that we dreamed,

And the immortal music of the Day and Night,
Leaving the echo of their wonder and their might

Deep in our hearts and minds. How could the dust
Of superstitions taught in schoolrooms, lust

In love's shape, dim our beauty? What dark lie,
Or cruelty's voice, could drown this God-made harmony?

For we knew naught of prison-worlds man built
Around us that we may not know man's guilt—

The endless vistas of the goatish faces
Echoing each other, and the basis

Of clay, the plumeless wings of Destiny,
The vistas leading only to the grave where we must lie.

The Sleeping Beauty, Canto 11

Do, do,
Princess, do,
Like a tree that drips with gold you flow.
Soon beneath that peaceful shade
The whole world dreaming will be laid.
Do, do,
Princess, do,
The years like soft winds come and go.

The Sleeping Beauty, Canto 15

Night passed, and in that world of leaves
The Dawn came, rustling like corn-sheaves;

And a small wind came like little Boy Blue
Over the cornfield and rustling through
The large leaves . . . Oh, how very deep
The old queen is sighing in her sleep:

'Alas, blue wind,
Bluebeard unkind,
Why have you blown so far from me,
Through the jewelled blue leaves that sound
    like the sea,

The lady Margotte,
The goosegirl Gargotte
Agog with curiosity?

They played Troy Town on the palace wall . . .
Like small grape hyacinths were their curls
And thin as the spring wind were those girls—
But now they never come if I call.'

The kingly cock with his red-gold beard,
And his red-gold crown had crowed unheard

While his queens ruffled down
Each feathered gown
Beside the waterfall's crystal town;

The cock, the dawn-fruits, the gold corn,
Sing this aubade, cold, forlorn:

'Jane, Jane,
Forget the pain
In your heart. Go work again.

Light is given that you may
Work till owl-soft dusk of day.

The morning light whines on the floor . . .
No one e'er will cross the door,

No one ever cares to know
How ragged flowers like you do grow.

Like beaux and belles about the Court
King James the Second held, athwart

The field the sheep run—foolish graces,
Periwigs, long Stuart faces,

While ragged-robin, cockscomb flowers
Cluck beneath the crystal showers.

51

A far-off huntsman sounds his horn
That sounds like rain, harsh and forlorn;

Pink as his coat, poor-robin seems . . .
Jane, no longer lie in dreams.

The crude pink stalactites of rain
Are sounding from the boughs again.

Each sighs the name of Harriet, Mary,
Susan, Anne, grown cold and wary—

Never your name. Bright and gay,
They used to whisper, "Come away,"

But now they have forgotten why.
Come, no longer sleeping lie.

Jane, Jane,
Forget the pain
In your heart. Go work again!'

No answer came. No footsteps now will climb
Down from Jane's attic. She forgets the time,
Her wages, plainness, and how none could love
A maid with cockscomb hair, in Sleep's dark grove.

.   .   .   .

And now the brutish forests close around
The beauty sleeping in enchanted ground.

All night the harsh bucolic winds that grunt
Through those green curtains. help me in my hunt.

Oh, the swinish hairy beasts
Of the rough wind
(Wild boars tearing through the forests)!
Nothing they will find

But stars like empty wooden nuts,
In leaves green and shrill.
Home they go to their rough stye
The clouds . . . and home go I.

Above the wooden shutters
Of my room at morn,
Like bunches of the country flowers
Seem the fresh dawn hours.

And the young dawn creeps
Tiptoe through my room . . .
Never speaks of one who sleeps
In the forest's gloom.

The Sleeping Beauty, Cantos 24, 25

1900–1913

I remember thinking when I was a schoolgirl how delightful it must be to enjoy oneself. I wished, definitely, to enjoy myself. I thought it would be fun.

But now I understand why my nurse preferred visiting the cemetery to any other visits. We cannot have misunderstandings with tombstones; but, especially if we have good manners, the misunderstandings when we are enjoying ourselves, are without end.

My Awkward Moments, 1927

It is true that there are many people who appear to find their happiness in being uncomfortable, people who will even distrust the moral value of the performance of a duty, if, by any chance, the duty becomes a pleasure, but I doubt very much if any normal person regards these victims of their own tastes as anything better than cranks, and maddening cranks at that. Also, I have heard of people who find a pleasure in quarrelling, 'because it is so nice to make friends again', but that has always appeared to me to be a peculiarly unpleasant point of view, and the warmest friendships might be expected to wear very thin in the process . . .

There is another type of person with whom it is impossible to have any kind of real peace; I mean those people who disagree instantly with any opinion that may be advanced on any subject, *not*, curiously enough, because they specially want to prove themselves to be in the right (which is a very usual and fairly pardonable failing) but because they want, with a feeling that amounts almost to violence, to prove that the other person is wrong.

At first glance these two attitudes of mind may seem to be the same, but, as a matter of fact, they are very, very wide apart. A person who always wants to be in the right, may be quite good natured in very many other ways; the person who particularly wishes to prove that you are in the wrong, is nearly always disagreeable in everything else.

Here, I think, we get to what makes the great difference between what is 'stimulating' and what is merely 'irritating'. Bickering is not an expression of a genuinely held opinion; it is a premeditated and spiteful attitude of disapproving dissent from anything and everything that some other person may say or do. It is the outward expression of a mental attitude of displeasure, of discontent, and of petty resentment, and I find it quite impossible to see how that can conduce happiness, even to the bickerer.

I cannot.

'The (Dis)Pleasures of Bickering', *Good Housekeeping*, 1936

The young Edith Sitwell looked for an antidote to discord and found it. On the shelves of the library at Wood End was a volume of Pope. This she read 'secretly at night when my governess was at dinner—sitting up in bed, bending over it, poring over it'. She had discovered poetry and:

The whole world was transformed for me—became a living heavenly thing, of heavenly joys and sorrows.

'Why Not Like Poetry?'

By the time she was thirteen her father had bought Montegufoni, the Italian castle near Florence that had once been the home of the Dukes of Athens and which became the family wintering place. On the long train journeys there and back Edith Sitwell memorized The Rape of the Lock:

That miracle of summer air, airy and glittering as the nets of the summer light and early dew over the strawberry beds—a poem so airy that it might have been woven by the long fingers of the sylphs in their dark and glittering Indian gauzes, floating like a little wind among the jewelled dark dews on the leaves of the fruit-trees.

Alexander Pope

The fact that she could recite the whole of this long poem did not compensate for her refusal to memorize The Boy Stood on the Burning Deck. *Disgrace reached its apotheosis when she vanished overnight from her grandmother's home in Bournemouth. Edith had made the discovery of Swinburne and, with her maid as companion, journeyed to the Isle of Wight to pour a libation of milk over his grave and leave upon it her tribute of roses. Her behaviour was considered to be even more disgraceful since the object of her adoration was a poet condemned by family friends as 'licentious' and therefore tabu.*

Outside a stuffy bookshop, two maiden ladies were on the pavement lost in speculation . . .

The younger maiden lady, then aged about eighteen, had the remote elegance and distinction of a very tall bird. Indeed, her gown had the feathery quality of a bird's raiment, and one would not have been surprised, at any moment, if she had preened her quills. She stood there, in the delicate, leafless cold, with her long thin legs poised upon the wet pavement, as some great bird stands in a pool.

She had not the look of one who has many acquaintances—not more, perhaps, than a few leafless flowering boughs and blackthorn boughs and the early and remote flakes of the snow. Her only neighbour was the silence, and her voice had more the sound of a wood-wind instrument than of a human voice. She was plain and knew it.

'An eighteenth-century memoir, Edith,' the older lady was saying, 'is what your Grannie would like—giving the life of the times.'

'Give me if you please,' she said shyly, as she entered the shop, 'some eighteenth-century memoirs', and retired with the works of Casanova. Memoirs indeed, but the life of the times eventually failed to please the eldest lady for whom the life was intended.

'And I should like, if you please,' said the youngest lady, 'some poems of Swinburne . . . Have you? . . .'

'Oh no Miss,' said the shopman, flustered and shocked—'we have nothing of that kind. But should you care for the works of Laurence Hope, which are also full of love interest . . .'

The youngest lady did not think she would care for these and, aunt and niece, they floated out again.

The notebooks of Edith Sitwell

The Princess:

'Upon the infinite shore by the sea
The lovely ladies are walking like birds,
Their gowns have the beauty, the feathery
Grace of a bird's soft raiment; remote
Is their grace and their distinction—they float
And peck at their deep and honeyed words
As though they were honeyed fruits; and this
Is ever their life, between sleep and bliss,
Though they are winged for enchanted flight,
They yet remain ever upon the shore
Of Eternity, seeking for nothing more,
Until the cold airs dull their beauty
And the snows of winter load those dazzling
Wings, and no bird-throat can sing!'

The Governante:

'Look not on the infinite wave,
Dream not of the siren cave,
Nor hear the cold wind in the tree
Sigh of worlds we cannot see.'

The Sleeping Beauty, Canto 12

She grew within his heart as the flushed rose
In the green heat of the long summer grows
Deep in the sorrowful heaven of her leaves.
And this song only is the sound that grieves
When the gold-fingered wind from the green veins
Of the rich rose deflowers her amber blood,
The sharp green rains.
Such is the song, grown from a sleepy head,
Of lovers in a country paradise—
You shall not find it where a songbird flies,
Nor from the sound that in a bird-throat grieves;
—Its chart lies not in maps on strawberry leaves.

* * *

How old, the small undying snake that wreathes
Round lips and eyes, now that the kiss has gone?
In that last night, when we, too, are alone
We have, for love that seemed eternity
The old unchanging memory of the bone—
That porphyry whence grew the summer rose.

Most ancient is the Worm—more old than Night
Or the first music heard among the trees
And the unknown horizons' harmonies
Where the huge suns come freshened. Shrunk and cold
Is he, like Venus blackened, noseless, old.

Yet all immensities lie in his strong
Embrace, horizons that no sight hath known,
The veins whose sea had heard the siren song
And worlds that grew from an immortal kiss.

And still their love amid this green world grieves:
'The gold light drips like myrrh upon the leaves
And fills with gold those chambers of the South
That were your eyes, that honeycomb your mouth.

And now the undying Worm makes no great stir,
His tight embrace chills not our luxuries,
Though the last light perfumes our bones like myrrh
And Time's beat dies.'

* * *

How should I dream that I must wake alone
With a void coffin of sad flesh and bone:—
You, with the small undying serpent's kiss,
You, the dull rumour of the dust's renown—
The polar night, a boulder rolling down
My heart, your Sisyphus, to that abyss
Where is nor light, nor dark, nor soul, nor heart to eat—
Only the dust of all the dead, the sound of passing feet.

* * *

So winter fell; the heart shaped like the rose
Beneath the mountain of oblivion lies
With all death's nations and the centuries.
And this song ending fades like the shrill snows,

Dim as the languid moon's vast fading light
That scatters sparkles faint and dim and chill
Upon the wide leaves round my window-sill
Like Æthiopia ever jewelled bright . . .

So fading from the branches the snow sang
With a strange perfume, a melodious twang
As if a rose should change into a ghost—
A ghost turn to a perfume on the leaves.

Romance

A few years later, the adolescent Edith Sitwell made a second pilgrimage, this time to the house of the poet W. B. Yeats, to offer another tribute of roses which she laid on his doorstep.

61

She summoned the courage to ring the bell, but not to wait until the door was opened.

About these, the passions of her mind, she has made no secret. About the more romantic passions she has said nothing.

Did she fall in love? Constance Sitwell, a cousin and friend of her girl-hood, said that she did, a statement borne out by the first two of her poems to be published. A decade passed before they appeared, and the credit for their appearance, goes perhaps surprisingly, to the Daily Mirror.

Serenade

The tremulous gold of stars within your hair
Are yellow bees flown from the hive of night,
Finding the blossom of your eyes more fair
Than all the pale flowers folded from the light.
Then, Sweet, awake, and ope your dreaming eyes
Ere those bright bees have flown and darkness dies.

Drowned Suns

The swans more white than those forgotten fair
Who ruled the kingdoms that of old-time were,
Within the sunset water deeply gaze
As though they sought some beautiful dim face,
The youth of all the world; or pale lost gems,
And crystal shimmering diadems,
The moon for ever seeks in woodland streams
To deck her cool faint beauty; thus in dreams,
Belov'd, I seek lost suns within your eyes
And find but wrecks of love's gold argosies.

It is Constance Sitwell, in her memoir Bright Morning, *who has left us this portrait of the adolescent Edith Sitwell, evoking an aura of aesthetic, if romantic, intensity.*

'The warm days of idleness passed by amidst the scents and sounds of summer . . . Edith was playing Chopin in the ballroom; later on she came out and we sat on the rim of the fountain on the lawn, while she talked to us about Yeats, who was not well known then, and

Swinburne. At that time [she] described a great many things in terms of music and musicians; she played a lot of Brahms then, and this, she said, was a "Brahms garden" . . . the terraces, fountains of Verona marble, and square yew hedges enclosing little lawns with round and square beds of carnations and lavender . . . long grass paths, and a delicate wrought iron gate at the far end of one of them. A wooden gate on another side opened on to a dark wood path which led through trees to the lake at the bottom of the park . . .

'Ghosts and flowers and songs were woven into the texture of those days; music and echoing rooms. To me there seemed to be a slightly malign spell upon the place, accentuated by its beauty and Edith's extreme sensibility, and it is to the remote, the half melancholy emotion, the sound of a Brahms intermezzo and the faint notes of a Chopin prelude floating out of the windows of the ball-room that my memory returns. The tapestry in that room had frames of dark red leather, the piano stood at one end, and if, lured by the sound of music, one went in quietly, one saw Edith's pale gold hair and her bent absorbed face as she played; it returns to her reading D'Annunzio to us, as we lay on the grass under the lime trees in the languid afternoon . . .'

And yet, it is only August, the pompous high meridian, the Augustan month. The August noon burning on the water. For there is the whole day to waste. The August noon glittering on the waters, the flashing of the oars, when it is too hot to look. For we have come here to think of this, away from poverty or riches. And who is this first phantom? A tall thin young woman in a pelisse of green sheep-skin and a wide-brimmed hat, who walks between the hedges upon the smoother grass. She has long, thin hands, and jet black rings and bracelets. She has sloping shoulders, and picks her way among the fallen twigs. And from her shadow the wood leads on into poetry. For her love is poetry, she lives within a phrase. Look at her once more for there will never be her like again among women!

This is the world of those who have transcended life, and been kept outside it. Of those who will never live again, for they have an immortality that is not physical. In this wood, this place of waiting, one will not speak to another, all are solitary. Their own world holds them. For her, the goat-foot waterfalls leap from rock to rock; the reflections in the water of cupolas and gables are the lake, itself, become a Georgian stables; the shadows are manteaux espagnoles over the long and the light summer land. Her ghost is a personal spectre: but why should I not speak of her? This is my master from whom I learned and there can never be her like again. But look into her features and see their tragic bones, her Dantesque profile in the mirror pane. We wrote in communion with one another and mine will always be the freedom of her world.

But we must be open and less melancholy! For this is the world as it has been, and as it might have been. Let us go quickly to where we breathe its air. Once more we may find that tall thin young woman, lying, this time, under a fruit tree that is in blossom and reading a book of poetry in the long, lush grass. Or sitting, it may be, in the garden of a London square. The pear tree is in flower and the long grass waves above the page. How lovely to be young and to feel poetry running in your veins! It will be Swinburne or William Morris that she reads: August, or In the Orchard, from *Poems and Ballads*; Anactoria; Golden Wings, or The Blue Closet. Such are the poems of pear or apple blossom to be read in the springtime of one's life. But, as well, the Fleurs du Mal darken this paradise, as though with lines of rain. It is poetry of the blood's decline. And her own images begin to form. Metaphors of a bony personality, of hard dry brilliance, nothing soft nor milky, of dogskin leaves and furry buds, of landscapes and persons that have never been before. And then, Ah! then, my world begins to grow. This wood leads on into infinity. I wander in the orange grove and feel the red-gold globes. I hear a barrel organ, and know they dance to it. Then, Actæon, stag antlered, comes out through the trees; we hear the horn of Orion: Krishna dances with the milkmaids: Midas and his men pick cherries, standing on long ladders: Cupid and Campaspe play their game of cards for kisses. Fantasies of the hot South come like tunes from the mind that made them. For, now, it is another world. And we must have the whole earth before it sinks, or burns.

'Profile in a Window Pane', from
The Homing of the Winds by Sacheverell Sitwell

Rain

Beside the smooth black marble sea
You and I drift aimlessly.

Each blade of grass springs pale, alone,
Tuneless as a quartertone . . .

Remote your face seems, far away,
Beneath the ghostly water, Day,

That laps across you, as again
We move across the endless plain.

We are two ghosts today, each ghost
For ever wandering and lost;

No yesterday and no tomorrow
Know we, neither joy nor sorrow,

For this is the hour when like a swan
The silence floats, so still and wan

That bird-songs, silver masks to hide
Strange faces, now all sounds have died,

Find but a curdled sheepskin flower
Embodied in this ghostly hour.

A Sylph's Song

The cornucopia of Ceres
I seek not, fading not for this,

But fair Pomona, gardener's daughter,
Laughing like bird-feathered water.

Amid this hot green glowing gloom
A word falls with a raindrop's boom;

And baskets of ripe fruit in air
The bird-songs seem, suspended where

Those goldfinches, the ripe warm lights,
Peck slyly at them, take quick flights.

I bring you branches green with dew
And fruits that you may crown anew

Your waspish-gilded hair until
That cornucopia doth spill

Dew, and your warm lips bear the stains,
And bird-blood leap within your veins.

Pomona, lovely gardener's daughter,
Fruits like ripples of the water

Soon will fade . . . then leave your fruits,
Smooth as your cheek or the birds' flutes,

And in this lovelier, smoother shade
Listen to my serenade.

Beneath a wan and sylvan tree,
Whose water-flowing beauty our tired eyes
Can feel from very far, two travellers lie;
And one is swarthy as the summer wind—
A man who travelled from a far countree;
The other Soldan in his pomp and panoply
Seems like le Roi Soleil in all his pride
When his gold periwig is floating wide.
They talked together, those dark kings beneath the bough,
And their songs mingled with soft winds that flow.

The Soldan (sings)

'When green as a river was the barley,
Green as a river the rye,
I waded deep and began to parley
With a youth whom I heard sigh.
"I seek", said he, "a lovely lady,
A nymph as bright as a queen,
Like a tree that drips with pearls her shady
Locks of hair were seen;

And all the rivers became her flocks,
Though their wool you cannot shear,
Because of the love of her flowing locks.
The kingly sun like a swain
Came strong, unheeding of her scorn,
Wading in deeps where she has lain,
Sleeping upon her river lawn
And chasing her starry satyr train.
She fled, and changed into a tree—
That lovely fair-haired lady . . .
And now I seek through the sere summer
Where no trees are shady!"

They say that Daphne never was more fair
With all the shaken pearls of her long hair—
The lovely tree that was Apollo's love,
To whom he brought his richest spoils—than she!
And oh, that other Soldan, the hot sun
Burns not with love as I, with my dark pomp,
My helmet thick-plumed as a water-god's,
Whose cornucopia filled with dripping jewels
Is not so rich as treasuries I bear—
Dark spices, nard and spikenard, ambergris . . .
No maid will change into a tree before my kiss!'

The Man from a Far Countree

'But I will be content with some far-lesser maid,
Who feeds her flocks beneath a fair-haired tree
And listens to the wind's song; she shall be
My soldanesse, and rule my far countree.

(He sings)
Rose and Alice,
Oh the pretty lassies,
With their mouths like a calice
And their hair a golden palace—
Through my heart like a lovely wind they blow.

Though I am black and not comely,
Though I am black as the darkest trees,

67

I have swarms of gold that will fly like honey-bees,
By the rivers of the sun I will feed my words
Until they skip like those fleecèd lambs
The waterfalls, and the rivers (horned rams):
Then for all my darkness I shall be
The peacefulness of a lovely tree—
A tree wherein the golden birds
Are singing in the darkest branches, O!'

Thus sang those plumed kings, and the winds that flow
Whispered of lands no waking heart may know.

The Sleeping Beauty, Canto 19

By the Lake

Across the flat and the pastel snow
Two people go . . . 'And do you remember
When last we wandered this shore?' . . . 'Ah no!
For it is cold-hearted December.'
'Dead, the leaves that like asses' ears hung on the trees
When last we wandered and squandered joy here;
Now Midas your husband will listen for these
Whispers—these tears for joy's bier.'
And as they walk, they seem tall pagodas;
And all the ropes let down from the cloud
Ring the hard cold bell-buds upon the trees—codas
Of overtones, ecstasies, grown for love's shroud.

At seventeen she was eligible for the marriage market and was duly sent along to a dinner party given by her aunt, Lady Londesborough, to find herself seated beside an eligible baronet.

But, in my first [evening] dress of white tulle, lightly spangled and streaming with waterlilies, with my face remorselessly 'softened' by my hair being frizzed and then pulled down over my nose, I resembled a caricature of the Fairy Queen in a pantomime.

'A Self-Developed Person', *Yorkshire Weekly Post*, 1936

The pantomime Fairy Queen added insult to the injury of her appearance by talking to the baronet about Brahms. The baronet complained and Edith was sent home in disgrace.

The county, like the rich, became a target for attack.

The County Calls

They came upon us like a train—
A rush, a scream, then gone again!
With bodies like a continent
Encased in silken seas, they went

And came and called and took their tea
And patronised the Deity
Who copies their munificence
With creditable heart and sense.

Each face a plaster monument
For some beloved aliment.
Whose everlasting sleep they deign
To cradle in the Great Inane;

Each tongue, a noisy clockwork bell
To toll the passing hour that fell;
Each hat, an architect's device
For building churches, cheap and nice.

I saw the County Families
Advance and sit and take their teas;
I saw the County gaze askance
At my thin insignificance:

Small thoughts like frightened fishes glide
Beneath their eyes' pale glassy tide:
They said: 'Poor thing! we must be nice!'
They said: 'We knew your father'—twice.

Funerals

Beneath umbrellas I can see
Pink faces sheened with stupidity,

With whiskers spirting from them (days
Of boredom, black and sentient days

From other personalities.)
And, mourners too, white-bearded seas

Walk slowly by them as they come,
Sing hymns to the wind's harmonium.

Old men shake hands; their clawing grasp
Seems like a door without a clasp—

That gapes on slow black emptiness . . .
Now—vanished is her cracked black dress,

The house grows tall from vacancy,
And in the kitchen I take tea

While the furry sun creeps out—that raw
Life—sheathes its murderous claw

And lets its tongue slink out to lap
The silence—(a slow-leaking tap) . . .

Solo for Ear-Trumpet

The carriage brushes through the bright
Leaves (violent jets from life to light).
Strong polished speed is plunging, heaves
Between the showers of bright hot leaves.
The window-glasses glaze our faces
And jarr them to the very basis,—
But they could never put a polish
Upon my manners, or abolish
My most distinct disinclination
For calling on a rich relation!
In her house, bulwark built between
The life man lives and visions seen,—
The sunlight hiccups white as chalk,
Grown drunk with emptiness of talk,
And silence hisses like a snake,
Invertebrate and rattling ache.

  .   .   .   .

Till suddenly, Eternity
Drowns all the houses like a sea,
And down the street the Trump of Doom
Blares,—barely shakes this drawing-room
Where raw-edged shadows sting forlorn
As dank dark nettles. Down the horn
Of her ear-trumpet I convey
The news that: 'It is Judgement Day!'
'Speak louder; I don't catch, my dear.'
I roared: *'It is the Trump we hear!'*
'The *What?*'—'THE TRUMP!' . . . 'I shall complain—
The boy-scouts practising again!'

Plutocracy at Play

From gilded house to gilded play
Plutocracy has paid its way
To sip that well-confectioned soul—
The vanille-tainted Barcarolle,

The iced veneer that violins made;
Great mirrors green as lemonade
Show tiers on tiers of gilded curls
Rococo profiles, rows of pearls.

Submerged within a wavy sea
Of plush, our great Plutocracy
Once more like swan-white water-girls
Prepare to catch the notes as pearls.

Portentous women splash like whales
Amid the froth of talk: and scales
Of lights glance on their surface, wink
And wish their jewels were good to drink;

And in the music's tepid seas
Bald heads seem red anemones
With gold fringe swelling on the tide;
The froth of conversation died.

71

The music's glutinous sweet flood
Crawls in their veins instead of blood;
Eyes glitter like the scales of fish
With some half-formed Hebraic wish;

And on the airs that proudly swell
Each plutocratic Ariel
(Wafted upon a half-formed sigh)
Finds heavenly courts are not too high;

Whose pastoral life befits their rank
With field of commerce, marbled bank,
Where seated, the Eternal Nose
Finds out the worm within the rose:

'Let those exalted be brought low'—
And noses follow suit, you know—
So on the cushioned ecstasy
Of music, our Plutocracy

Exudes the glucose of its soul—
The vanille-tainted Barcarolle
Mid tiers on tiers of gilded curls—
Rococo profiles, rows of pearls.

It should be noted that despite the tone of this poem Edith Sitwell was far from anti-Semitic. This poem is included as an example of her satire at its best.

'Help was on the way,' wrote Osbert Sitwell in his Memoir *The Scarlet Tree.* Helen Rootham, faithful friend and champion . . . 'the first grown up person to seize the quality of this young girl,' arrived at Renishaw as governess to the recalcitrant Edith. And,

'In six months, I found my sister a changed person . . . I noticed an alteration in her way of looking at things, for her absence from home—and as a result, the discontinuance of the perpetual nagging to which for years she had been obliged to submit—had lifted the whole range of her spirits. She knew now, that she would be going away again before long and the result was to make her much more amenable, because hopeful. In the peace she now obtained for the first time, no longer fearing every moment that she would be found fault with, able to attend concerts and go to galleries with her governess, and come back home without having to face scenes, all her interests had blossomed in the short interval that had elapsed, and music and poetry burned in her blood like fire. She had become the most exhilarating and inspiring as well as understanding of companions. And, in spite of her disfiguring though expensive clothes, the brown plumage, physically as well as mentally, of the cygnet had gone, and the swan's green white ruffling surge of feathers had come to replace it.'

Helen Rootham, translator of Rimbaud and acclaimed by at least one critic of the day as a poet of talent, pointed the way towards worlds unknown.

Through Helen Rootham, Edith Sitwell made the discovery of the French symbolists, Verlaine, Baudelaire, Rimbaud, who, said the critic Jack Lindsay, declared that 'the word has to be broken open, so that the new nexus of meaning can get inside it. And then from this broken thing burst new radioactive forces, knitting together and organising in unpredictable patterns.'

The word had come alive; poetry had emerged from the past to be placed in the context of the present. The young Edith Sitwell caught her first glimpse of the years of experiment ahead of her.

Stopping Place

The world grows furry, grunts with sleep . . .
But I must on the surface keep.
The jolting of the train to me
Seems some primeval vertebrae
Attached by life-nerves to my brain—
Reactionary once again,
So that I see shapes crude and new
And ordered—with some end in view,
No longer with the horny eyes
Of other people's memories.
Through highly varnished yellow heat,
As through a lens that does not fit,
The faces jolt in cubes, and I

Perceive their odd solidity
And lack of meaning absolute:
For why should noses thus protrude,
And to what purpose can relate
Each hair so oddly separate?
Anchored against the puff of breeze,
As shallow as the crude blue seas,
The coloured blocks and cubes of faces
Seem Noah's arks that shelter races
Of far absurdities to breed
Their queer kind after we are dead.
Blue wooden foliage creaks with heat
And there are woollen buns to eat—
Bright-varnished buns to touch and see
And, black as an Inferno, tea.
Then (Recketts' blue) a puff of wind . . .
Heredity regains my mind
And I am sitting in the train
While thought becomes like flesh—the brain
Not independent, but derived
From hairy matter that half lived—
Identities not round or whole.
A questing beast who thirsts for soul,
The furry vegetation there—
Purring with heat, sucks in the air;
And dust that's gathered in the train,
Protecting flesh, seems almost brain—
(That horny substance altering sight);
How strange, intangible is light
Whence all is born, and yet by touch
We live—the rest is not worth much . . .
Once more the world grows furred with sleep—
But I must on the surface keep
While mammoths from the heat are born—
Great clumsy trains with tusk and horn
Whereon the world's too sudden tossed
Through frondage of our mind, and lost.

It was proper for a gently brought up young girl to leave her family provided that she was suitably chaperoned. With Helen Rootham as a buffer against the charge of impropriety, Edith Sitwell escaped from the suffocation of parental disapproval and rented a cheap flat in Bayswater on the fourth floor of Pembridge Mansions.

Miss Sitwell had come to London.

1913–1922

The old are young, the young are old,
The sunlight pours all whiskey-gold!
 Houp–la! the world is gay!

I was so young and debonair;
My gay feet trod the summer air,
 Houp–la! the world is gay!

Duckie

Edith Sitwell went to concerts, visited the galleries, read, worked and was happy. If her first poems were not published until she was in her late twenties, it is because she had not entirely surrendered her adolescent ambition to become a concert pianist. But in Pembridge Mansions there was no room for a piano and, although she had escaped from home, she had not been provided with enough money on which to live. During the year 1913, for the first and only time in her life, she worked in an office, 'signing on' at nine in the morning and earning the sum of 25/– a week. She was poor, and unused to work.

But this ineptitude on my part was, gradually, cured. I am the crane-tall Jane of my poem Aubade—although in the poem, I had changed my situation to that of a poor young country servant.

The poem was written like this: it was about a year after I had emerged from a longish period of poverty in London (I am the poor member of a rich family). One of the minor things I hated most was getting up at six in the morning to lay and light the sulky bad-tempered fire. That is how the poem started. Then I thought, no! that'll be a dull poem. I wanted rain in it, but rain in London is ugly, and dull, and anyhow, what do I know about London? I am a country woman. So I must fuse my experience with somebody else's.

Selected Letters

Aubade

Jane, Jane,
Tall as a crane,
The morning light creaks down again;

Comb your cockscomb-ragged hair,
Jane, Jane, come down the stair.

Each dull blunt wooden stalactite
Of rain creaks, hardened by the light,

Sounding like an overtone
From some lonely world unknown.

But the creaking empty light
Will never harden into sight,

Will never penetrate your brain
With overtones like the blunt rain.

The light would show (if it could harden)
Eternities of kitchen garden,

Cockscomb flowers that none will pluck,
And wooden flowers that 'gin to cluck.

In the kitchen you must light
Flames as staring, red and white,

As carrots or as turnips, shining
Where the cold dawn light lies whining.

Cockscomb hair on the cold wind
Hangs limp, turns the milk's weak mind . . .

Jane, Jane,
Tall as a crane,
The morning light creaks down again!

A year after her move to London, war was declared. Edith Sitwell had the painful experience of saying goodbye to her brother Osbert who left to rejoin his regiment. She was not a pacifist, but neither then nor later did she yield to the blandishment of the chauvinists.

Nothing will ever make me believe that war is either a good thing, or a wise thing, or that there can be any possible justification for sending out some millions of men for the avowed purpose of killing each other.

The hypocritical talk about the 'virtues' which are produced by war sickens me. Has one any right to torture a man in order to admire his 'fortitude' in enduring his agony or his 'charity' in easing a fellow sufferer?

It is my sincere conviction that war is a beastly thing, and that it is brought about by greed and fear, and by nothing else.

'It Is Fear That Breeds War', *Sunday Referee*, 7 April 1935

*Her answer to the 'beastly thing' was an outburst of poetic energy. In
1915* The Mother, *her first collection of poems, appeared. It was ten
pages, privately printed and, she told Sir Maurice Bowra, brought her
'the summit of happiness'.*

This was followed by Twentieth Century Harlequinade and Other
Poems *published jointly with her brother Osbert. But her most significant
challenge came in the form of an anthology called* Wheels *of which she
was editor:*

'*Wheels*, an anthology of poems edited by Edith Sitwell, appeared
in six annual cycles from 1916 to 1921. Apart from Edith, Osbert,
and Sacheverell Sitwell, the contributors included Nancy Cunard,
Aldous Huxley, Alan Porter, Iris Tree, and Sherard Vines. All the
contributors were young, and some of them were members of families
well known in society and in the fashionable artistic world. *Wheels* was
intended to be an act of defiance, a deliberate rebellion against the
stuffy canons of respectable, conservative society. It mocked explicitly
or implicitly the standards of poetic decorum and middle-class
romanticism associated with [Eddie] Marsh and his Georgians; it
undermined the dignified postures of academic men of letters; its
tone was anti-militaristic, sophisticated and cynical. Not surprisingly,
it evoked abusive hostility and delighted applause.'

John Press, *A Map of Modern English Verse*

'Harpies like nightingales, and nightingales like harpies, chirping
balefully upon the walls of old Babylon'—*The Nation*
'The vanguard of British poetry. They are a portent'—*The Saturday
Review*
'The publication of *Wheels* is regarded by all right-minded people as
more a society event than a literary one'—*Weekly Dispatch*
'Mr Osbert and Miss Edith Sitwell we can imagine as anxiously
asking ourselves: "What can we do to be original?" '—*The Literary
World*

*The edition of 1919 was distinguished by its dedication to the soldier
poet Wilfred Owen who had been killed the year before.*

I have at length, after infinite thought and care, decided to ask
you if *Wheels* may have the great privilege and the sacred honour of
producing 'The Show', 'Terre à terre', 'Strange Meeting', 'The

Sentry Disabled', 'The Dead Beat', 'The Chances' [wrote Edith to Mrs Owen] . . . these poems should overwhelm anybody who cares really for poetry.

Selected Letters

The critics could hardly be described as overwhelmed, but one paper risked a prophecy which can now be claimed to have been justified:

'Fifty years hence, the publication of *Wheels* will be remembered as a notable event in the inner history of English literature.'

Pedagogues

The air is like a jarring bell
That jangles words it cannot spell,
And, black as Fate, the iron trees
Stretch thirstily to catch the breeze.

The fat leaves pat the shrinking air;
The hot sun's patronising stare
Rouses the stout flies from content
To some small show of sentiment.

Beneath the terrace shines the green
Metallic strip of sea, and sheen
Of sands, where folk flaunt parrot-bright
With rags and tags of noisy light.

The brass band's snorting stabs the sky
And tears the yielding vacancy—
The imbecile and smiling blue—
Until fresh meaning trickles through;

And slowly we perambulate
With spectacles that concentrate
In one short hour, Eternity,
In one small lens, Infinity.

With children, our primeval curse,
We overrun the universe—
Beneath the giddy lights of noon,
White as a tired August moon.

The air is like a jarring bell
That jangles words it cannot spell,

And, black as Fate, the iron trees
Stretch thirstily to catch the breeze.

Déjeuner sur l' Herbe

Green apples dancing in a wash of sun—
Ripples of sense and fun—
A net of light that wavers as it weaves
The sunlight on the chattering leaves;
The half-dazed sound of feet,
And carriages that ripple in the heat.
The parasols like shadows of the sun
Cast wavering shades that run
Across the laughing faces and across
Hair with a bird-bright gloss.
The swinging greenery casts shadows dark,
Hides me that I may mark
How, buzzing in this dazzling mesh, my soul
Seems hardening it to flesh, and one bright whole.
O sudden feathers have a flashing sheen!
The sun's swift javelin
The bird-songs seem, that through the dark leaves pass;
And life itself is but a flashing glass.

Springing Jack

Green wooden leaves clap light away
From the young flowers as white as day—

Clear angel-face on hairy stalk
(Soul grown from flesh, an ape's young talk).

The showman's face is cubed, clear as
The shapes reflected in a glass

Of water (Glog, glut, a ghost's speech
Fumbling for space from each to each).

The fusty showman fumbles, must
Fit in a particle of dust

The universe, for fear it gain
Its freedom from my box of brain.

Yet dust bears seeds that grow to grace
Behind my crude-striped wooden face,

As I, a puppet tinsel-pink,
Leap on my strings, learn how to think,

Then, like the trembling golden stalk
Of some long-petalled star, I walk

Through the dark heavens, until dew
Falls on my eyes and sense thrills through.

TWO ORCHARD POEMS

1. *The Satyr in the Periwig*

The Satyr Scarabombadon
Pulled periwig and breeches on:
'Grown old and stiff, this modern dress
Adds monstrously to my distress.
The gout within a hoofen heel
Is very hard to bear; I feel
When crushed into a buckled shoe
The twinge will be redoubled, too.
And when I walk in gardens green
And, weeping, think on what has been,
Then wipe one eye—the other sees
The plums and cherries on the trees.
Small bird-quick women pass me by
With sleeves that flutter airily,
And baskets blazing like a fire
With laughing fruits of my desire:
Plums sunburnt as the King of Spain,
Gold-cheeked as any Nubian,
With strawberries all goldly-freckled,

84

Pears fat as thrushes and as speckled.
Pursue them? . . . Yes, and squeeze a tear!
"Please spare poor Satyr one, my dear!"
"Be off, sir! Go and steal your own!"
—Alas, poor Scarabombadon,
Trees rend his ruffles, stretch a twig,
Tear off a satyr's periwig!'

ii. *The Muslin Gown*

With spectacles that flash,
Striped foolscap hung with gold
And silver bells that clash,
(Bright rhetoric and cold),
In owl-dark garments goes the Rain,
Dull pedagogue, again.
And in my orchard wood
Small song-birds flock and fly,
Like cherubs brown and good,
When through the trees go I
Knee-deep within the dark-leaved sorrel.
Cherries red as bells of coral
Ring to see me come—
I, with my fruit-dark hair
As dark as any plum,
My summer gown as white as air
And frilled as any quick bird's there.
But oh, what shall I do?
Old Owl-wing's back from town—
He's skipping through dark trees: I know
He *hates* my summer gown!

The Spider

The fat light clings upon my skin,
Like grease that slowly forms a thin
And foul white film; so close it lies,
It feeds upon my lips and eyes.

The black fly hits the window-pane
That shuts its dirty body in;
So once, his spirit fought to quit
The body that imprisoned it.

He always seemed so fond of me,
Until one day he chanced to see
My head, a little on one side,
Loll softly as if I had died.

Since then, he rarely looked my way,
Though he could never know what lay
Within my brain; though iron his will,
I thought, he's young and teachable.

And often, as I took my drink,
I chuckled in my heart to think
Whose dark blood ran within his veins;
You see, it spared me half my pains.

The time was very long until
I had the chance to work my will;
Once seen, the way was clear as light,
A father's patience infinite.

He always was so sensitive;
But soon I taught him how to live
With each day, just a patch of white,
A blinded patch of black, each night.

Each day he watched my gaiety.
It's very difficult to die
When one is young . . . I pitied him,
The glass I filled up to the brim,

His shaking fingers scarce could hold;
His limbs were trembling as with cold . . .
I waited till from night and day
All meaning I had wiped away.

And then I gave it him again;
The wine made heaven in his brain,
Then spider-like, the kindly wine
Thrust tentacles through each vein,

And knotted him so very fast
I knew I had him safe at last.
And sometimes in the dawn, I'd creep
To watch him as he lay asleep,

And each time, see my son's face grown
In some blurred line, more like my own.
A crumpled rag, he lies all night
Until the first white smear of light;

And sleep is but an empty hole . . .
No place for him to hide his soul,
No outlet there to set him free:
He never can escape from me.

Yet still I never know what thought
All fly-like, in his mind lies caught:
His face seems some half-spoken word
Forgot again as soon as heard,

Beneath the livid skin of light;
Oh, just an empty space of white,
Now all the meaning's gone. I'll sit
A little while, and stare at it.

Switchback

By the blue wooden sea,
Curling laboriously,
Coral and amber grots
(Cherries and apricots),
Ribbons of noisy heat,
Binding them head and feet,
Horses as fat as plums
Snort as each bumpkin comes:
Giggles like towers of glass
(Pink and blue spirals) pass;
Oh, how the Vacancy
Laughed at them rushing by!
'Turn again, flesh and brain,

Only yourselves again!
How far above the Ape,
Differing in each shape,
You with your regular,
Meaningless circles are!'

By Candlelight

Houses red as flower of bean,
Flickering leaves and shadows lean!
Pantalone, like a parrot,
Sat and grumbled in the garret,
Sat and growled and grumbled till
Moon upon the window-sill,
Like a red-geranium,
Scented his bald cranium.
Said Brighella, meaning well—
'Pack your box and—go to Hell!
Heat will cure your rheumatism.'
Silence crowned this optimism.
Not a sound and not a wail—
But the fire (lush leafy vale)
Watched the angry feathers fly.
Pantalone 'gan to cry—
Could not, *would* not, pack his box,
Shadows (curtseying hens and cocks)
Pecking in the attic gloom,
Tried to smother his tail-plume . . .
Till a cock's comb candle-flame,
Crowing loudly, died: Dawn came.

Clowns' Houses

Beneath the flat and paper sky
The sun, a demon's eye,
Glowed through the air, that mask of glass;
All wand'ring sounds that pass

Seemed out of tune, as if the light
Were fiddle-strings pulled tight.
The market-square with spire and bell
Clanged out the hour in Hell;

The busy chatter of the heat
Shrilled like a parokeet;
And shuddering at the noonday light
The dust lay dead and white

As powder on a mummy's face,
Or fawned with simian grace
Round booths with many a hard bright toy
And wooden brittle joy:

The cap and bells of Time the Clown
That, jangling, whistled down
Young cherubs hidden in the guise
Of every bird that flies;

And star-bright masks for youth to wear,
Lest any dream that fare
—Bright pilgrim—past our ken, should see
Hints of Reality.

Upon the sharp-set grass, shrill-green,
Tall trees like rattles lean,
And jangle sharp and dizzily;
But when night falls they sigh

Till Pierrot moon steals slyly in,
His face more white than sin,
Black-masked, and with cool touch lays bare
Each cherry, plum, and pear.

Then underneath the veilèd eyes
Of houses, darkness lies,—
Tall houses; like a hopeless prayer
They cleave the sly dumb air.

Blind are those houses, paper-thin;
Old shadows hid therein,
With sly and crazy movements creep
Like marionettes, and weep.

Tall windows show Infinity;
And, hard reality,
The candles weep and pry and dance
Like lives mocked at by Chance.

The rooms are vast as Sleep within:
When once I ventured in,
Chill Silence, like a surging sea,
Slowly enveloped me.

Fireworks

Pink faces (worlds or flowers or seas or stars)—
You all alike are patterned with hot bars

Of coloured light; and, falling where I stand,
The sharp and rainbow splinters from the band

Seem fireworks, splinters of the Infinite
(Glitter of leaves the echoes). And the night

Will weld this dust of bright Infinity
To forms that we may touch and call and see:

Pink pyramids of faces: tulip-trees
Spilling night perfumes on the terraces.

The music, blond airs waving like a sea,
Draws in its vortex of immensity

The new-awakened flower-strange hair and eyes
Of crowds beneath the floating summer skies.

And against the silk pavilions of the sea
I watch the people move incessantly

Vibrating, petals blown from flower-hued stars
Beneath the music-fireworks' waving bars;

So all seems indivisible, at one:
The flow of hair, the flowers, the seas that run—

A coloured floating music of the night
Through the pavilions of the Infinite.

Small Talk

II

Upon the noon Cassandra died
The harpy preened itself outside.

Bank Holiday put forth its glamour,
And in the wayside station's clamour

We found the cafe at the rear,
And sat and drank our Pilsener beer.

Words smeared upon our wooden faces
Now paint them into queer grimaces;

The crackling greeneries that spirt
Like fireworks, mock our souls inert,

And we seem feathered like a bird
Among those shadows scarcely heard.

Beneath her shade-ribbed switchback mane
The harpy, breasted like a train,

Was haggling with a farmer's wife:
'Fresh harpy's eggs, no trace of life.'

Miss Sitwell, cross and white as chalk,
Was indisposed for the small talk,

Since, peering through a shadowed door,
She saw Cassandra on the floor.

Eventail

Lovely Semiramis
Closes her slanting eyes:
Dead is she long ago.

From her fan, sliding slow,
Parrot-bright fire's feathers,
Gilded as June weathers,
Plumes bright and shrill as grass
Twinkle down; as they pass
Through the green glooms in Hell
Fruits with a tuneful smell,
Grapes like an emerald rain,
Where the full moon has lain,
Greengages bright as grass,
Melons as cold as glass,
Piled on each gilded booth,
Feel their cheeks growing smooth.
Apes in plumed head-dresses
Whence the bright heat hisses—
Nubian faces, sly
Pursing mouth, slanting eye,
Feel the Arabian
Winds floating from the fan:
Salesmen with gilded face
Paler grow, nod apace;
'Oh, the fan's blowing
Cold winds . . . It is snowing!'

What the Dean said to Silenus

Excuse me, Sir, *my* plums, I think!
Amid thick leaves I saw the wink
Of bird-black eyes, where on the brink

Of water, trees seem pale as rain,
With watery sounds—and marked with pain
That you were—at it—once again.

No really, Sir, I must protest;
For you and each shy-footed guest
Have quite deprived me of my rest:

The sap of trees within my veins
And sleepy frondage of my brains
Hurts quite as much as growing pains;

My trees that hung above a pool
Like sleepy clouds of cotton-wool
No longer seem to me so cool.

And on my lawns of parrot-green
Where plumed leaves have a bird-quick sheen,
Young persons are distinctly seen,

In colour, really, scarcely nice—
Like centaur waves that drip with spice
From Indian isles of ambergris;

Their wilderness of glittering hair
Seems fire-plumed devils of the air.
My sheep, those sparkling clouds, pass there;

And while the heat, red Harlequin,
Plays on the airs for mandoline,
Each in an air-white crinoline

With points like coloured dust of stars—
Confetti, or the wavering bars
From sharpened strings of light that mars

The fruit-trees, (cataracts of fire
That in those nets of golden wire
Catch bird-voices to light the pyre

Of cherries)—teach my sheep to buck;
My apples, red with sleep, they pluck,
And cherries, plums and grapes they suck.

Then, mirage-waters as they flow
Or dream-perfumes, they fade and go
With movements like a ship and slow.

You'd scarce believe, but till of late
You came, between a man and mate
I scarce could differentiate,

And always thought a double-chin
Was incompatible with sin.
And at my age, one can't begin

To study men instead of bees!
My gaiters seem like trunks of trees—
Not pillars of the Church that freeze

To stalactites of boredom through
Long centuries of sermons.—No,
I really think, Sir, you must go!

*Materialism: or; Pastor—takes the Restaurant Car
for Heaven*

Upon sharp floods of noise there glide
The red-brick houses, float, collide

With aspidistras, trains on steel
That lead us not to what we feel.

Hot glassy lights fill up the gloom
As water an aquarium—

All mirror-bright; beneath these seen,
Our faces coloured by their sheen,

Seem objects under water, bent
By each bright-hued advertisement

Whose words are stamped upon our skin
As though the heat had burnt them in.

The jolting of the train that made
All objects coloured bars of shade,

Projects them sideways till they split
Splinters from eyeballs as they flit.

Down endless tubes of throats we squeeze
Our words, lymphatic paint to please

Our sense of neatness, neutralize
The overtint and oversize.

I think it true that Heaven should be
A narrow train for you and me,

Where we perpetually must haunt
The moving oblique restaurant

And feed on food of other minds
Behind the hot and dusty blinds.

Portrait of a Barmaid

Metallic waves of people jar
Through crackling green toward the bar,

Where on the tables, chattering white,
The sharp drinks quarrel with the light.

Those coloured muslin blinds, the smiles,
Shroud wooden faces; and at whiles

They splash like a thin water (you
Yourself reflected in their hue).

The conversations, loud and bright,
Seem spinal bars of shunting light

In firework-spirting greenery.
O complicate machinery

For building Babel! Iron crane
Beneath your hair, that blue-ribbed mane

In noise and murder like the sea
Without its mutability!

Outside the bar, where jangling heat
Seems out of tune and off the beat,

A concertina's glycerine
Exudes and mirrors in the green

Your soul, pure glucose edged with hints
Of tentative and half-soiled tints.

Contributors to Wheels *were not only poets. The endpapers for the second number were designed by a young Chilean painter who was already making his name in London. Alvaro Guevara, who had met Edith Sitwell when Roger Fry was painting her portrait, began work on another, which he called* The Editor of Wheels. *Guevara, seven years younger, darkly handsome, immensely attracted, became the first acknowledged love of Edith's life. Seen together at various social functions, their names were linked by the gossip press. But Guevara was already infatuated by another contributor to* Wheels, *Nancy Cunard. In 1921 he left London for Chile. By the time he returned, in 1925, Edith Sitwell had accepted his place in her life as an admiring and affectionate friend.*

Instead of marriage had come fame. Miss Sitwell was asked to read her poems to literary groups, to lecture at universities. Miss Sitwell's Saturday afternoon tea parties had begun to attract the Bloomsburys, the avant-garde, poets, painters and philosophers. Aldous Huxley, T. S. Eliot, Virginia Woolf, Mrs Patrick Campbell—these among others toiled up the five flights of stone steps to her three rooms in Pembridge Mansions.

Among the younger poets was Brian Howard, whose memory of his visit is as unflattering as Allanah Harper's is enthusiastic.

Here are their two accounts, in contrast with one another.

'I went to see Edith [Sitwell] and was very disappointed indeed. I arrived at Moscow Road—an uninviting slum—and toiled up flights and flights of bare Victorian stairs (very narrow stairs). From outside, Pembridge Mansions looked like a dirty and inexpensive hospital. I arrived at a nasty green door, which was opened by Edie herself. She has a very long thin expressive face with a pale but good complexion. She looks rather like a refined Dutch medieval madonna. She had on an enlarged pilu hat of grey fur, an apple green sheepswool jacket, and an uninteresting 'old gold' brocade dress. Her hair is thin, but of a pleasant pale gold colour, bobbed at the sides and bunned at the hind. I do not care for the people she usually has around her—to Saturday teas, for example, at all. They are common little nobodies. Also I don't like her teas—as teas at all. Tell William I got one penny bun, and three quarters of a cup of rancid tea in a dirty cottage mug. Also I don't like her apartments, or rather, room. It is small, dark and, I suspect, dirty. The only interesting things in the room are an etching by Augustus John and her library, which is most entertaining. The remainder seems to consist of one lustre ball and a quantity of bad draperies. Miss Helen Rootham, whom she lives with, is one of those terrifyingly forceful women—she proffered me a picture by Kandinsky—an incoherent smudge of colour, and murmured with great vim into my ear, "Isn't that pure beauty?" I replied in the affirmative. I always do that when I meet muscle.'

Rather different is Allanah Harper's account. Allanah Harper, editor of the Review *Echanges in Paris, had written an article on the poetry of Edith Sitwell, published in* Le Flambeau. *The result was an invitation to tea.*

'Climbing flight after flight of bare stone stairs, I waited at the door, before having the courage to knock. Edith Sitwell opened the door herself, teapot in hand.

' "How splendid," she said, "we meet at last. I am making tea."

'So she made tea herself in a brown kitchen pot. Indian tea, too. I had expected a Queen Anne tea service with a Chinese design. I did not know that Edith Sitwell, having escaped to London from the tyranny of her parents, was very poor . . .

'There was a noise of cross voices on the stairs. "That must be Tom," Edith said. In walked T. S. Eliot and his first wife. I remembered his lines "I should have been a pair of ragged claws scuttling across the floors of silent seas." He looked like a curate who would later become a Bishop . . .

'I listened, with awe, to the two most creative of contemporary poets discussing the evolution of poetry, rooted as it is in the great tradition, yet an essentially living and developing organism . . .

'They spoke of the loosening of tradition in order to admit new dimensions and deeper questioning . . . They spoke of the fruitful unrest which is life itself and from which all creative art is born . . . They discussed several culture vultures, whom I shall not name . . .'

And they exchanged stories of their various 'pests', the admirers who besieged them with letters, for the most part unwelcome:

I have received, from a doctor at Ipswych (I can't spell) the photograph of fourteen children (presumably his) who have been brought up on my poetry. They are dressed in Highland costume, and above them is printed 'Scots wha hae.' Imagine my unbounded horror and disgust.

Letter to Harold Acton,
Selected Letters

'I'm having such trouble with the lady who will write me letters about her chef. However, I've written her pages—with quotations—about the destructive qualities of the Wombat—one of the species has, apparently, prevented Melbourne from getting a drop of water for six weeks, and has also caused a landslide—by persisting in burrowing. I have said that will she let me have *at once* any information she may possess about the Wombat, and will she tell me also if an *ordinary* bat could or would do such a thing.

Letter to Virginia Woolf,
Selected Letters

By 1920 Wheels *was in its fifth cycle and* Clowns' Houses *had appeared, to be followed by* The Wooden Pegasus.

In The Wooden Pegasus *were her 'Seven Nursery Songs' of which the most successful was* The King of China's Daughter. *Yeats, who admitted that he preferred her work 'when she seems to be a child', wrote to ask permission to have* The King of China's Daughter *set to music for a performance at the Abbey Theatre, in Dublin. The fee he offered was one pound, but Edith Sitwell, who did not consider her Nursery Songs worthy of serious consideration, was mortified more by his choice than by his parsimony.*

But in his Essays and Introductions, *Yeats declared her to be 'an important poet' and went on to analyse his reactions to her early work:*

'Her language is the traditional language of literature, but twisted, torn, complicated, jerked here and there by strained resemblances, unnatural contacts, forced upon it by terror or by some violence beating in her blood, some primitive obsession that civilization can no longer exorcise. I find her obscure, exasperating, delightful.'

The King of China's Daughter

The King of China's daughter,
She never would love me
Though I hung my cap and bells upon

Her nutmeg tree.
For oranges and lemons,
The stars in bright blue air
(I stole them long ago, my dear)
Were dangling there.
The Moon did give me silver pence,
The Sun did give me gold,
And both together softly blew
And made my porridge cold;
But the King of China's daughter
Pretended not to see
When I hung my cap and bells upon
Her nutmeg tree.

One o'Clock

Great Snoring and Norwich
A dish of pease porridge!
The clock of Troy town
Sounds one o'clock; brown
Honey-bees in the clover
Are half the seas over,
And Time is a-boring
From Troy to Great Snoring.
But Time, the grey mouse,
Can't wake up the house,
For old King Priam
Is sleepy as I am!

Trams

Castles of crystal,
Castles of wood,
Moving on pulleys
Just as you should!
See the gay people

Flaunting like flags,
Bells in the steeple,
Sky all in rags.
Bright as a parrot
Flaunts the gay heat—
Songs in the garret,
Fruit in the street;
Plump as a cherry,
Red as a rose,
Old Mother Berry—
Blowing her nose!

Madame Mouse Trots

*'Dame Sourie trotte grise dans
le noir,'*—Verlaine.

Madame Mouse trots,
Grey in the black night!
Madame Mouse trots:
Furred is the light.
The elephant-trunks
Trumpet from the sea . . .
Grey in the black night
The mouse trots free.
Hoarse as a dog's bark
The heavy leaves are furled . . .
The cat's in his cradle,
All's well with the world!

Came the Great Popinjay

Came the great Popinjay
Smelling his nosegay:
In cages like grots
The birds sang gavottes.
'Herodiade's flea
Was named sweet Amanda,

100

She danced like a lady
From here to Uganda.
Oh, what a dance was there!
Long-haired, the candle
Salome-like tossed her hair
To a dance tune by Handel.' . . .
Dance they still? Then came
Courtier Death,
Blew out the candle flame
With civet breath.

Said King Pompey

Said King Pompey, the emperor's ape,
Shuddering black in his temporal cape
Of dust, 'The dust is everything—
The heart to love and the voice to sing,
Indianapolis
And the Acropolis,
Also the hairy sky that we
Take for a coverlet comfortably.'
Said the Bishop,
Eating his ketchup:
'There still remains Eternity
Swelling the diocese,
That elephantiasis,
The flunkeyed and trumpeting sea.'

By 1920 London had become Edith Sitwell's spiritual home. She could even afford a char who, she wrote, 'was surprised that with so many available window ledges, I had no boxes of flowers.

"You could fancy yourself in the country, Miss," she would urge.
"But I don't want to fancy myself in the country," I would reply. "I hate the country and I like to be surrounded with proofs that I am in London." '

Naturally enough, since in London, she had discovered—herself.

101

'Every poet must find out what is his own personality, *and then act upon it,' she wrote to Harold Acton—a theme which she was later to expand into an article for the press.*

I believe the greatest thing in life to be true self development.

At once I can hear cries of 'egoism', 'individuality', 'lack of altruism' arising from all sides. But wait until I have explained what I mean by 'true' self development . . . to find the true use of one's powers and use them, and this, I believe, is the greatest thing in life.

At first sight this may appear platitudinous; but how many people are there who will give the same careful thought, the same discriminating sense of proportion and balance, to the finding out of their own potencies as they will give, let us say, to the potencies of a recipe for a new cocktail?

Not everyone has the same powers . . . but every person who is capable of mental development must carry, within himself or herself, a power of some kind . . . it is in the discovery of this power that true intelligence is shown; and it is in the fostering and proper development of it that happiness lies.

By 'happiness' I do not mean worldly success or outside approval, though it would be priggish to deny that both these things are most agreeable. I mean the inner consciousness, the inner conviction that one is doing well the thing that one is best fitted to do by nature.

It is a much better thing to be a good carpenter than a bad artist . . .

Several parties have been given in recent times which have been described as 'freak' parties, and at one of these each guest had to appear as someone else. Where is the 'freakishness' in this?

In these days of standardised faces, standardised clothes, standardised voices, I think the real 'freak' party would be the one at which all were forced to appear as their own idea of themselves.

It is this lack of personality, this entire absence of any knowledge of what 'personality' really means, which is at the bottom of nearly all the bad work which is done today.

Just as every young girl wants to look like every other young girl and every grandmother wants to be mistaken for her own granddaughter, so most workmen are content . . . to turn out 'sections' which will fit into any 'whole' and artists are pleased and flattered to be called 'another so and so'.

Yet should not everyone be burningly anxious to be himself or herself because of an intense and intimate conviction that no one else can be that 'self'? Can one imagine Shakespeare or Beethoven being flattered at being acclaimed 'another' anyone at all? Were they not the creators of Shakespeare and Beethoven and as such unique and unrepeatable?

Because the world cannot be populated by Titans, and because the smallest is as necessary as the greatest in every well proportioned scheme, then, no matter how small the place to be filled, the person who is called upon to fill it should be convinced that it is a better place by the mere fact of his presence and his work; that it is he himself and not another person who is a necessity there.

'A Self Developed Person', *Yorkshire Weekly Post*, 1936

Edith Sitwell had become—Edith Sitwell.

Painters were magnetized by her. Portraits were painted by most of the painters of the day—Roger Fry, Wyndham Lewis and Alvaro Guevara. A young photographer had also come on the scene. Through Allanah Harper, Edith Sitwell met Cecil Beaton. The result was photographs unusual enough to attract attention to the photographer as well as to his subject. Edith Sitwell was photographed in her coffin à la Bernhardt; in repose, hands folded, on a tiled floor; taking tea in a canopied bed, dressed in a turban and gown, wearing her jet bracelets, and attended by a negress. Cecil Beaton, quite as much as Wyndham Lewis or Alvaro Guevara, appreciated the gothic elegance of this latter day Plantagenet, who, with the help of her brother Osbert, had draped her six feet of slender bone structure with brocades decorated by semi-precious jewels, like a tall tree in flower.

She accepted her reputation for eccentricity, not with resignation but with a comment from Pope, reserved for her denigrators: 'God comfort thy capacity', deflecting criticism with the rapier of her wit, as her two self portraits show:

Since many of her friends—and they are for the most part persons of intelligence—have claimed that the subject of this treatise is an eccentric, I can only accept their verdict, whilst retaining the impression that, in all probability, I know her better than they do.

Why she should have gained this reputation for eccentricity, or in what her eccentricity consists, it is difficult for me to judge. The reputation may have been gained, in part, by her appearance, which strongly resembles that of a tall bird who has been blown by some vast wind.

And her adventures add to this resemblance. On one occasion, when returning from Venice to Paris, the sleeping car attendant was startled by piercing bird-like shrieks issuing from one of the compartments.

On entering, he saw a tall figure in a loose gown with winged sleeves, and slippers edged with long trailing ostrich plumes, apparently in the act of flying through the window.

It was Miss Sitwell, who, trying to shut the window, had become involved in such a hurricane that, unable to let go the blind, she was being dragged by the wind, in the wake of the blind, through the window.

Disengaging her with some difficulty from the blind, the astounded attendant placed her upon a seat, and mopping his brow, murmured: 'Mais qu' est-ce que vous faites là, Madame?'

It was, no doubt, such incidents as these, and the fact that, whenever she travelled, she invariably arrived at her destination accompanied by one widow or several, of whom she had taken charge on the journey, or who had taken charge of her (for widows had an extraordinary fascination for her) that led to this reputation.

She has a horror of 'arty' clothes, of sacks and chintz dresses and wooden beads, and of hair plaited round the ears, and these phenomena bore her even more than fashionable clothes, which look right on the persons for whom they are intended, but do not look right on Miss Sitwell.

In the evening, therefore, she wears either long, sweeping dresses of white velvet or of black velvet, or brocade gowns of the Elizabethan or James I style, because her appearance resembles that to be seen in the portraits of that time.

In the daytime she wears woollen dresses with the narrow bodice, long, flowing skirts, and wide sleeves reminiscent of the gown of an abbess; or, in the afternoon, if she goes to a party, a dress of light brocade, again with wide skirts, and a black hat with a veil under the chin, like those worn by the ladies whom Longhi painted.

Miss Sitwell was, as well, the first woman to paint her nails silver or mother-of-pearl, and she was the first to revive the fashion of wearing huge bracelets of carved jet or ivory, and necklaces and rings of the same.

In character, Miss Sitwell bears a certain resemblance to Dr Johnson, having the same predilection for strong tea, and for 'tossing' adversaries.

But she bears a yet stronger resemblance to Squire Waterton, her favourite eccentric, being impelled to odd behaviour by the same rather outrageous sense of fun, and having in the same measure a love of nearly all living creatures.

So great was this, indeed, that she made strenuous efforts to like brilliant black beetles, nosy, blustering blue-bottles and Mr Percy Wyndham Lewis, succeeding, eventually, in pitying them all.

They say that pity is akin to love . . . Perhaps!

Like Squire Waterton, Miss Sitwell has a strong and abiding love for a toad, inspired by his Garden of Eden trustfulness (shown in his swimming towards her and begging her, as clearly as eyes can beg, to rescue him from a pond full of arum lilies into which he had leaped incautiously) and by the age-old and unfathomable beauty of his black eyes with their ruby glitter; and when his long fingers were stroked by a friend, he stretched them out and clasped one of hers, holding on tightly as he was conveyed to a place of safety, and sighing deeply.

Miss Sitwell dislikes crowds, and the crowd-mind, seeing in the latter the terms of slavishness and of cruelty.

But to dislike crowds does not mean to dislike people, and Miss Sitwell has a genuine liking for the public, and confidence in their good sense as regards decency and fair play.

She has, however, the strongest possible contempt for what is known as 'public opinion'—or perhaps it would be more accurate to say that she pays no attention to it, since it is a result of the crowd-mind.

She is intensely irascible, and cruelty, the one wickedness which she judges harshly, arouses in her a fury which knows no bounds.

For the cruel she has no pity. Fools, whom she does not suffer gladly, are a different matter, and she never attacks unless she has first been the subject of an attack.

Having in many ways a feline nature, it amuses her to sharpen her wits upon the wooden heads of her adversaries as much as it amuses a cat to sharpen his claws upon the leg of a table.

And nearly all her battles are the result of this, or of her rather outrageous sense of fun. She has never wished to wound, and hopes that her adversaries are getting an equal amount of fun out of the battle.

Very few attacks made upon her work annoyed her—and those attacks were many. She was bored by them, and that was all.

Attacks of a personal nature were a different matter, and those that were made upon her were usually of a vile character.

Miss Sitwell has always regarded it as a disgrace for a man to make an attack upon the character of a woman, of a nature which he would not dare to make upon the character of a man for fear of a thrashing.

Miss Sitwell is used to being bothered by intrusive strangers in person, and by people wanting this or that, and thinking that Miss Sitwell was born for the purpose of giving it to them.

If they persist in pestering her she deals with them gently but firmly—as in the case of the gentleman from Johannesburg who insisted that she should send him an electric bore in order that he should be enabled to take on work as a sinker of bore-holes. In reply to his clamorous insistence, she replied that she was unable to send him an *electric* bore, but would be delighted to send him hundreds of an ordinary kind.

In conclusion: she wages war unremittingly against blood-sports; and she is unable to resist teasing bad poets and persons who, with no knowledge of prosody, give their opinions about poetry.

In spite of this, however, and in spite of the many oddities of her character, she has as many friends as any woman alive.

'That English Eccentric Edith Sitwell', *Sunday Referee*, 1936

From time to time, a loud cry arises from certain portions of the Press: 'There she goes! *She's* sighted! Heave something at her!'

Then will follow, either a sympathetic description (under the heading 'Plain Jane makes good') of my sufferings, as one not gifted by Providence with anything causing the eye to dwell willingly upon me.

When I am not being called 'Plain Jane', a description is given of me that seems to have been culled from a medieval description of sea-monsters.

I can never quite understand why my appearance is the affair of anyone except my friends, but since it seems to be becoming a national problem, we will go into it . . .

If one has an aquiline profile, one should *never* try to soften it—it only looks ridiculous.

Why not be one's self? That is the whole secret of a successful appearance. If one is a greyhound, why try to look like a Pekingese?

Those days are far behind. Now I have the look that is natural to me, and my clothes, I trust, look as if they grew on me.

They say I look strange (to some people this is regarded as a misfortune, to others a very great asset).

I am as highly stylised as it is possible to be—as stylised as the music of Debussy or Ravel.

That I know, because it is my nature. I have, if I may say so, my own particular elegance (which every human being ought to have).

If people *will* try to look different from their character, change their appearance, nobody is deceived for a moment. It only makes the onlooker think they are ashamed of both.

'Why I Look As I Do', *Sunday Graphic*

I cannot sit and suck my thumb
As certain other poets do:
I wish I could . . . but I am dumb
Save when I find out something new.

Though I am plain, no longer young,
And am of quite astounding size—
Yet I can never quite attain
To looking through ancestral eyes.

The penalty of fame was social success. But from the world of Lady Cunard she retreated with alarm as she retreated from the more intellectual, but equally permissive embrace of Bloomsbury.

I've been having a lot of trouble with silly little Bloomsburys lately. They all think that it matters to me if they, and people like

Desmond MacCarthy, like my poetry. It doesn't. I don't expect them to. They've civilised all their instincts away. They don't any longer know the difference between one object and another, or one emotion and another. They've civilised their senses away, too. People who are purely 'intellectual' are an awful pest to artists. Gertrude Stein was telling me about Picasso, when he was a boy, nearly screaming with rage when the French version of the Bloomsburys were 'superior' to him.

'Yes yes,' he said. 'Your taste and intellect is so wonderful. But who does the work? Stupid tasteless people like me!'

How irritating it is, though. In the 1890's 'superior' people discovered that ugliness is beauty. But the modern intellectual is a bigger fool than that. He has discovered that everything is ugly.

Letter to Allanah Harper,
Selected Letters

The nymphs are dead,—Syrinx and Dryope
And that smooth nymph that changed into a tree.
But though the shade, that Æthiopia, sees
Their beauty make more bright its treasuries,

Their amber blood in porphyry veins still grows
Deep in the dark secret of the rose,
Though dust are their bright temples in the heat,
The nymph Parthenope with golden feet.

My glittering fire has turned into a ghost,
My rose is now cold amber and is lost;
Yet from that fire you still could light the sun,
And from that amber, bee-winged motes could come;

Though grown from rocks and trees, dark as Saint Anne,
The little nun-like leaves weep our small span,
And eyeless statues in the garden weep
For Niobe who by the founts doth sleep,

In gardens of a fairy aristocracy
That lead downhill to mountain peaks of sea,
Where people build like beavers on the sand
Among life's common movements, understand

That Troy and Babylon were built with bricks;
They engineer great wells into the Styx
And build hotels upon the peaks of seas
Where the small trivial Dead can sit and freeze.

·   ·   ·   ·   ·   ·   ·   ·   ·   ·

And there, with Fortune, I too sit apart,
Feeling the jewel turn flower, the flower turn heart,
Knowing not goddess's from beggar's bones,
Nor all death's gulf between those semitones.

Elegy On Dead Fashion

Then through the broad green leaves the gardener came
With a basket filled with honeyed fruits of dawn
Plucked from the thickest leaves. They heard him sing
As he walked where that pillared avenue
Of tall clear-fruited ripe trees grew
(For so the Palace seemed); and sweet
His song fled, soft as wind and fleet:

'Now the dawn lights seem
Ripe yellow fruits in a dream
Among the great green leaves
Of dawn and rustling sheaves.

The vast sun's rays like sheaves of wheat
Are gold and dry,
All bound together, growing yet—
An early offering. I

Heard the old King's lullabies
That his nurse, the South Wind, sighs,
As she heaps the honeycombs
Where he lies; the fruit-ripe domes

All around him, clear and sweet . . .
And now the old King's cockscomb crown
Is nodding, falls a-down, a-down . . .
Till the golden sheaves of the sun shall be mown
He will lie in the palace above the wheat.

The dew all tastes of ripening leaves;
Dawn's tendril fingers heap
The yellow honeyed fruits whose clear
Sounds flow into his sleep.

Those yellow fruits and honeycomb . . .
"Lulla-lullaby,"
Shrilled the dew on the broad leaves—
"Time itself must die—
$\qquad$ (—must die)."

Now in the palace the maidens knead
And bake the little loaves of the bread,
Gold as the sun; they sighing said,
"When will the sun begin to seed
And waken the old Dead—
$\qquad$ (—cold Dead)?" '

The Sleeping Beauty, Canto 3

The Little Ghost Who Died For Love

'Fear not, O maidens, shivering
As bunches of the dew-drenched leaves
In the calm moonlight . . . it is the cold sends quivering
My voice, a little nightingale that grieves.

Now Time beats not, and dead Love is forgotten . . .
The spirit too is dead and dank and rotten,

And I forget the moment when I ran
Between my lover and the sworded man—

Blinded with terror lest I lose his heart.
The sworded man dropped, and I saw depart

Love and my lover and my life . . . he fled
And I was strung and hung upon the tree.
It is so cold now that my heart is dead
And drops through time . . . night is too dark to see

110

Him still . . . But it is spring; upon the fruit-boughs of
    your lips,
Young maids, the dew like India's splendour drips;

Pass by among the strawberry beds, and pluck the berries
Cooled by the silver moon; pluck boughs of cherries

That seem the lovely lucent coral bough
(From streams of starry milk those branches grow)
That Cassiopeia feeds with her faint light,
Like Æthiopia ever jewelled bright.

Those lovely cherries do enclose
Deep in their sweet hearts the silver snows,

And the small budding flowers upon the trees
Are filled with sweetness like the bags of bees.

Forget my fate . . . but I, a moonlight ghost,
Creep down the strawberry paths and seek the lost

World, the apothecary at the Fair.
I, Deborah, in my long cloak of brown
Like the small nightingale that dances down
The cherried boughs, creep to the doctor's bare
Booth . . . cold as ivy is the air,

And, where I stand, the brown and ragged light
Holds something still beyond, hid from my sight.

Once, plumaged like the sea, his swanskin head
Had wintry white quills . . . "Hearken to the Dead . . .
I was a nightingale, but now I croak
Like some dark harpy hidden in night's cloak
Upon the walls; among the Dead, am quick;
Oh, give me medicine, for the world is sick;
Not medicines, planet-spotted like fritillaries
For country sins and old stupidities,
Nor potions you may give a country maid
When she is lovesick . . . love in earth is laid,
Grown dead and rotten" . . . so I sank me down,
Poor Deborah in my long cloak of brown.
Though cockcrow marches, crying of false dawns,
Shall bury my dark voice, yet still it mourns

111

Among the ruins—for it is not I
But this old world, is sick and soon must die!'

Her own view of life she set out clearly enough in an article written for
The Spectator:

Modern Values

The dictionary gives the following as one of the definitions of the word 'value': 'the desirability of a thing, especially as compared with other things'.

If one regards modern life with the contemplative eye of an artist, the worth and desirability of much that one sees, especially as compared with other things that one has little hope or chance of seeing, does make one pause and think.

An artist is one whose mind dwells principally in a world which is not wholly visible to the unaided physical sight of the ordinary person, but which is none the less as real as the world of the astronomer (who uses special instruments of vision in order to be in a position to describe it to the ordinary man) and as real as the elemental world of the chemist, who frequently does not see the actual elements of his world at all, but deduces their presence and uses by the reactions of other substances to them.

It is true that even scientists do not always live together in harmony, and have been known to denounce each other with as much acrimony as that with which the ordinary person denounces the artist. But so far as the general public is concerned, scientists are supposed to stand on solid ground, whilst it is notorious that artists live in the clouds, which is perhaps the reason why they are so often expected to live on air. (It is well known that the higher the scientist's fee, no matter in what branch of science he exercises, the more the scientist is respected; whilst, on the other hand, directly an artist gets a living wage for his—or her—work, it is at once assumed that he—or she—has no ideals, and from then on will do bad work. An artist is supposed to be at his best when he starves; in fact, it is regarded as one of his duties to starve—perhaps because that is a means of getting him out of the way more quickly.)

The artist observes many things which are often invisible to, and unsuspected by, the ordinary person. But these things are none the less realities, and the artist has as much right as the scientist to make his deductions and advance his theories about the things which he observes. And the mode of expression of a skilful artist is not any more obscure than the mode of expression of a skilful scientist. Both use images and symbols which are proper to their own needs, but which are not always immediately intelligible to the untrained mind. Thus the artist creates real values, real 'desirabilities', working in a spiritual world, and bringing his values from spiritual sources. How many of these values can be found in the world of today?

Modern values could be summed up in two words—Speed and Money; and both these things have ceased to have any relation to reality, though their attendant evils form a large part of our everyday life. Speed is only useful to me (so far as I can remember at the moment) on two kinds of occasion. The first of these is on the occasion of what is known as speeding the parting guest; and the other occasion is when I myself am going home again, after one of those delightful evenings we all spend in other people's houses sometimes. But even so, I want to get home alive—not dead, nor yet in bits.

So far as I can judge—and I confess that I am a child in these matters—speed as calculated in modern terms means the elimination of most of the senses. The person at the wheel of the speed-record car cannot possibly see very far beyond the tip of his nose, and we all know how such persons were made to appear to us in our childhood. He cannot hear anything excepting the roar of his engine; he cannot smell or taste anything but dust and oil, and his touch becomes a matter of grip. He does not even go anywhere which it takes a complete and ordinary hour of sixty minutes to reach; he just goes somewhere in four—five—or six minutes *at the rate of* some hundred miles an hour. I call this purely fictitious travelling.

Perhaps the day will come when we shall try 'record-living' for fifteen minutes, at the rate of several hundred years an hour. We have surely started the idea in our social pleasures and amusements already. Speed, on the whole then, and as a thing in itself, does not attract me. And now, what about money? I confess that when I do get a little money there are some things about it which I like. But I do not wish it to get beyond my mental grasp; I do not wish to have to think of money in millions. Partly because my wants are simple, and I do not wish to be forced to make them complicated in response to a swollen income, and partly because I think exaggerated money records are quite as mad as exaggerated speed records. Just as I am not impressed by the making of speed records, so I am not impressed by the making, or the holding, of money records. The qualities which go to the making of them, though admirable in themselves, do not appeal to me in this connexion. Endurance, perseverance, concentration and industry, all these things are acknowledged to be virtues, but I do not think they remain virtues *no matter to what object* they are applied.

I cannot see that any real benefit accrues to the world at large, simply because someone has sufficient nervous endurance and concentration to go from one place of no importance to another place of no importance in sixty seconds less time than it took someone else to do the same thing a few weeks before. I do not find anything specially meritorious in the mere fact of going from where you are to somewhere else, even if you do go at lightning speed—any merit to be obtained depends upon what you do when you get there, and so far as I can gather, no one does anything when they get there. They simply come back again, if they are still alive. Nor does it rouse any enthusiasm in me to know that some day in the dim future it may be possible for me to travel during some hours—or days—of deafening roars and explosions from here to Mars. I get into quite enough trouble trying to write about what I see on this earth of ours; goodness only knows what would happen to me if I started writing about any other planet.

In the same way I cannot see that the world in general is benefited by the presence of multi-millionaires. I do not wish multi-millionaires any ill—but, as I say, I cannot take any real interest in them. They come into the category of 'face-value only', and as such have no true meaning for me. They are, to me, much like paper-money, which has no intrinsic value, but is dependent for the esteem in which it is held upon the numbers printed on its surface. It is a long time since I last saw gold sovereigns, but I remember how they looked, and what they felt like, and I remember that there was an impression of concrete reality about them, which it pleases me to look back upon.

Paper-money seems to me now as fictitious as the short journeys taken 'at the rate of' so many miles an hour. Money has no relation to life at present; it has no relation to anything real; it has no true relation to the things which it buys. It has got outside human control altogether; it is a Frankenstein monster dominating the unhappy world which created it. Where Charity once spread a cloak which was permitted to cover venial faults, this Frankenstein monster now offers the one garment which is allowed not only to cover, but to glorify, any kind of mortal sin. Nothing matters if you can spend more money than your neighbour; and if you can spend it in such a way that no one who really needs it benefits by it, then so much the better.

We no longer realize our needs; and our wants, inflated and unbalanced by a perpetual inrush of fevered air, have ceased to bear any relation to any known reality, either material or spiritual.

It seemed a low-hung country of the blind,—
A sensual touch upon the heart and mind;
Like crazy creaking chalets hanging low
From the dark hairiness of bestial skies
The clouds seem, like a potting-shed where grow
The flower-like planets for the gay flower-show:
Gold-freckled calceolarias,
Marigolds, cinerarias,
African marigolds, coarse-frilled,
And cherries, apricots, all chilled
With dew, for thus the bright stars seemed
To cottage windows where none dreamed.
But country gentlemen who, from their birth,
Like kind red strawberries, root deep in earth
And sleep as in the grave, dream far beyond
The sensual aspects of the hairy sky
That something hides, they have forgotten why!
And so they wander, aiming with their gun
At mocking feathered creatures that have learnt
That movement is but groping into life,—
Under rough trees like shepherds' goatish tents.

And only Midsummer's wide country Fair
Seem to them heaven and hell, and earth and air.

The people ride in roundabouts; their hair
Is like the gardens of the Pleiades,
Or the first impulse from which music sprung,
And the dark sound in the smooth growth of trees;
They sparkle like the sea; their love is young
Forever, they are golden as the boy
Who gave an apple smoother than the breeze
To Lady Venus, lovely as the seas;
Their lips are like the gold fires burning Troy.

Like harsh and crackling rags of laughter seems
The music, bright flung as an angel's hair—
Yet awful as the ultimate despair
Of angels and of devils . . . Something dreams
Within the sound that shrieks both high and low
Like some ventriloquist's bright-painted show
On green grass, shrill as anger, dulled as hate:
It shrieks to the dulled soul, 'Too late, too late!'
Sometimes it jangles thin as the sharp wires
Whereon the poor half-human puppets move;
Sometimes it flares in foliage like hell's fires,
Or whispers insincerities for love.
A little hurdy-gurdy waltz sounds hollow
And bright-husked as the hearts of passing people,
Whose talk is only of the growth of plums
And pears: 'Life goes, Death never comes,'
They sigh, while the bright music like a wave
Sings of far lands and many a siren cave.

The Sleeping Beauty, Canto 16

Although she seldom, if ever, admitted to the influence of other poets, Edith Sitwell acknowledged her debt to composers such as Debussy and Ravel:

When I first heard Debussy as a girl it upset me to listen to him. It was like having a squint. Then after a while I got used to it and I began to listen to him all the time.

The Last Years of a Rebel by
Elizabeth Salter

But it was to Stravinsky, more than to any other composer, that she acknowledged her debt. It was in 1920 that Stravinsky came to live in Paris. Diaghilev commissioned him to write a score for his Russian Ballet. Through her brother Sacheverell, Edith met the company when they arrived in London. Their work excited her and she admitted their influence on all artists of their day. To Stravinsky she attributed her 'Dark Song', which, she said, had been inspired by a song of his:

The fire was furry as a bear
And the flames purr . . .
The brown bear rambles in his chain
Captive to cruel men
Through the dark and hairy wood . . .
The maid sighed, 'All my blood
Is animal. They thought I sat
Like a household cat;
But through the dark woods rambled I . . .
Oh, if my blood would die!'
The fire had a bear's fur;
It heard and knew . . .
The dark earth furry as a bear,
Grumbled too!

But the Russian ballet was also responsible for a prose book, Tales From the Russian Ballet, *retold by Edith Sitwell. This extract from her introduction, an example of her prose at its best, shows the extent of her feeling for this art form, her understanding of it and its implications.*

Before the arrival of the first company of the Russian ballet in England, the average person had never dreamt that movement could convey a philosophy of life as complete and rounded as any world could be. We had been galvanised by the vitality of the music-hall stage, but this is often a mechanical life, animating a slightly masked world; or rather, let us say, it is not so much life itself as a distorting mirror of life, in which we see our faces and our natures broadened into a grin—sometimes merely sardonic, sometimes tragic. For underneath the distorted good-humour of the 'turns', heaven knows what bitter hatred may not hide itself. Laughter itself seems mechanical as a switchback; it swings from a height to unutterable depths, and it has the same inevitable movement as the switchback. And the rouge on the laughing masks is, from time to time, not a little like blood. Thus, under the violent rays of a many-coloured sun, that dissects our hypocrisies bone from bone, we move somnambulently through this mirror-bright world, and cling into some mournful patterning; while the harsh mordant music strips off our flesh and shows us, marionettes that we are, clothed only in our primal lust. Performing animals mimic our tricks, our poor impertinences against the Infinite, such as we mimic those of a higher order of being; and we feel a vague unhappiness. We know that the red volcano mouths of these women posturing before us, are one with the life that burned Troy; but they have forgotten that, long ago, now that

> Brain has changed the old Obscene
> Into a complicate machine
> With breasts to feed the starry nation
> With milk of cold imagination . . .

And now we, too, have almost forgotten. Life is a perpetual Can-Can, and underneath the rays of the stage, seas, buildings, gush from the crude, blue planes and cubes of faces as though they were fiery astral manes. This terrible gaiety is nothing but a rope ladder up which we must climb to escape from bottomless pits. But in what air and under what skies we shall find ourselves when we have climbed to the topmost rung of that ladder, I dare not guess.

Then came the Russian ballet, and with it, our clearer philosophy. These movements, and the bright shrilling of the colour which is part of their speech, are an interpretation, not of a mood alone, but often of life itself. Seen with the clearness of a dream, these bright magical movements have, now the intense vitality of the heart of life, now the rigidity of death; and for speech they have the more universal and larger language of music, interpreting still more clearly these strange beings whose life is so intense, yet to whom living, seen from the outside, is but a brief and tragic happiness upon the greenest grass, in some unknown flashing summer weather. 'Dames qui tournaient sur les terrasses voisines de la mer, enfantes et géantes, superbes, noires dans la mousse vert-de-gris, bijoux debout sur le sol gras des bosquets et des jardinets dégelés, jeunes mères et sœurs aux regards pleins de pèlerinages, sultanes, princesses de démarche et de costumes tyranniques, petites étrangères et personnes doucement malheureuses,'[1] all these pass before our eyes, sometimes building sand-castles upon the shores of eternity, sometimes chasing the music like butterflies in the ephemeral life of the stage. For indeed, their tragedies seem but the tragedy of two painted butterflies who, intent upon their play, have floated all unawares into the courts of Hell. Strange eyes may stare at them, 'simian faces, green flowers streaked with encre de chine' look askance at them chattering in an unknown tongue; they may float through those jewelled green gardens for ever—but they scarcely care, and we care not at all. Life is so ephemeral. Their tragedies pierce us, yet leave no scar, for we understand them only as children understand; we are protected by our own individuality—so unalterably different from theirs; and all the while we are as remote from the world in which these alien beings move as are the children dressed in mourning of whom Arthur Rimbaud writes in his prose poem, 'Après le Déluge'; like these, 'from our great glass house we look at the marvellous pictures.' So we sit, in the loneliness of identity, watching the movements growing and ripening like fruit, or curling with the fantastic inevitability of waves seen by a Chinese painter; and thought is never absent from these ballets. In *Petrouchka* we see mirrored for us, in those clear sharp outlines and movements, all the philosophy of Laforgue, as the puppets move somnambulently through the dark of our hearts. For this ballet, alone among them all, shatters our glass house about our ears and leaves us terrified, haunted by its tragedy. The music, harsh, crackling rags of laughter, shrieks at us like some brightly-painted Punch and Judy show, upon grass as shrill as anger, as dulled as hate. Sometimes it jangles thin as the wires on which those half-human puppets move; or a little hurdy-gurdy valse sounds hollow, with the emptiness of the hearts of the passing people, 'vivant de can-cans de clochers, disant: "Quel temps fera-t-il demain," "Voici l'hiver qui vient," "Nous n'avons pas eu de prunes cette année".'[2] But sometimes the music has terrible moments of darkness, as when the Magician gropes in the booth for his puppet Petrouchka. And there is one short march, quick and terrible, in which the drum-taps are nothing but the anguished beat of the clown's heart as he makes his endless battle against materialism. And we know that we are watching our own tragedy. Do we not all know that little room at the

[1] Arthur Rimbaud
[2] Laforgue: *Les Moralités Légendaires*

back of our poor clown's booth—that little room with the hopeful tinsel stars and the badly-painted ancestral portrait of God? Have we not all battered our heads through the flimsy paper walls—only to find blackness? In the dead Petrouchka, we know that it is our own poor wisp of soul that is weeping so pitifully to us from the top of the booth, outside life for ever, with no one to warm him or comfort him, while the bright-coloured rags that were the clown's body lie, stabbed to the heart, in the mire of the street—and, with Claudius, we cry out for 'Lights, lights, more lights.'

In *Parade* again (whose tall lodging-houses with black windows hide from us, perhaps nothingness, perhaps half-human creatures, landladies scuttling like crabs) that white blankness of sea, as seen through the portals of the travelling theatre, that mechanism of showmen (all cubes of houses and no flesh) and the lonely child-dancer playing upon the sand to the sound of the wheezing wind's harmonium—this gives us the eery loneliness of each identity. The wheezing wind's harmonium oozes out cold memories of ancient ragtime tunes; they are blown hither and thither, whirling quick and light and inhuman, looking for the dancing lovers whom we shall never see . . . but the salt water has got into these ragtimes, till they are dead out of tune, no longer human and warm; and we are tired and not a little frightened by these exteriors—always exteriors. The Chinese mandarin in his red and gold dress is blown in upon us by the cold wind, increasing our sense of segregation; and our Pegasus itself becomes like the broken-kneed horse, tattered with age, that, flapping in the breeze, blows through the portals of the travelling theatre. And the actors themselves are even more chilled and pitiable than we, for they are outside life for ever, in some deserted pleasure-land. They beckon, but there is no one to come, for nobody realises that these turns upon the sand are merely a foretaste of what we should enjoy if we dared venture through those vast portals and become part of the white blankness that seems to our limited vision like some endless sea . . . Our brains echo with the words 'There is nothing beyond; we have seen all there is to see' . . . The audience has been blown away, or perhaps has never been; everything is as empty as the tunes that blow in and out of the wind's inconsequent mind; and all the while these poor players have played their tricks for the benefit of nothingness . . . This world is a pitiful catchpenny.

Two of these ballets deal with the life of a child—the ballet which is the subject of this essay, and another, *La Boutique Fantasque*; but, in this latter, we do not find a chart of the child's limitless mind, as realised by itself, but a little bright-coloured corner as realised by the grown-up person.

When the curtain is raised, we find ourselves in the afternoon of a hot day, and, leaving the steamer in which we have crossed the lake, we pass through dark leaves and great mauve cactus flowers dripping with sleep, and walk upon a broad pathway beside the lake . . . What is this toy-shop in which we find ourselves suddenly; or does it really exist? The younger of the two shopmen, with his queer, sly silence, and his fantastic movements curling with the inevitability of a wave—he only covets these pennies because they will bring him closer to being human. He fawns upon these Real People in their loud clothes glazed by the heat; for how real vulgarity makes them: perhaps they will help him to be real also. And these dolls, too, dancing to tunes that are happy and blatant and yellow as calceolarias —how they covet humanity; how they long to alter the heart-strings that are only the echoes of the worn-out and jangling strings of a piano on some hot afternoon; how they long to alter the brains that are nothing but little musical-boxes, tinkling out a little vacant tune.

In the ballet, *Children's Tales*, there is no fierce movement of life against a fairy tale that knowledge has turned to tragedy—only life as seen by the eyes of a child—life as rounded, cool and clear as the cheek of an apple. The very name *Children's Tales* evokes memories of nursery afternoons when we listened to the Snow's little old musical box, giving out half-forgotten tunes; afternoons when our old nurse told us stories that fell with the same tinkling notes as the Snow's tunes . . . 'Long ago, and once upon a time'. But these tales of the Ballet are warm as summer itself, are as rounded and glowing as fruit.

Stravinsky, Debussy, Ravel, Matisse, Picasso—these were names too important to be bandied about by the 'culture vultures' of society. Edith Sitwell began to understand that London, which had offered her freedom, was also a threat. To keep her individuality intact, she knew that she must reject the invasion of materialism. Her target now became the prosaic, the worldly, and above all the false, epitomized by Bohemia 1922:

Who were the Bohemians of former days?

David had certain of the peculiarities of a Bohemian. But he was a good king, and the father of Solomon, who was a great poet.

Lucrezia Borgia, I think, was a Bohemian. Yes, I think she may be included in our list. And she had beauty.

Nell Gwynn was one. And she had wit.

Verlaine, Swinburne (in one sense of the word) and William Morris were Bohemians. And they had genius.

Whom have we today? My goodness! *Miss Tomkins and Little Mr Smithers.*

Bohemians began to go downhill in the 'nineties, what with bad poetry of a limp but neat description, and drinking coffee at cab-shelters. The fact is that the minute a habit ceases to be natural and becomes *voulu*, it becomes, also, a bore; and Bohemianism in these days was becoming *voulu*.

But never in their wildest dreams could the Bohemians of the 'nineties, however weak-kneed, have dreamt of the horrors of today, of the 'smart' Bohemians, of the little tight hens' heads, giggling and pecking at great reputations, at all the idle admiring chatter which, if we would let it, would spoil the new art for us.

'Are There Still Bohemians?' *Daily Chronicle*, 1923

Life in this epoch has become a too-familiar gesture; the soul is a midwife perpetually assisting at the birth of usefulness, and there is nowhere to go, for all the ways are known. The 'musicians of silence' are dead, and I do not like reading the books of the time, for they are too loud; they shout in my ear till I am nearly deafened.

This was my complaint as I walked down Bond Street on a hot and gilded day. Where the shadows fell like dark agates falling through water, the street became transformed into a sparsely growing, dwarf Japanese forest. How sand-like was the gold light beneath those large black leaves of the shadow; it lay, that dusty gold, untouched by any air, in the clear mirage noon! With hard faces round as dead-sea fruit carved in cornelian, men walked by . . .

Red and white lacquer Chinoiserie ghosts were driving on their way to Bohea and the latest philosophy and the latest religion . . . Yet what, I ask myself, would they do if they were confronted suddenly with the realities which have been served up for them like exotic fruits? They would be terrified as a negro king seeing for the first time the delicate, the evanescent, the so-unexplainable and untouchable snow. They would be struck silent by the cold of the spirit, that is not like the cold of any winter they have known (muted winds singing Palestrina, snows falling like little tunes on the Virginals—that instrument whose tinkling sound is bright, sour and unripe as budding fruit-point lace hanging from the trees, women like little ermines walking between dark bushes that bear only the pearl-berries of the snow, under skies that are like the bitter, gilded rind of some rare and unattainable fruit).

Readers and Writers, 1922

When the hot gilded day will reach
A restful close,
A Japanese dwarf forest on the beach,
With dark trees of the shadow, the street grows.
How sand-like quivers the gold light
Under the large black leaves of shadow; mirage-bright
It lies, that dusty gold,
Untouched of any air;
Like Dead Sea fruit carved in cornelian, bold,
The faces of a man and Pleasure's mournful daughter

Show lovely in the light, a moment flare,
Then shadows fall again—dark agates through clear water.

Then these Chinoiseries, old ghosts of red and white
Smooth lacquer, in their palanquins take flight

For tea, and the last esoteric rage
Whose plumes may soften age, that harpy's cage.

Their smile is like Death's trap . . . a little gilded dust
Of valueless beauty from the sun soon must

Brush, for a fading while, each feathered cheek
That paradisal airs will never sleek—

And round them, as they move, the unfading sea, Eternity,
With its cool feathered airs of beauty, sighs of no horizons they can
    see.

What would these ghosts do, if the truths they know,
That were served up like snow-cold jewelled fruits
And the enfeathered airs of lutes,
Could be their guests in cold reality?

They would be shivering,
Wide-eyed as a Negro king
Seeing the evanescent mirage snow—
They would be silenced by the cold
That is of the spirit, endlessly
Unfabled and untold.

The swan's-breath winter these have known is finer
Fading than the early snows of China,

The poems of Queen Marguerite of Navarre
(Narcissus-petalled, perfumed like a star),

Or the Pleiades' citron-scented poems, fading like the snows,
Perfuming their long fingers till their eyelids close.

The winters these have known have been too kind,
With skies that seemed the bitter gilded rind

Of unattainable fruits; small women go
As white as ermines, and small winds are slow

As tunes upon a lute; the point-lace on the trees
And the pearl-berries of the snow upon dark bushes freeze,

And the snow falls, as sharp and bright, unripe and sour,
As the budding grapes' bright perfume or the sweet grape-flower.

The daughters of the Silence now are dead,
And these Chinoiserie ghosts,
These mummies in dim hosts,
Tread the long mournful avenues instead;
Alarm the soul by their cold interest—
For what can be the purpose of their quest?

When spring begins, in China and Tibet
Through bell'd lime-avenues a springe is set
To catch the softly-smiling wind,
The cherubim to catch and blind
As cruel men blind a singing-bird;
They trap them with the sound of lutes
And the softest smiles of fruits,
That these old ghosts may prove the feathered creatures real to hold,
And make them sing upon a perch of gold
In cages with a foolish bell-hung gable,
Amid the powders on their dressing-table;
Till, trapped by our mortality, they die, and their small bones,
Sounding as sweetly as the west wind's tones,
Are sold because they sound like a small music-box;
Their slayers sell for silver the bright plumes in flocks,
To make the pillows for a sleepy head
That never dreams of heaven, but the lonely Dead.

And still they dwindle the bright world down to the gilded glooms
Of dust, these mummies, hieing, harrying fast
The Soul, their quarry, through the deserted tombs—
Or lying, lotus-eaters in a dreamful ease,
Perfuming their cold lips with silence and the past
Beneath the Asian darkness of smooth trees . . .
Thus spoke the men; then sleep came colder than the rose
Blooming in desolation . . . No one knows
The end there is to dust—it is the soul that shall survive them at the
    last.

The Sleeping Beauty, Canto 17

At the sight of these Chinoiserie ghosts, I want to leave this dwarf forest, and to exist in the perfume of an early literature that is half forgotten—poems that fade like the snows of China; the citron-smelling poems of Queen Marguerite of Navarre; the starry narcissus of the Pleiade, falling softly as music ('Jonquilles dont on fit les cils purs de tant de blondes filles'). For I should be safe there, and alone.

These Chinoiseries would never pursue their chase through the tombs. But indeed I am terrified by the new and mysterious interest that these people take in the spirit . . . for where may it not lead us? Those men of the species who are drawn to the hunting of big game may, suddenly, travel into the plains of Thibet and of China, and there, in avenues of lime trees where the wind sounds like that forgotten seventeenth-century court instrument the Chapeau Chinas, they will shoot cherubim—to prove their reality! . . .

But perhaps this will not happen, for I think there is very little left to sell, or to explore in this age. Springes for dreams have been set up in all the avenues of the wind; these poor feathered creatures are caught and dissected in every laboratory of science; yet in literature, which should be the aviary wherein they are preened and comforted, they are, on the contrary, disliked and suspected . . .

As for myself, it is time for me to be gone; for I am essentially 'de l'Outre-tombe; et pas de commissions'!

Readers and Writers, 1922

1922-1929

One of the reasons for which I was made was to give 'Public suscepti-
bilities' a good shaking, and, if possible, to get them on their feet
instead of on their heads.

Selected Letters

It was in 1922 that I wrote *Façade*, the then much derided poems for which nobody else is in the least to blame. William Walton and I were in closer collaboration than is usual when poems are set to music, because he was then sharing a house with my two brothers. The idea that we should collaborate originated with them and the first performance took place privately and peacefully at their house in January, 1922.

But in June, 1923, the first public performance, at the Aeolian Hall, was anything but peaceful. Never, I should think, was a larger and more imposing shower of brickbats hurled at any new work. These missiles have now been exchanged for equally large and imposing bouquets. But at that time there was not a bouquet to be seen. Indeed, the attitude of certain of the audience was so threatening that I was warned to stay on the platform, hidden by the curtain, until they got tired of waiting for me and went home.

Certain newspaper critics, enraged and alarmed by the performance, rushed from the hall and, lassoing a passing postman, asked him what he thought. Dashing back to the hall they waylaid a fireman and anxiously asked his opinion. These modern substitutes for the Delphic Oracle replied promptly, and in no uncertain terms. They opined that we were mad.

Taken Care Of

With the performance in the Aeolian Hall the greatest of the Sitwell controversies had begun.

The attack was led by a talented young actor-writer, Noël Coward, who discovered in Façade *food for satire abounding.*

'The Swiss Family Whittlebot, an accurate if uncharitable send-up of a family of contemporary poets', made its appearance in a Revue called London Calling. *This was followed by a reading on the radio by Mr Noël Coward of Miss Hernia Whittlebot's poems; sandwiched in between Chamber Music and a talk by the secretary of the Folk Dance Society on The Sword Dance Through the Ages. Later Miss Whittlebot*

herself began to make regular appearances in the gossip columns, to which Noël would feed such information as 'Hernia is busy preparing for publication of her new book, Gilded Sluts and Garbage. *She breakfasts on onions and Vichy Water'* (A Talent To Amuse *by Sheridan Morley).*

Edith Sitwell replied:

The fierce light that beats upon the throne is nothing to that which shows up Mr Coward.

Indeed such are the illuminations of his advertisement that he bears a strong resemblance to Piccadilly Circus at night-time. But I admire, particularly, those photographs taken of him in the morning, looking more than ever like the lilies and langours of virtue, sipping his breakfast and obviously about to break into one of those heart breaking brittle little ditties (sung in a voice with a catch in it) in which an elephantine wit lumbers and scampers breathlessly after an emotion frail and destructive as a clothes moth.

Sunday Referee, 10 April 1936

Another feud had begun; another chance to sharpen her claws, this time on the far from wooden head of Noël Coward, who was now bracketed with Alfred Noyes as a literary antagonist. But, however sharp the claws, the pain of failure was sharper. Edith Sitwell's reaction to the hostility roused by Façade *was to retire to bed with an attack of jaundice. For the first and perhaps the only time in her life, she listened to the counsel of caution:*

I am feeling miserably disappointed. I've seen Osbert who tells me it is impossible for me to do *Façade* at Oxford . . . he says that after *London Calling,* I cannot risk it, as probably little Coward's supporters (being far in excess of intelligent people in number) would flock to the performance to insult me, and that it would be too undignified to expose oneself to it.

Letter to Harold Acton,
Selected Letters

Years later, after Coward's apology had been received and accepted, she gave her own explanation for 'a work of gaiety' at which 'the audience was meant to laugh' but which was also the result of technical experiments on the part of an artist totally serious in relation to her craft.

At the time I began to write, a change in the direction, imagery, and rhythms in poetry had become necessary, owing to the rhythmical flaccidity, the verbal deadness, the dead and expected patterns, of some of the poetry immediately preceding us.

Rhythm is one of the principal translators between dream and reality. Rhythm might be described as, to the world of sound, what light is to the world of sight. It shapes and gives new meaning.

The poems in *Façade* are *abstract* poems—that is, they are patterns in sound. They are too, in many cases, virtuoso exercises in technique of an extreme difficulty, in the same sense as that in which certain studies by Liszt are studies in transcendental technique in music.

My experiments in *Façade* consist of inquiries into the effect on rhythm and on speed of the use of rhymes, assonances, and dissonances, placed at the beginning and in the middle of lines, as well as at the end, and in most elaborate patterns. I experimented, too, with the effect upon speed of the use of equivalent syllables—a system that produces great variation.

Some Notes On My Own Poetry

Hornpipe

Sailors come
To the drum
Out of Babylon;
    Hobby-horses
Foam, the dumb
Sky rhinoceros-glum

Watched the courses of the breakers' rocking-horses and with Glaucis,
Lady Venus on the settee of the horsehair sea!
Where Lord Tennyson in laurels wrote a gloria free,
In a borealic iceberg came Victoria; she
Knew Prince Albert's tall memorial took the colours of the floreal
And the borealic iceberg; floating on they see
New-arisen Madam Venus for whose sake from far
Came the fat and zebra'd emperor from Zanzibar
Where like golden bouquets lay far Asia, Africa, Cathay,
All laid before that shady lady by the fibroid Shah.
Captain Fracasse stout as any water-butt came, stood

131

With Sir Bacchus both a-drinking the black tarr'd grapes' blood
Plucked among the tartan leafage
By the furry wind whose grief age
Could not wither—like a squirrel with a gold star-nut.
Queen Victoria sitting shocked upon the rocking-horse
Of a wave said to the Laureate, 'This minx of course
Is as sharp as any lynx and blacker-deeper than the drinks and quite as
Hot as any hottentot, without remorse!
                    For the minx,'
                        Said she,
                    'And the drinks,
                        You can see,
Are hot as any hottentot and not the goods for me!'

Mariner Man

'What are you staring at, mariner man,
Wrinkled as sea-sand and old as the sea?'
'Those trains will run over their tails, if they can,
Snorting and sporting like porpoises! Flee
The burly, the whirligig wheels of the train,
As round as the world and as large again,
Running half the way over the Babylon, down
Through fields of clover to gay Troy town—
A-puffing their smoke as grey as the curl
On my forehead as wrinkled as sands of the sea!—
But what can that matter to you, my girl?
(And what can that matter to me?)'

Trio for Two Cats and a Trombone

Long steel grass—
The white soldiers pass—
The light is braying like an ass.
See
The tall Spanish jade
With hair black as nightshade

Worn as a cockade!
Flee
Her eyes' gasconade
And her gown's parade
(As stiff as a brigade).
Tee-hee!
The hard and braying light
Is zebra'd black and white,
It will take away the slight
And free
Tinge of the mouth-organ sound,
(Oyster-stall notes) oozing round
Her flounces as they sweep the ground.
The
Trumpet and the drum
And the martial cornet come
To make the people dumb—
But we
Won't wait for sly-foot night
(Moonlight, watered milk-white, bright)
To make clear the declaration
Of our Paphian vocation,
Beside the castanetted sea,
Where stalks Il Capitaneo
Swaggart braggadocio
Sword and mustachio—
He
Is green as a cassada
And his hair is an armada.
To the jade 'Come kiss me harder'
He called across the battlements as she
Heard our voices thin and shrill
As the steely grasses' thrill,
Or the sound of the onycha
When the phoca has the pica
In the palace of the Queen Chinee!

'Through gilded trellises
Of the heat, Dolores,
Inez, Manuccia,
Isabel, Lucia,
Mock Time that flies.
"Lovely bird, will you stay and sing,
Flirting your sheenèd wing—
Peck with your beak and cling
To our balconies?"
They flirt their fans, flaunting—
"O silence, enchanting
As music!" then slanting
Their eyes,
Like gilded or emerald grapes,
They take mantillas, capes,
Hiding their simian shapes.
Sighs
Each lady, "Our spadille
Is done . . . Dance the quadrille
From Hell's towers to Seville;
Surprise
Their siesta," Dolores
Said. Through gilded trellises
Of the heat, spangles
Pelt down through the tangles
Of bell-flowers; each dangles
Her castanets, shutters
Fall while the heat mutters,
With sounds like a mandoline
Or tinkled tambourine . . .
Ladies, Time dies!'

The Sleeping Beauty, Canto 19

Lullaby for Jumbo

Jumbo asleep!
Grey leaves thick-furred
As his ears, keep
Conversations blurred.

Thicker than hide
Is the trumpeting water;
Don Pasquito's bride
And his youngest daughter
Watch the leaves
Elephantine grey:
What is it grieves
In the torrid day?
Is it the animal
World that snores
Harsh and inimical
In sleepy pores?—
And why should the spined flowers
Red as a soldier
Make Don Pasquito
Seem still mouldier?

Black Mrs Behemoth

In a room of the palace
Black Mrs Behemoth
Gave way to wroth
And the wildest malice.
Cried Mrs Behemoth,
'Come, court lady,
Doomed like a moth,
Through palace rooms shady!'
The candle flame
Seemed a yellow pompion,
Sharp as a scorpion;
Nobody came . . .
Only a bugbear
Air unkind,
That bud-furred papoose,
The young spring wind,
Blew out the candle.
Where is it gone?
To flat Coromandel
Rolling on!

I Do Like To Be Beside The Seaside

When
        Don
Pasquito arrived at the seaside
Where the donkey's hide tide brayed, he
Saw the banditto Jo in a black cape
Whose slack shape waved like the sea—
Thetis wrote a treatise noting wheat is silver
    like the sea; the lovely cheat is sweet as
    foam; Erotis notices that she
            Will
            Steal
            The
Wheat-king's luggage, like Babel
Before the League of Nations grew—
So Jo put the luggage and the label
In the pocket of Flo the Kangaroo.
Through trees like rich hotels that bode
Of dreamless ease fled she,
Carrying the load and goading the road
Through the marine scene to the sea.
'Don Pasquito, the road is eloping
With your luggage, though heavy and large;
You must follow and leave your moping
Bride to my guidance and charge!'

When
        Don
Pasquito returned from the road's end,
Where vanilla-coloured ladies ride
From Sevilla, his mantilla'd bride and young
    friend
Were forgetting their mentor and guide.
For the lady and her friend from Le Touquet
In the very shady trees upon the sand
Were plucking a white satin bouquet
Of foam, while the sand's brassy band
Blared in the wind. Don Pasquito
Hid where the leaves drip with sweet . . .

But a word stung him like a mosquito . . .
For what they hear, they repeat!

Tarantella

Where the satyrs are chattering, nymphs with their flattering
Glimpse of the forest enhance
All the beauty of marrow and cucumber narrow
And Ceres will join in the dance.
Where the satyrs can flatter the flat-leaved fruit
And the gherkin green and the marrow,
Said Queen Venus, 'Silenus, we'll settle between us
The gourd and the cucumber narrow.'
See, like palaces hid in the lake, they shake—
Those greenhouses shot by her arrow!
The gardener seizes the pieces like Croesus, for gilding the
    potting-shed barrow.
There the radish roots,
And the strawberry fruits
Feel the nymphs' high boots in the glade.
Trampling and sampling mazurkas, cachucas and turkas,
Cracoviaks hid in the shade
Where in the haycocks the country nymphs' gay flocks
Wear gowns that are looped over bright yellow petticoats,
Gaiters of leather and pheasants' tail feathers
In straw hats bewildering many a leathern bat.
There, they haymake, cowers and whines in showers
The dew in the dogskin bright flowers;
Pumpkin and marrow
And cucumber narrow
Have grown through the spangled June hours.
Melons as dark as caves have for their fountain waves
Thickest gold honey. And wrinkled as dark as Pan,
Or old Silenus, yet youthful as Venus
Are gourds and the wrinkled figs
Whence all the jewels ran.

Said Queen Venus, 'Silenus
We'll settle between us
The nymphs' disobedience, forestall
With my bow and my quiver
Each fresh evil liver:
For I don't understand it at all!'

Country Dance

That hobnailed goblin, the bobtailed Hob,
Said, 'It is time I began to rob.'
For strawberries bob, hob-nob with the pearls
Of cream (like the curls of the dairy girls),
And flushed with the heat and fruitish-ripe
Are the gowns of the maids who dance to the pipe.
Chase a maid?
She's afraid!
'Go gather a bob-cherry kiss from a tree,
But don't, I prithee, come bothering me!'
She said
As she fled.
The snouted satyrs drink clouted cream
'Neath the chestnut-trees as thick as a dream;
So I went,
And I leant,
Where none but the doltish coltish wind
Nuzzled my hand for what it could find.
As it neighed,
I said,
'Don't touch me, sir, don't touch me, I say!
You'll tumble my strawberries into the hay.'
Those snow-mounds of silver that bee, the spring,
Has sucked his sweetness from, I will bring
With fair-haired plants and with apples chill
For the great god Pan's high altar . . . I'll spill
Not one!

So, in fun,
We rolled on the grass and began to run
Chasing that gaudy satyr the Sun;
Over the haycocks, away we ran
Crying, 'Here be berries as sunburnt as Pan!'
But Silenus
Has seen us . . .
He runs like the rough satyr Sun.

                              Come away!

Polka

'Tra la la la la la la la
La
La!
    See me dance the polka,'
Said Mr Wagg like a bear,
'With my top-hat
And my whiskers that—
(Tra la la la) trap the Fair.

Where the waves seem chiming haycocks
I dance the polka; there
Stand Venus' children in their gay frocks,—
Maroon and marine,—and stare

To see me fire my pistol
Through the distance blue as my coat;
Like Wellington, Byron, the Marquis of Bristol,
Buzbied great trees float.

While the wheezing hurdy-gurdy
Of the marine wind blows me
To the tune of "Annie Rooney", sturdy,
Over the sheafs of the sea;

And bright as a seedsman's packet
With zinnias, candytufts chill,
Is Mrs Marigold's jacket
As she gapes at the inn door still,

Where at dawn in the box of the sailor,
Blue as the decks of the sea,
Nelson awoke, crowed like the cocks,
Then back to the dust sank he.

And Robinson Crusoe
Rues so
The bright and foxy beer,—
But he finds fresh isles in a Negress' smiles,—
The poxy doxy dear,

As they watch me dance the polka,'
Said Mr Wagg like a bear,
'In my top-hat and my whiskers that,—
Tra la la la, trap the Fair.

Tra la la la la—
Tra la la la la—
Tra la la la la la la la la
La
La
La!'

Four in the Morning

Cried the navy-blue ghost
Of Mr Belaker
The allegro Negro cocktail-shaker,
'Why did the cock crow,
Why am I lost,
Down the endless road to Infinity toss'd?
The tropical leaves are whispering white
As water; I race the wind in my flight.
The white lace houses are carried away
By the tide; far out they float and sway.
White is the nursemaid on the parade.
Is she real, as she flirts with me unafraid?
I raced through the leaves as white as water . . .
Ghostly, flowed over the nursemaid, caught her,
Left her . . . edging the far-off sand

Is the foam of the sirens' Metropole and Grand.
And along the parade I am blown and lost,
Down the endless road to Infinity toss'd.
The guinea-fowl-plumaged houses sleep . . .
On one, I saw the lone grass weep,
Where only the whimpering greyhound wind
Chased me, raced me, for what it could find.'
And there in the black and furry boughs
How slowly, coldly, old Time grows,
Where the pigeons smelling of gingerbread,
And the spectacled owls so deeply read,
And the sweet ring-doves of curded milk
Watch the Infanta's gown of silk
In the ghost-room tall where the governante
Gesticulates lente, and walks andante.
'Madam, Princesses must be obedient;
For a medicine now becomes expedient,—
Of five ingredients,—a diapente,'
Said the governante, fading lente . . .
In at the window then looked he,
The navy-blue ghost of Mr Belaker,
The allegro Negro cocktail-shaker,—
And his flattened face like the moon saw she,—
Rhinoceros-black (a flowing sea!).

Waltz

Daisy and Lily,
Lazy and silly,
Walk by the shore of the wan grassy sea,—
Talking once more 'neath a swan-bosomed tree.
Rose castles,
Tourelles,
Those bustles
Where swells
Each foam-bell of ermine,
They roam and determine
What fashions have been and what fashions will be,—

What tartan leaves born,
What crinolines worn.
By Queen Thetis,
Pelisses
Of tarlatine blue,
Like the thin plaided leaves that the castle crags grew;
Or velours d'Afrande:
On the water-gods' land
Her hair seemed gold trees on the honey-cell sand
When the thickest gold spangles, on deep water seen,
Were like twanging guitar and like cold mandoline,
And the nymphs of great caves,
With hair like gold waves
Of Venus, wore tarlatine.
Louise and Charlottine
(Boreas' daughters)
And the nymphs of deep waters,
The nymph Taglioni, Grisi the ondine,
Wear plaided Victoria and thin Clementine
Like the crinolined waterfalls;
Wood-nymphs wear bonnets, shawls;
Elegant parasols
Floating were seen.
The Amazons wear balzarine of jonquille
Beside the blond lace of a deep-falling rill;
Through glades like a nun
They run from and shun
The enormous and gold-rayed rustling sun;
And the nymphs of the fountains
Descend from the mountains
Like elegant willows
On their deep barouche pillows,
In cashmere Alvandar, barège Isabelle,
Like bells of bright water from clearest wood-well.
Our élégantes favouring bonnets of blond,
The stars in their apiaries,
Sylphs in their aviaries,
Seeing them, spangle these, and the sylphs fond
From their aviaries fanned

With each long fluid hand
The manteaux espagnoles,
Mimic the waterfalls
Over the long and the light summer land.

.   .   .   .

So Daisy and Lily,
Lazy and silly,
Walk by the shore of the wan grassy sea,
Talking once more 'neath a swan-bosomed tree.
Rose castles,
Tourelles,
Those bustles!
Mourelles
Of the shade in their train follow.
Ladies, how vain,—hollow,—
Gone is the sweet swallow,—
Gone, Philomel!

Popular Song

Lily O'Grady,
Silly and shady,
Longing to be
A lazy lady,
Walked by the cupolas, gables in the
Lake's Georgian stables,
In a fairy tale like the heat intense,
And the mist in the woods when across the fence
The children gathering strawberries
Are changed by the heat into Negresses,
Though their fair hair
Shines there
Like gold-haired planets, Calliope, Io,
Pomona, Antiope, Echo, and Clio.
Then Lily O'Grady,
Silly and shady,
Sauntered along like a
Lazy lady.

143

Beside the waves' haycocks her gown with tucks
Was of satin the colour of shining green ducks,
And her fol-de-rol
Parasol
Was a great gold sun o'er the haycocks shining,
But she was a Negress black as the shade
That time on the brightest lady laid.
Then a satyr, dog-haired as trunks of trees,
Began to flatter, began to tease,
And she ran like the nymphs with golden foot
That trampled the strawberry, buttercup root,
In the thick gold dew as bright as the mesh
Of dead Panope's golden flesh,
Made from the music whence were born
Memphis and Thebes in the first hot morn,
—And ran, to wake
In the lake,
Where the water-ripples seem hay to rake.
And Adeline,
Charlottine,
Round rose-bubbling Victorine,
And the other fish
Express a wish
For mastic mantles and gowns with a swish;
And bright and slight as the posies
Of buttercups and of roses,
And buds of the wild wood-lilies
They chase her, as frisky as fillies.
The red retriever-haired satyr
Can whine and tease her and flatter,
But Lily O'Grady,
Silly and shady,
In the deep shade is a lazy lady;
Now Pompey's dead, Homer's read,
Heliogabalus lost his head,
And shade is on the brightest wing,
And dust forbids the bird to sing.

Jodelling Song

We bear velvet cream,
Green and babyish
Small leaves seem; each stream
Horses' tails that swish,

And the chimes remind
Us of sweet birds singing,
Like the jangling bells
On rose-trees ringing.

Man must say farewell
To parents now,
And to William Tell,
And Mrs Cow.

Man must say farewells
To storks and Bettes,
And to roses' bells,
And statuettes.

Forests white and black
In spring are blue
With forget-me-nots,
And to lovers true

Still the sweet bird begs
And tries to cozen
Them: 'Buy angels' eggs
Sold by the dozen.'

Gone are clouds like inns
On the gardens' brinks,
And the mountain djinns,—
Ganymede sells drinks;

While the days seem grey
And his heart of ice,
Grey as chamois, or
The edelweiss,

And the mountain streams
Like cowbells sound—

Tirra lirra, drowned
In the waiter's dreams

Who has gone beyond
The forest waves,
While his true and fond
Ones seek their graves.

Scotch Rhapsody

'Do not take a bath in Jordan,

                  Gordon,

On the holy Sabbath, on the peaceful day!'
Said the huntsman, playing on his old bagpipe,
Boring to death the pheasant and the snipe—
Boring the ptarmigan and grouse for fun—
Boring them worse than a nine-bore gun.
Till the flaxen leaves where the prunes are ripe
Heard the tartan wind a-droning in the pipe,
And they heard MacPherson say:
'Where do the waves go? What hotels
Hide their bustles and their gay ombrelles?
And would there be room?—Would there be *room*?
    Would there be room for me?'
There is a hotel at Ostend
Cold as the wind, without an end,
Haunted by ghostly poor relations˙
Of Bostonian conversations
(Bagpipes rotting through the walls).
And there the pearl-ropes fall like shawls
With a noise like marine waterfalls.
And 'Another little drink wouldn't do us any harm'
Pierces through the Sabbatical calm.
And that is the place for me!
So do not take a bath in Jordan,

                  Gordon,

On the holy Sabbath, on the peaceful day—
Or you'll never go to heaven, Gordon MacPherson,

And speaking purely as a private person
That is the place—*that* is the place—that is the *place* for me!

✵

Fox Trot

Old
　　Sir
　　　　Faulk,
Tall as a stork,
Before the honeyed fruits of dawn were ripe, would walk
And stalk with a gun
The reynard-coloured sun,
Among the pheasant-feathered corn the unicorn has torn, forlorn the
Smock-faced sheep
Sit
　　And
　　　　Sleep;
Periwigged as William and Mary, weep . . .
'Sally, Mary, Mattie, what's the matter, why cry?'
The huntsman and the reynard-coloured sun and I sigh;
'Oh, the nursery-maid Meg
With a leg like a peg
Chased the feathered dreams like hens, and when they laid an egg
In the sheepskin
Meadows
Where
The serene King James would steer
Horse and hounds, then he
From the shade of a tree
Picked it up as spoil to boil for nursery tea,' said the mourners. In the
Corn, towers strain,
Feathered tall as a crane,
And whistling down the feathered rain, old Noah goes again—
An old dull mome
With a head like a pome,
Seeing the world as a bare egg
Laid by the feathered air; Meg
Would beg three of these

For the nursery teas
Of Japhet, Shem, and Ham; she gave it
Underneath the trees,
Where the boiling
Water
  Hissed,
Like the goose-king's feathered daughter—kissed
Pot and pan and copper kettle
Put upon their proper mettle,
Lest the Flood—the Flood—the Flood begin again through these!

Sir Beelzebub

When
Sir
Beelzebub called for his syllabub in the hotel in Hell
    Where Proserpine first fell,
Blue as the gendarmerie were the waves of the sea

  (Rocking and shocking the barmaid).

Nobody comes to give him his rum but the
Rim of the sky hippopotamus-glum
Enhances the chances to bless with a benison
Alfred Lord Tennyson crossing the bar laid
With cold vegetation from pale deputations
Of temperance workers (all signed In Memoriam)
Hoping with glory to trip up the Laureate's feet

  (Moving in classical metres) . . .

Like Balaclava, the lava came down from the
Roof, and the sea's blue wooden gendarmerie
Took them in charge while Beelzebub roared for his rum.

  . . . None of them come!

The years between 1923 and 1929 saw the full flowering of creative energy. Bucolic Comedies (1923) *was followed by* The Sleeping Beauty (1924) *and* Troy Park (1925). *In 1926* Façade *appeared in a third edition, the Augustan Books of Modern Poetry included selections*

from Edith Sitwell, and Duckworth brought out Elegy on Dead
Fashion. *This was followed in 1927 by* Rustic Elegies, *in 1928 by* Five
Poems, *and in 1929 by* Gold Coast Customs.

For many she had become 'the High Priestess' of modern poetry.

'A hieratic figure in Limoges enamel [wrote Harold Acton] . . .
the pale oval face with its almond eyes and long thin nose had often
been carved in ivory by true believers. Her entire figure possessed a
distinction seldom to be seen outside the glass cases of certain
museums.'

'In her appearance, as in her poetry, she was triumphantly herself,
yet endlessly reaching beyond herself into other people and other
times' [*Autobiography* by Stephen Spender].

*For the High Priestess these were days of public triumph and personal
sadness. In 1924, to escape the attentions of her admirers, she moved to
Paris to 'hide' in the flat of Madame Wiel, sister of Helen Rootham, and
to write in peace. Two years later, when she was thirty-eight years old,
she met the second and greatest love of her life, Pavel Tchelitchew.*

*As a friend of Allanah Harper and of Sylvia Beach, it was inevitable
that Edith Sitwell should be introduced to Gertrude Stein. The two
women had much in common. Both were dedicated to the renewal of the
language. Edith Sitwell declared Gertrude Stein to be 'one of the most
important living pioneers of the language', and arranged for her to
lecture at Oxford. Gertrude Stein, in return, invited her to her Saturday
evening soirées in order to introduce her to the poets, musicians and painters
who were living in Paris at the time. Through Gertrude Stein, Edith
Sitwell met Picasso and Matisse, the painter Stella Bowen and her de
facto 'husband', Ford Madox Ford, and she met the young Russian
painter who owed his budding reputation to the support of Gertrude Stein:
Pavel Tchelitchew.*

*She was warned. 'If I present Pavlik to you,' said Gertrude Stein,
'it's your responsibility because his character is not my affair.'*

*Tchelitchew, like Roger Fry, Alvaro Guevara, Wyndham Lewis and
Stella Bowen, painted her portrait.*

' "This morning I painted the face of Edith Sitwell," he said to
William Carlos Williams. "What do you think?"

'It was a white-looking woman in a nun's habit. She was sitting as
if in a straightback, medieval chair, completely self absorbed, ascetic,

severe. It was a shock to me after what I thought I had known of the woman's verse.

' "She is like that," he said. "A very beautiful woman. She is alone. She is very positive and very emotional. She takes herself very seriously and seems to be as cold as ice. She is not so." '

An Afternoon with Pavel Tchelitchew by
William Carlos Williams

'Pavel Fyodorovitch discovers in her a beautiful sheltered eroticism, the purely passive female sensibility that lives forever, a glass flower under glass, behind the opaque façade so remarkable in itself. While this discovery gives him the feeling he can do what he likes with her (she will declare he threatened to kill her), it also frightens him half out of his wits.'

The Divine Comedy of Pavel Tchelitchew by
Parker Tyler

In all Edith Sitwell sat to Tchelitchew for six portraits and a sculpture in wax on wire. Guevara was forgotten. Her new and abiding love was given to 'Pavlik' Tchelitchew.

She was also his patron, arranging an exhibition for him at the Claridge Galleries in London. The Graphic of 28 July 1928 carried what it called her 'eulogy' of his work.

London has been introduced to a really great new painter, Tchelitchew . . . I can say with honesty that the day on which I first began to realise [his] pictures was one of the most important days in my artistic life. They opened out to me a whole new world of revelation and beauty . . . what at first appears as subtlety soon takes on the aspect of sublimity.

Tchelitchew, like Guevara, responded with passion, but it was aesthetic; the passion of a painter, in love with her beauty, grateful for her patronage. Like Guevara, he was already infatuated. A homosexual, he shared a house with the pianist Allan Tanner.

In this more enlightened age, this fact alone would have constituted a warning. But Edith Sitwell neither recognized, nor, in fact, understood the implication of such a relationship. In describing her visit to Swin-

burne's grave on the Isle of Wight she observed that 'this, of course, was in the days when at seventeen, one must be clamped to an older female or one's name was mud.' Brought up in this tradition of chaperonage, it did not occur to her to question the relationship of two people of the same sex living together.

'Artists should not marry,' she said. It was a comforting philosophy but not one that exempted her from suffering. In retrospect her years in Paris were remembered as 'unmitigated hell'. The theme of betrayal manifested itself in her poetry, culminating in her Gold Coast Customs, *the poem which, wrote the critic Cyril Connolly, 'reached a pitch of despair, written with a controlled savagery and a sense of personal betrayal, like* King Lear *or* Troilus and Cressida.'

Gold Coast Customs, *inspired, she said, by the hunger marches, was an attack on fashionable society. Lady Bamburgher was the hostess who gave her champagne parties while men starved, and so the 'Mayfair jungle' is linked with the cannibal rites of King Munza of Ashanti.*

Awareness of poverty, which had stirred quick sympathy for her governesses and later became a personal experience, was now expanded into a crusade, outlined in more detail in two articles written years later.

In what sort of a position is a man who is suffering the unending pangs of hunger, can buy no food, because he can get no work which will enable him to earn money, cannot take food without paying for it, because that is against the law, and cannot take his own life, because that is against two laws—the moral and the judicial?

He is, in actual fact, the property and the victim of two systems, neither of which, while claiming his obedience, fulfils its own obligations towards him. The prosperity of the nation is no more beneficial to that man than is the prosperity of the slave-owner to the slave.

A good many ideas have got falsified in the course of ages, and one of the worst examples of this is the idea of poverty.

There is a tendency on the part of those who are not poor, to regard poverty as a beautiful ideal, as a high 'religious ideal'—for the others.

But what is known as 'holy poverty' is a state that is *voluntarily* embraced by those who profess it, and it is done for a definite religious purpose.

I have yet to learn what is the religious purpose concealed behind the economic system which makes 'hunger marches' necessary and semi-starvation a permanent condition of being for many millions of people.

Can any meaner, more abject person be imagined than that person who needs the stimulant of a 'charity ball', with 'champagne included', to drag his, or her guineas out of her pocket, to help in a charitable object?

Have we not got the extreme swing back of the pendulum in the ugly curve of the slave-system, when it swings from the 'hunger-marcher', with his banner-inscription: 'Feed us, or shoot us,' to the charity-dancer, with his card of admittance, and its 'champagne included'?

'What Is Slavery?' *Sunday Referee*, 1935

In the wonderful golden weather, we drove, first, into the Chinese quarter, with its fantastic houses painted on the roof with dragons. Here, in spite of the poverty, everyone looked happy. Friendship seemed to be universal. Nothing looked dirty; one could not see any vestiges of despair—perhaps because there had been no ambition; and there were even signs of a humble luxury—fruit shops, for instance, filled with lovely golden, exotic-looking fruits like great moons.

But from Chinatown we emerged into the most appalling slum I have ever seen.

The street was enormously wide. It would take, I think, five minutes to cross it. And that was one of its horrors. For on one pavement a derelict might be dying, friendless, from hunger, and on the other pavement, the passing half-dead creatures would be quite unaware of this, or else, dazed by their own misery, uncaring.

As we emerged from Chinatown we saw, leading out of that monstrous road, on the left, a narrow street going God knows where. Perhaps nowhere, excepting some limbo of Death, where all identity would be forgotten.

In spite of the golden weather, that terrible narrow street seemed as if it were enveloped in spangled black gauze. And at the entrance to the street stood a shop that had no windows and no door, and was hung with unspeakable black rags that looked as if they had been stolen from the dead.

There were a number of lodging houses that seemed as if they were inhabited by ghosts and rats only. And there were numerous missions. These were shaped like coffins, and the derelicts who were utterly starving entered these terrible places and were given a cup of coffee and a doughnut as a reward for listening to a sermon and saying a prayer. There were also horrible-looking Music Halls, at the entrance to which were enormous bloated figures, grotesquely tall and coarse, dressed as cowboys.

The people who crawled along the pavements looked as if they were made of either red rags or grey rags. Those made up of red rags coughed all the time. The others merely stared.

There is no contact between one human being and another. If you die of starvation, that is *your* affair. You must not expect me, menaced with the same fate, to care.

I had seen Skid Row gilded by a false spring light. But now, in my sleepless nights, I walk through that long street again, ungilded by that light, but as it exists in reality, in a world fallen into winter. And I was a part of that winter world.

Winter is the time for comfort, for good food and warmth, for the touch of a friendly hand and for a talk beside the fire: it is the time for home. It is no season in which to wander the world as if one were the wind blowing aimlessly along the streets without a place to rest, without food, and without time meaning anything to one, just as time means nothing to the wind. All that means anything to the wind is beginning and ending. And coldness. But here, in the city's circles of Hell, sunk beneath the world-height of empty houses, twenty thousand persons creep who have neither friend nor shelter. All through the day, under the Bedlam daylight's murderous roar, changing to the enormous Tartarean darkness of a fog, through the deepest circles of Hell all forms of misery loomed and faded, monstrous shapes, their sightless faces turned to the unheeding sky, tapping upon the ground with a hollow noise that seemed to echo down millions of fathoms to the very centre of the ball of the earth. For in this city of universal night, only the blind can see. Along the wide pavements that were long and hard as Hell's huge polar street, cold as the universal blackness of Hell's day, the towers of rags and bones were swept—each a universe of misery, a world of hunger and polar wastes, shut off from all others. Some were young, and these had nothing between their one outer covering of rags and their skin, so that it seemed they had early been made ready for the grave. With those who were older, it was as if all the nations of the dead with their million-year-old rags about them, had risen to denounce us. A whisper would pierce my sleeplessness. 'What have we done? What have we done? Now it's always night, and winter. And we have been thrown down into Hell. Night after night! Week after week, month after month, year after year . . . How many moments go to an hour, how many hours go to a night, how many nights go to a year, how many years go to a life? And every night an eternity of cold.'

Taken Care Of

Gold Coast Customs, *in the opinion of her contemporaries, brought a new dimension to her work:*

'I felt that something absent from all literature was back again [wrote W. B. Yeats], and in a form rare in the literature of all generations, passion ennobled by intensity, by endurance, by wisdom. We had such a man once. He lies in St Patrick's now, under the greatest epitaph in history.'

My actual experiments led eventually to the poem *Gold Coast Customs*. It is a poem about the state that led up to the Second World War. It is a definite prophecy of what would arise from such a state— what *has* arisen. [It was written in 1929.]

> . . . Do we smell and see
> The sick thick smoke from London burning . . .?

In this poem the bottom of the world has fallen out.

The organisation of the poem, speaking of this world that has broken down, but where a feverish, intertwining, seething movement, a vain seeking for excitement, still existed, presented considerable difficulty. I tried to give a concentrated essence of that world through a movement which at times interweaves like worms intertwining, which at times has a jaunty wire-jerked sound, or rears itself up like a tidal wave rushing forward, or swells like a black sea-swell by means of violently stretching vowels . . . We see everything reduced to the primal mud—the 'Rich man Judas, Brother Cain', and the epitome of his civilisation, Lady Bamburgher, are at one with the slum-ignorance and superstition of the African swamp. The beating of their fevered hearts and pulses is no more than the beating of the drums that heralded the Customs, as they were called in Ashantee, a hundred and fifty years ago, when, at the death of any rich or important person, slaves and poor persons were killed so that the bones of the dead might be washed by human blood. So, the spiritual dead-in-life cry, in our time, for a sacrifice—that of the starved. And these, sacrificed, are watched by the appalling dumb agony of

> . . . the rat-eaten bones
> Of a fashionable god that lived not
> Ever, but still has bones to rot.

Throughout the poem, I have tried to produce not so much the record of a world, as the wounded and suffering soul of that world, its living evocation, not its history, seen through the eyes of a protagonist whose personal tragedy is echoed in that vaster tragedy . . .

My time of experiments was done.

Some Notes On My Own Poetry

> I only know one half of my heart
> Lies in that terrible coffin of stone,
> My body that stalks through the slum alone.
> And that half of my heart
> That is in your breast
> You gave for meat
> In the sailor's street
> To the rat that had only my bones to eat.
>
> But those hardened hearts
> That roll and sprawl,
> In a cowl of foul blind monkey-skin,
> Lest the whips of the light crash roaring in—
> Those hearts that roll

Down the phantom street
They have for their beat
The cannibal drums
And the cries of the slums,
And the Bamburgher parties—they have them all!

One high house flaps . . . taps
Light's skin drum—
Monkey-like shrunk
On all fours now come
The parties' sick ghosts, each hunting himself—
Black gaps beneath an ape's thick pelt,

Chasing a rat,
Their soul's ghost fat,
Through the Negro swamp,
Slum hovel's cramp,
Of Lady Bamburgher's parties above
With the latest grin, and the latest love,
And the latest game:
To show the shame
Of the rat-fat soul to the grinning day
With even the rat-skin flayed away.

Now, a thick cloud floating
Low o'er the lake,
Millions of flies
Begin to awake,
With the animation
Of smart conversation:
From Bedlam's madness the thick gadflies
Seek for the broken statue's eyes.

.   .   .   .

Lady Bamburgher airs
That foul plague-spot,
Her romantic heart.
From the cannibal mart,
That smart Plague-cart,
Lady Bamburgher rolls where the foul news-sheet
And the shambles for souls are set in the street.

And stuck in front
Of this world-tall Worm,
Stuck in front
Of this world's confession—
Like something rolled
Before a procession,
Is the face, a flimsy worm-skin thing
That someone has raked
From the low plague-pit
As a figure-head
For Corruption dead,
And a mask for the universal Worm.

Her ape-skin yellow
Tails of hair
Clung about her bone-white bare
Eyeless mask that cackled there:

The Worm's mask hid
Her eyeless mud,
Her shapeless love,
The plot to escape
From the God-ordained shape

And her soul, the cannibal
Amazon's mart,
Where in squealing light
And clotted black night
On the monkey-skin black and white striped dust they
Cackle and bray to the murdered day.

And the Amazon queen
With a bone-black face
Wears a mask with an ape-skin beard; she grinds
Her male child's bones in a mortar, binds
Him for food, and the people buy. For this,

Hidden behind
The Worm's mask, grown
White as a bone
Where eyeholes rot wide

And are painted for sight,
And the little mouth red as a dead Plague-spot
On that white mask painted to hide Death's rot,

For this painted Plague-cart's
Heart, for this
Slime of the Worm that paints her kiss
And the dead men's bones round her throat and wrist,
The half of my heart that lay in your breast
Has fallen away
To rot and bray
With the painted mud through the eyeless day.

The dust of all the dead can blow
Backwards and forwards, to and fro,
To cover the half of my heart with Death's rot,
Yet the dust of that other half comes not
To this coffin of stone that stalks through the slum;
Though love to you now is the deaf Worm's lust
That, cloven in halves, will re-unite
Foulness to deadness in the dust
And chaos of the enormous night.

.   .   .   .

'Starved silly Sally, why dilly and dally?'
The dummies said when I was a girl.
The rat deserts a room that is bare,
But Want, a cruel rat gnawing there,
Ate to the heart, all else was gone,
Nothing remained but Want alone.
So now I'm a gay girl, a calico dummy,
With nothing left alive but my feet
That walk up and down in the Sailor's Street.

.   .   .   .

What is that whimpering like a child
That this mad ghost beats like a drum in the air?
The heart of Sal
That once was a girl
And now is a calico thing to loll

158

Over the easy steps of the slum
Waiting for something dead to come.

.   .   .   .

Rich man Judas,
Brother Cain,
The rich men are your worms that gain
The air through seething from your brain;
Judas, mouldering in your old
Coffin body, still undying
As the Worm, where you are lying
With no flesh for warmth, but gold
For flesh, for warmth, for sheet:
Now you are fleshless, too, as these
That starve and freeze,
Is your gold hard as Hell's huge polar street,
Is the universal blackness of Hell's day so cold?

.   .   .   .

When, creeping over
The Sailor's Street
Where the houses like rat-skin
Masks flap, meet
Never across the murdered bone
Of the sailor, the whining overtone
Of dawn sounds, slaves
Rise from their graves,
Where in the corpse-sheet night they lay
Forgetting the mutilating day,
Like the unborn child in its innocent sleep.
Ah Christ, the murdered light must weep—
(Christ that takest away the sin
Of the world, and the rich man's bone-dead grin)
The light must weep,
Seeing that sleep
And those slaves rise up in their death-chains, part
The light from the eyes,
The hands from the heart,
Since their hearts are flesh for the tall
And sprawling

159

Reeling appalling
Cannibal mart,
But their hands and head
Are machines to breed
Gold for the old and the greedy Dead.

I have seen the murdered God look through the eyes
Of the drunkard's smirched
Mask as he lurched
O'er the half of my heart that lies in the street
'Neath the dancing fleas and the foul news-sheet.

Where (a black gap flapping,
A white skin drum)
The cannibal houses
Watch this come—
Lady Bamburgher's party; for the plan
Is a prize for those that on all fours ran
Through the rotting slum
Till those who come
Could never guess from the mud-covered shapes
Which are the rich or the mired dire apes,
As they run where the souls, dirty paper, are blown
In the hour before dawn, through this long hell of stone.

Perhaps if I too lie down in the mud,
Beneath tumbrils rolling
And mad skulls galloping
Far from their bunches of nerves that dance
And caper among these slums, and prance,
Beneath the noise of that hell that rolls
I shall forget the shrunken souls,
The eyeless mud squealing 'God is dead',
Starved men (bags of wind) and the harlot's tread,
The heaven turned into monkey-hide
By Lady Bamburgher's dancing fleas,
Her rotting parties and death-slack ease,
And the dead men drunken
(The only tide)
Blown up and down

And tossed through the town
Over the half of my heart that lies
Deep down, in this meaner Death, with cries.

The leaves of black hippopotamus-hide
Black as the mud
Cover the blood
And the rotting world. Do we smell and see

The sick thick smoke from London burning,
Gomorrah turning
Like worms in the grave,
The Bedlam daylight's murderous roar,
Those pillars of fire the drunkard and the whore,
Dirty souls boiled in cannibal cookshops to paper
To make into newspapers, flags? . . . They caper
Like gaping apes. Foul fires we see,
For Bedlam awakes to reality

The drunkard burning,
The skin drums galloping,
In their long march still parched for the sky,
The Rotten Alleys where beggars groan
And the beggar and his dog share a bone;
The rich man Cain that hides within
His lumbering palaces where Sin
Through the eyeless holes of Day peers in,
The murdered heart that all night turns
From small machine to shapeless Worm
With hate, and like Gomorrah burns—
These put the eyes of Heaven out,
These raise all Hell's throats to a shout,
These break my heart's walls toppling in,
And like a universal sea
The nations of the Dead crowd in.

.   .   .   .

Gomorrah's fires have washed my blood—
But the fires of God shall wash the mud
Till the skin drums rolling

The slum cries sprawling
And crawling
Are calling
'Burn thou me!'
Though Death has taken
And pig-like shaken,
Rooted, and tossed
The rags of me.
Yet the time will come
To the heart's dark slum
When the rich man's gold and the rich man's wheat
Will grow in the street, that the starved may eat,—
And the sea of the rich will give up its dead—
And the last blood and fire from my side will be shed.
For the fires of God go marching on.

Gold Coast Customs

1929–1942

Nobody would have guessed at the vulnerability concealed behind that mighty shield and buckler.

Stella Bowen

After Gold Coast Customs *Edith Sitwell wrote no more poetry for a decade.*

First of her prose books was her Alexander Pope, *notable to this day because of the empathy felt by the author for her subject, about whom she wrote:*

I do not know how anyone could fail to be saddened by the tragedy of this man, whose body was too frail for the terrible burden of genius, and whose life was one long torture of pain and weakness and the humiliation caused by the knowledge of his deformity—a knowledge that had been forced upon him at a most impressionable age by the unspeakable Dennis. Pope had a heart like other men: he was young and romantic-minded, and from the moment of Dennis's attack upon him he saw himself doomed to live his life through without love. (He had, perhaps, the most subtle and sensitive feeling for beauty of form possessed by any artist that our race has produced, and his feeling for texture was so phenomenally sensitive that had the verses been transformed into flowers, he could have told lily from rose, buttercup from cowslip, in no matter how starless and moonless a night, merely by touching one petal. He gives us a million ecstasies of the differences between summer air and the summer breath of wind, between the secrecy of dew falling and the poignancy of the first heavy drops of rain. And these differences are not produced by imagery, or by a change of *structure*, but by *texture*.) Yet he realised that his own outward form raised feelings of mocking amusement or coarse pity in the beholders. Indeed, his very weakness was a subject for ridicule.

I do not know why the unhappy Pope's underlying beauty of character and kindness have not been more commented upon, since his life's record is one of loyalty to his friends, unchanging love where that love was not betrayed, financial generosity, and, where that generosity was extended, the most extraordinary delicacy and kindness. Was this man filled with nothing but hatred and malice?

The instances of his kindnesses are not recorded as actions worthy of praise, but as the ordinary business affairs of every day. We are not allowed by his biographers to think of him as a good man.

It is imagined for some reason, that it is perfectly right and proper for persons of small wit, and a dreadful little slick talent, or indeed, for persons of no wit, and not even that pimpish talent, to attack, and try to injure, any creature possessed of genius. It does not matter how low and foul the attack, it does not matter by what cunning, hatred, and malice it may be prompted, nor how under-brained and dirty the attacker may be. The quarry is possessed of genius, and is therefore meant to be hunted and half-killed. But let a man of genius reply, and the whole populace rises up to protect the original aggressor. The man of genius, it is understood, in protecting himself, and consequently his work, or in protecting his personal reputation, is a creature actuated by malice. He is cold-hearted, he is serpent-like. He should have allowed himself to be hunted into the grave, like Keats; starved into the grave, like Chatterton; driven out of England, like Shelley. And the malice is proved by the fact that, being a man of genius, he is naturally able to deliver harder blows when attacked, than the majority of his aggressors are able to administer to him.

Again, his bodily martyrdom and the cruel and humiliating sneers to which martyrdom exposed him, made him liable to bursts of fury which would have been held within bounds by a stronger frame. There is nothing cold about Pope's poetry; we are buried beneath a torrent of lava, but we are not walled up in ice. The effects of his rage, and this I cannot deny, were terrible towards his enemies, and even towards some quite harmless persons whom he believed to cherish designs against him. For the lamentable fact is that he loathed bad poetry—that the cause of poetry affected him as the sound of a bugle is supposed to affect a war horse. The fact that he was almost a more perfect artist (by which I mean a man formed for nothing but his art) than any other artist of our race, did not help to make so frail a body less subject to fits of irascibility.

It seems as if Pope's character has been misunderstood because he was, primarily, a great artist, and lived first and foremost for his art. One of his biographers has said that no man ever lived more for fame than he. I can find no evidence of it, nor any evidence that he thought fame worth having. It seems that even his whole-hearted, fiery-souled devotion to poetry had to be subjected to the same calumny as the rest of that most unhappy life.

Alexander Pope

After Alexander Pope *came four more major prose works:* Bath, The English Eccentrics, Victoria of England *and finally, in 1937, her novel* I Live Under a Black Sun. *Though she wrote almost no new poetry, she wrote about it. In 1934 came her* Aspects of Modern Poetry, *a book of criticism sharper, perhaps, because of her own frustration, and beginning with an attack on those writers whose standing in the literary world she questioned: Dr Leavis, professor of literature at Cambridge University, and destined to be the strongest critical influence on the thinking of the next generation; Geoffrey Grigson, co-editor of 'A Paper Called New Verse, of Inordinate and Notorious Funniness', and her old enemy Wyndham Lewis, painter, and author of* The Apes of God.

Here are samples of her attacks.

On Dr Leavis: The Doctor has a transcendental gift, when he is writing sense, for making this appear to be nonsense . . .

The sound of a great deal of Milton . . . affects Dr Leavis much as the sound of a motor bicycle affects my less sensitive nervous system . . . as for his interpretation of the stressing, it is sad to see Milton's great lines bobbing up and down in the sandy desert of Dr Leavis's mind with the grace of a fleet of weary camels.

On Geoffrey Grigson: Mr Grigson is not as amusing as Dr Leavis, but there is still considerable pleasure to be derived from contemplating him . . . Of the Poem in Seven Spaces 'enthroned' by Mr and Mrs Grigson in *New Verse* . . . I can only say that I wish there had been more Spaces: in short, I wish there had been nothing excepting Space.

On Wyndham Lewis: Mr Lewis suffers from various other little troubles that he would like us to understand and to sympathise with. There is for instance the worry about back and fronts . . . and this, at moments, grows to such a pitch that **he** seems scarcely to know if he is coming or going.

[This in reference to the poem beginning:

Try and walk backwards: you will quickly see
How you were meant only one-way to be!

167

Attempt to gaze out of your bricked-up back:
You will soon discover what we one-ways lack!]

The situation you describe must be most trying, but these little things will occur, you know. And we want you not to fret about the seriousness of the symptoms.

Edith Sitwell had been enjoying herself: 'I laughed till I nearly cried as I was writing it,' she told Christabel Aberconway [Selected Letters]. But the objects of her mirth were not so amused.

Dr Leavis observed—in print—that the Sitwells 'belonged to the history of publicity'.

Wyndham Lewis, whose critique for Time and Tide *was headed 'Sitwell Circus', finished it with this sentence:*

'. . . the patter is frankly poor, the jests are "old favourites" indeed: and with so much wild stuff hurtling about in the air, there is, it must be confessed, a certain danger for the public—or there would be if there *were* a public.'

Defenders of the three pondered their defence, and decided upon plagiarism as their most effective weapon. G. W. Stonier, reviewing the book for the New Statesman and Nation, *accused her of borrowing from both Leavis and Grigson without acknowledging the fact.*

Edith Sitwell returned to the attack in the correspondence pages of the New Statesman and Nation:

Sir, With regard to Mr G. W. Stonier's review of my book *Aspects of Modern Poetry*, may I reply that had I known that Dr Leavis was the author of Andrew Lang's sonnet *The Odyssey* (and I think him capable of it), I should have acknowledged my debt to him. Had I known that he was the author of Mr Arthur Symons's book on the French Symbolists, of Villiers de l'Isle Adam's *Axel*, of Mr Yeats's *Autobiographies* and *Essays*, and of the *Oxford Book of English Verse*, I should have acknowledged my debt. But this is the first I have heard of it. Before we know where we are, we shall find that Dr Leavis is the Dark Lady of the Sonnets!

Again, Mr Stonier says that, whilst attacking Mr Grigson, I 'appropriate, without acknowledging' (*sic*) 'an exceedingly apt quotation from Yeats's *Packet for Ezra Pound*, which Mr Grigson used in a review in *New Verse*, October, 1933 . . .'

I have not read Mr Grigson's review. Mr Yeats, with great kindness, sent me the *Packet for Ezra Pound* when it first appeared, with most interesting annotations in his own handwriting. The book is one of my most treasured possessions. I was unaware that I had to thank Mr Grigson for this. I thought my debt was to Mr Yeats, who sent me the book!

It is right and natural that Mr Stonier should admire Dr Leavis. It reminds me of Miss Nellie Wallace's appeal to her slightly denuded feather boa: 'For God's sake, hold together, boys!'

As, Sir, you have published Mr Stonier's quite unwarranted remarks about me, I hope that you will also publish my letter, without alterations.

Geoffrey Grigson added to the charge of plagiarism; Edith, bolstered by a letter from Osbert Sitwell, answered it. The correspondence columns of the New Statesman and Nation *were bright, but not as bright as those of* The Sunday Times, *in 1936. A new controversy had begun, longer this time, as Edith Sitwell was writing, not in her own defence, but in defence of one of her discoveries.*

In January of the year she sent this letter to an unknown young poet called Dylan Thomas:

Though we have never met, I am unable to resist writing to tell you, however inadequately, with what deep admiration and delight I have read your very beautiful poem which begins with the line 'A Grief ago', and the beautiful and strange poem in this quarter's *Life and Letters*. It is no exaggeration to say that I do not remember when I have been so moved, profoundly so excited, by the work of any poet of the younger generation, or when I have felt such a deep certainty that here is a poet with all the capabilities and potentialities of greatness.

Selected Letters

It was the beginning of a friendship which was to last a lifetime. It was also the beginning of the controversy, as it was followed by her review of his 25 Poems, *the cause of letters of protest by the score.*

'The main outcry was against his obscurity. "Clarity", as one correspondent expressed it, "is a perennial characteristic of all great poets . . . I concede that poetry will never appeal to the plain 'man in the street'. It should, however, appeal to the man in Intellectual or Beautiful Street."

'Edith, never loth to take up a challenge, sent back a spirited reply, to the effect that the argument seemed to be developing into a beauty competition. Her letter finished with the tart comment that if she wanted to be taught her job by somebody who wrote for *Poetry Review*, she would send in a request, but that she would as soon ask a writer in the *Poultry Gazette* to teach her to train eagles to fly.'

The Last Years of a Rebel
by Elizabeth Salter

By 1937 the controversy had died down, but Edith Sitwell's name was far from absent in the columns of the literary press. By October, her novel I Live Under a Black Sun *had been reviewed in most of the serious newspapers. Though it was generally recognized to be based on the life of Jonathan Swift, there was this time no accusation of plagiarism. On the contrary, critical opinion ranged from the approving to the ecstatic:*

'Miss Sitwell's novel is impressive, profoundly felt, wonderfully produced, witty, vehemently just; but the main effect is one of almost unbearable beauty' [wrote R. Ellis Roberts for the News Chronicle*]. It was 'a passacaglia, having such subtle counterpoint, such rare decoration, that it should urge still further her acceptance as the most unique musician in literature of our time' [Pamela Hansford Johnson in* The Sunday Times*].*

Edith, who had complained of working 'seven hours a day on this confounded book on Eccentrics' to Veronica Gilliat, and to Tom Driberg about 'that old bore Queen Victoria', could now declare herself pleased. She wrote to Ree Gorer:

My novel is getting on well. It is the only prose book (excepting for criticism) that I've ever been pleased with. (I mean, naturally, the only prose book of *mine*!!)

Even so she was 'nearly dead with fatigue'.

My usual time for starting work is 5.30 a.m. I'm never later than 6. It is the only time when I can be sure of being quiet.

Selected Letters

The reason given for strenuous effort divorced from poetry, was the need to make money. It was in 1930 that Helen Rootham discovered the cancer from which she died in 1938. As her illness progressed, her needs became greater. Edith Sitwell was faced, not only with the expenses of illness, but with the practicalities of her new role as nurse.

She felt her responsibility towards Helen Rootham and she worked hard to make money. But can a poet cease to be a poet because of economic necessity? We, her anthologists, do not accept this. We consider that the reason lay deeper.

'I have always been a little outside life,' she wrote of herself. And again, in her preface to her last volume of poetry, The Outcasts, *she defined her concept of the poet:*

I do not mean—have never meant—that we must avoid the everyday world . . .

But: Poetry is, indeed, the deification of reality, and one of its purposes is to show that the dimensions of man are, as Sir Arthur Eddington said, 'Half way between those of an atom and a star.'

But the 'deification of reality' depends on perspective. Caught up in the illness of a friend, in the practical work associated with this; struggling with her thwarted passion for Tchelitchew in these, the difficult middle years of her life, she was enmeshed by the immediate. The long sight of the poet was focused, perforce, on the minutiae of daily living. These were her years of involvement. It was not until she was able to detach herself again, freed by the death of Helen Rootham, that the gift of poetry returned.

In the meantime she wrote prose. The world was presented with other manifestations of her talent: as journalist, biographer, lecturer, critic and novelist.

Her articles for the newspapers were many, often witty, usually reflecting her attitude towards life as it was lived in the thirties.

That part of the cinematographic art known as a 'close-up', and the unrivalled opportunity it gives to all students of facial expression to study their subject in its most exact and minute detail, is, perhaps, the principal reason for the strange progress made in the art of what is known as 'making faces'. For there is no doubt that what was once regarded as a bad habit has now become an important factor in the life of nations, and has really assumed the proportions of a political art.

I had been vaguely aware of this phenomenon for some time, more especially in the case of national—and international—celebrities of various kinds, but I had not given any real or serious attention to the matter until a day or two ago, when I was suddenly confronted with a Press photograph of the head of Signor Mussolini, carved by Italian soldiers on a particularly large piece of rock in Abyssinia, with a melodramatic caption to the effect that it is looking towards Addis Ababa.

Perhaps it is so, but what actually interests me is not the geographical detail, but the evident and reverential care with which Signor Mussolini's fellow-countrymen have carved, not so much a face, in the ordinary sense of the word, as a very skilful close-up of the Duce 'making' his well-known face at the world in general, and at Abyssinia in particular.

There was a time in the history of the world when careful nurses would warn their young charges not to 'make that face', lest the wind should suddenly change while they were doing it, and fix it on them for ever. It is not so now.

On the contrary, the wise and far-seeing have learned the psychological and political value of a really good face when 'made' by an expert, and the effect on affairs of international importance. Therefore, in case the wind of popularity should change suddenly and, instead of fixing it for ever, remove it altogether from the public view, they have it photographed on every available occasion, and under every conceivable circumstance, and disseminate it for purposes of propaganda.

No one with the most superficial acquaintance with Signor Mussolini's character can doubt for one moment that he knew exactly the full international significance of what he was doing the first time he made his famous face in public—that face that is now known to every newspaper reader and every cinema-goer throughout the world.

It is sad to think that we shall never be privileged to see photographs of all those he must have discarded in private before he achieved, and kept, the one that now gazes out of the rock across a section of Northern Abyssinia.

'Making Faces at the World',
Sunday Referee, 1936

Is liberty, wearing the robes in which she is presented to us today, really worth having?

I am aware that this is a very dangerous question to ask, and it entails a certain amount of courage to do it. In fact, I should not have asked it, if it were not for a certain quotation that I read a few days ago.

The quotation, the name of the book from which it is taken and the name of the author, will be given in due course; but, for the moment, I will devote myself to the extremely controversial subject of liberty.

It is controversial, owing to the fact that very few persons agree as to what constitutes liberty—or freedom, which is a word some people prefer to use for the same thing.

Liberty, now, in the urban districts, seems to be construed and boiled down into 'taking a liberty'. In fact, 'liberty' and 'licence' are practically indistinguishable, much to the detriment of the former.

I may as well say at once, that I have for a long time held the belief that the word 'liberty', though it may still retain its ideal significance in the pages of a dictionary, has lost all reality if it is judged from the standpoint of its practical application and subsequent results.

We are told, for instance, that a person who cannot write two lines of poetry may yet have buried in the recesses of what he calls his mind the finest poem that was ever not written, and which transcends in beauty and value any poem that ever has been written by a mere poet.

On the same principle, the best statues are those which have never been removed from the block of stone in which they lie hidden, and the finest symphonies are those which have never been put on paper—owing, no doubt, to the fact that their composer did not know his notes.

But even though we may grant that a theory cannot be entirely judged by its practical results (and perhaps there may be some truth in this), yet we may be allowed to feel a little amusement when we look at the discrepancy between the two things.

Putting the arts on one side, and returning to the subject of liberty, what does it mean, for instance, as a national ideal, and where does this ideal lead us, logically?

If we may judge by national symbolism—for every nation claims to possess its own ideal of liberty—it means to the English, roughly speaking, that God ordained that Britannia should rule the waves, in order that Britons never, never, never, etc. . . ., and that, by implication, what happened to the rest of the world could not possibly matter in the sight of Heaven.

The Germans take much the same view of their own divine prerogative in the matter of freedom, and the ensuing subordination of the rest of the world. 'Deutschland über alles in der Welt' (Germany above everything else in the world), is the leitmotif of their national anthem.

The Statue of Liberty welcomes all comers to America—via the Customs and Ellis Island.

We all know that perfect freedom of speech is one of the first essentials of liberty.

Everyone is allowed to say exactly what they like—and what happens to them, in consequence, is not allowed to be any concern of their relations.

With regard to France, and its inheritance of 'liberty, fraternity, equality' from the Revolution, I cannot do better than quote the Russian writer Soloviev (translated by Helen Rootham):

'. . . the working class, bare of all possessions, in spite of its Freedom, and Equal Rights, is, in reality, an enslaved proletariat, for whom Equality means an equality of poverty, and for whom Freedom often means nothing but the freedom to die of starvation.'

In these circumstances, does it appear as if 'liberty' were something which can be attained by every individual, or by every different *group* of individuals in a nation, at one and the same time?

Does it not appear as if its attainment were the result of might rather than of right? As if, in fact, there is in every nation, and in every group of nations, a top-dog and an under-dog, and only the former can have a semblance of liberty, and even that semblance only for so long as he can keep the other dog—or dogs—down by sheer force.

Therefore I ask, is such liberty really worth having?

And now, I will give the quotation which caused me to put the question which seems to me to put the whole matter of contemporary 'liberty' in a nutshell.

I have just been reading a short notice of an American edition of a book called *Rats, Lice, and History*, by Hans Zinsser, Professor of Bacteriology at Harvard. The notice includes the following quotation:

'The louse sacrifices liberty that signified chiefly the necessity for hard work, the uncertainty of food and shelter, and exposure to dangers from birds, lizards, and frogs; loses the fun of having wings, perhaps, but achieves, instead, a secure and effortless existence on a living island of plenty.

'In a manner . . . the louse has attained the ideal of bourgeois civilisation, though its methods are more direct than those of business or banking, and its source of nourishment is not its own species.'

'What Do We Mean by Liberty?'
Sunday Referee, 1935

It seems to me that nearly every criminal, no matter how 'clever' he may appear to be in the actual technique of his own crime—is a criminal because in everything that matters he is too densely stupid to be anything else.

I should like to say in parenthesis that I never understand why real criminals are regarded as being 'romantic'. If they resemble at all what we see on the films, or read about in detective stories, they are, for the most part, dull persons who cannot talk intelligibly excepting through the mouth of a revolver, and so little brave that they are afraid to move outside their own houses without a heavily-armed bodyguard and a machine-gun.

Also I cannot see why it is any more interesting, from the point of view of the beholder, to be a criminal than it is to cheat at cards or any other game.

Perhaps if a bridge player pointed a revolver at one of his opponents and said, 'Excuse me, I think you have an ace that would be useful to me,' bridge would then take on a romantic aspect which it lacks at present . . .

That there is something terribly wrong in the world's attitude towards crime, and its punishment, is clearly proved by the appalling number of crimes with violence that are committed.

Punishment, as it stands at present, does not appear to deter the criminal when he is still outside the prison, and, in the majority of cases, does not 'correct' or 'amend' him when he is inside.

Under more or less favourable circumstances, it appears to restore him to the world as a 'hardened offender'; in the case of certain notorious prisons, it turns him into a devil.

'Gangsters, Fraudulent Financiers, War Mongers',
Sunday Referee, 1936

The vagaries of human nature seem endless: we can, and do, find an unreasoning cowardice and a reckless bravery mixed, in almost equal degrees, in the same character.

And nowhere do women show these mixed characteristics more startlingly than in their choice of clothes.

There are but few women who will resist a fashionable idiocy, no matter how imbecile, how lacking in beauty, it may be—if they are told that it is *new*. Highly-priced scarves made of string, which is not a beautiful substance, dresses with a single huge lobster printed in front (and a lobster, though good to eat, has no decorative value)—these are new, therefore they must be worn.

Yet I ask myself, has newness alone, when unaccompanied by any other desirable quality, anything to recommend it? Is it really worth while to turn oneself into a string bag, or a dish for a lobster, in order to be new?

Women will appear without a qualm in these 'new' idiocies, but if you suggest to them that they should wear a dress because it is beautiful, unless every other woman in the world is wearing one too, they will refuse under the plea that 'It makes one look so odd, my dear.'

And yet there is no woman on earth who could not be, if not beautiful, at least interesting-looking—if she chose.

The trouble about most Englishwomen is that they *will* dress as if they had been a mouse in a previous incarnation, or hope to be one in the next. They do not want to attract attention, and therefore they try to soften their worst features. And that is what any French-woman who is clever with her appearance will tell you that you must never do. We can never soften our worst features without loss of character.

Were I enormously fat with multitudinous chins I should emphasise the fact. Nothing that I could do would alter it so I should pretend that I enjoyed it.

Were I a dwarf I would wear clothes of an incredible fantasy, founded upon those worn by the dwarfs painted by Velasquez.

I am not advocating the wearing of 'fancy dress', but I *am* advocating the heightening of character—and the use of a little intelligence . . .

One can have a great deal of fun if one is [very tall]—wearing, for the theatre, vast cloaks like ecclesiastic capes in a portrait by Titian, made of stiff brocade, over a perfectly simple dress falling in soft sculptural folds.

One can wear, at evening parties or at home (but this, of course, only if we have shoulders suitable for the purpose), velvet dresses of a medieval cut with long hanging sleeves and the whole of the shoulders bare—or wide skirted dresses of a stiff black silk as acrid as our profiles, tightly cut bodices, the whole of the shoulders bare, and immense puffs of the silk just below the shoulders, going into long tight sleeves . . .

Again, if one has black eyebrows and a swarthy complexion, one will look particularly striking dressed in a gown of acrid black silk, simply cut, and if one's hair is sufficiently abundant one should draw it back plainly to the head and do it in a bun, or a plait, behind.

At least that is what I should do if my appearance were of that kind. Black suits people of this aspect best, but gentian colour, and the colour of blue cinerarias, will also become them.

A woman whose main quality is *prettiness* is the most difficult of all people to dress. An ugly woman has far more possibilities of enhancing character by her clothes.

Purely pretty women (I do not mean women who are beautiful), and especially those who are of the fair-haired, blue-eyed, straw-berries-and-cream-skinned type, look best in the summer, in light, airy materials, when they can wear large, shady hats and carry elaborate parasols.

But the day for the pretty fair-haired woman was really in the time of *The Merry Widow* and of the late Mr George Edwardes, the happy, slight, silly, musical comedy era.

The clothes that were worn at that date were so fluffy, so lacy, so frilly that only a pretty woman could hope to look well in them.

Today all has changed. This is the era of the woman with character, and the cleverness to make the most of it.

'How to Wear Dramatic Clothes',
Daily Express

Probably all women, and the majority of men, would agree with me that the answer to the question, 'How old will you be next year?'

is not to be found on a birth certificate. So many things go to the making of 'how old are you?' and perhaps the least important of these things is the count of our actual years.

What would be an ideal in the way of age? In experience forty years old; in appearance twenty-five; in wisdom two million.

But, alas, it is a fact, sad or otherwise, according to the point of view from which you observe it, that actual years, experience and wisdom are three parallel lines which seldom find their point of meeting during our lifetime here on earth.

We are only too often forty years old in appearance, eighteen years in experience, and in wisdom an unborn baby, and the fact that we may be thirty years of age according to our birth certificate does not in any way help us to solve the difficulty as to how old we are in reality.

To the girl or boy of sixteen, thirty lies in the fastnesses of that which it seems unlikely we shall ever live to be; to the woman and the man of sixty, thirty is happy youth. Not callow youth, because to sixty callow youth is green fruit without flavour, but youth with understanding; and in the long run it is understanding which gives us happiness.

We all want to be young, and when I say that I do not mean that we all want to be eighteen years old for ever, but we all want to keep youth in our hearts, and most of us want to keep youth in our faces, too.

Why is this so? What is the special privilege of youth? It is, I think, the power of looking forward, the firm belief that the future holds something that is worth possessing, and that, therefore, one can let the present moment drop from one without regret and without fear. It is that which makes the eyes bright, and keeps the face unlined; it is the deep conviction that behind the tomorrow which we believe we know, and can more or less count upon, lie the endless unknown, hidden days and things, which are only waiting for us to come up to them and grasp them, to shed all manner of delights and blessings upon us.

Why do we go to beauty parlours, why are the relative merits of face-lifting and mud masks discussed in the daily papers, why do we try all the infallible remedies for keeping slim, and observe an asceticism of diet which would do credit to a nun or a monk for no other reason than that of conserving our figure and our complexion?

It is because a careful study of other people's woes has taught us that age, in itself, has no qualities which youth either envies or values, and that, as a general rule, the aged have learned no wisdom from the experience of their own personal years which youth can find any benefit in acquiring.

That is why my ideal in the way of age includes the experience of forty years and the wisdom of two million years. Wisdom (if we can believe the statements of those who claim to be wise) is frequently attained by observing the follies of others, but, so far as I know, no maker of statistics has as yet informed the world how many generations of fools it takes to produce one sage.

No one acquires wisdom out of their own experience—it may happen occasionally that a more than ordinarily intelligent person manages to acquire more common sense than he or she started with; but common sense is not the same thing as wisdom. A certain amount of experience has taught me, for instance, that time is elastic.

How often, when I have been dragged to a dinner party, have I left the house at my usual age, which is—well, never mind—and in the middle of dinner have felt myself aged at least a thousand.

At the end of the evening a thousand years seemed, comparatively speaking, young, and I left the house feeling and looking older than Cleopatra, but not, alas, nearly so good-looking.

On an occasion like that, common sense tells me that I am actually only a few hours older when I return home than I was when I left the house; but wisdom—the wisdom that has been acquired by the sufferings of other unknown and unsung martyrs throughout the ages, and which has been left as the heritage of the ages to me—tells me that harm has been done which no beauty parlour can repair.

Common sense says four hours are four hours, no matter how they are spent; wisdom says that four hours may be as forty centuries in their effect on my character and on my face.

But, you may ask, why look like twenty-five; why not look like thirty, or forty, or two million; why not be on equal terms with either your birth certificate, or your experience, or your wisdom? Because it takes away all one's fun.

Everyone likes to have a little fun—even the most serious-minded and the most highbrowed amongst us—and what better fun can there be than not being exactly what you appear to be? Financiers—statesmen—spiritual reformers, they all have their little jokes in

179

this direction, and the greater part of the time someone else is paying heavily for the privilege of being the object of the joke . . .

As I have already said, my ideal now, or next year, or at any moment of life, would be to have the worldly ability equal to forty years of personal experience, the moral support conferred by two million years of other people's hardly acquired wisdom, and the inner peace of mind and tranquillity which is attained by the fraudulent conversion of any age one happens to possess into the appearance of twenty-five.

Given favourable circumstances, that is how old I shall be next year.

'Why Worry About Your Age?'
Yorkshire Weekly Post, 1932

It had been related of the bees that, in some far-distant, pre-human epoch of the world's existence, they were endowed with Reason, and ordered their own daily lives, and the life of the hive, so well and so carefully under her rule, that at last they attained to a perfection of law and order which can be justly described as the Golden Age of the bees. In fact, they became so imbued with good habits that, by insensible degrees, they began to follow their daily pursuits without making the accustomed pauses to appeal to the Goddess of Reason for her counsel and advice. Sunk as they were in good habits, they took both her presence and her guidance for granted. In consequence of this, there followed on that Golden Age in the history of the bees, a period where voluntary and consciously-evolved good order degenerated into mere routine, and so, seeing no longer any place for her in their busy life, Reason deserted the bees. They were so confirmed in their habit of life, however, that they did not realize anything unusual had happened; they continued their outward existence exactly as before, and never realized there was a difference.

We are further told (but whether by a despondent and dis-illusioned bee, or by a vainglorious man, history does not relate) that at a still later stage of the world's evolution, the Goddess of Reason bestowed her gifts on man, and tried to help him in the ordering of his affairs. To the dispassionate observer this would seem to be empty bragging. I am not a student of history, but so far as I know there are no available data which would support this claim, or could state what was the exact epoch in the history of mankind when it was supposed to happen. It must have been at some period antecedent to the Neanderthal Man; but in any case it was so very long ago that the Golden Age of mankind, about which so much has been written, has become a fable.

We do know, however, from the evidence of our own senses, that our own Golden Age, unlike that of the bees, did not last long enough for good order to become a matter of routine with mankind. Unlike the bees, our habits of life have become so bad, that we are driven to the conclusion that either there never was a Golden Age, presided over by the Goddess of Reason, or that if there was, the difference is so great now, that Reason might just as well never have dwelt among us at all.

It is with an amazing disregard for both reason and verisimilitude that we talk about our modern civilization, and boast of the benefits accruing from it, as if any of this had any real foundation in fact.

What are the benefits of our much-vaunted civilization? Let us consider a few of them.

One of the things about which we boast most loudly, and, on the face of it, with some justice, is the great advance we have made in personal and public hygiene. Our modern hygiene, we are told, has brought about a marked decrease in contagious fevers and diseases. This would really seem to be an indisputable benefit; but, on the other hand, there is an increase in nearly every kind of nervous disorder, brought about by the racketing conditions of modern life . . .

Another of our boasts is in connection with our greatly increased facilities for travelling. Here, again, is something which at first would seem to be an obviously good thing in itself, and much is written and said about it. But against this benefit of quick and easy transport, of cheap tickets, and cheap motor-cars, there must be placed the fact that, as a direct result of it, there is now no spot on earth where one can be sure of finding either solitude or quiet. Even the North Pole, that strange Mecca of misanthropic tourists, can no longer be depended upon as a silent and deserted waste. Airships survey it, or talk about surveying it, and the softly-padding polar bear may find the ice cut from beneath his feet by an intrusive submarine, at any moment, whilst aerial engines throb and roar above his outraged head.

Thirdly, in spite of any complaints, justified or otherwise, which may be brought against the censorship as a system, we have great freedom of speech and action, in the ordinary affairs of life. Against this, we may place an inconceivable licence in manners, and a very marked increase in offences against conventions of speech and behaviour. I am not referring to criminal offences, but to those offences against taste which tend to make daily life intolerable. The lives of most people are not built up upon big, isolated events, but run along a continuous, closely-knitted chain of small social happenings, and it is against these that so many people sin today, making life unnecessarily difficult and unpleasant for those with whom they come in contact.

We could continue at length, to count the benefits of what we call with easy arrogance, our modern 'civilization'. In the history of the world many of them lie buried and hidden under jungle growth, some under sandy wastes; others have left mighty monuments by which to remind their successors that Death is a wider gate than Life. If we were to compare seriously, and with the guidance and counsel of 'reason', that which we have gained with all that which has been lost, I question if the balance would remain in our favour.

'Is Our Civilization a Benefit?'
Time And Tide, 1933

There always have been, and probably always will be, a certain number of persons who contrive to find amusement in the misfortune and the sorrows of others.

Dwarfs, misshapen creatures, freaks, and all the other pitiful 'exhibits' which used to be found in the side-shows of travelling circuses have been, in their time, a source of giggling amusement to certain of their more fortunate fellow-beings; but these latter formed a minority, and could scarcely be regarded as a social symptom.

More dangerously significant were the crowds who assisted at public torturings and public executions, and these were horribly significant as a social symptom, for the reason that all classes of society went to the composition of the crowd, and all kinds of intelligences.

We have got into the habit of regarding these sadistic, sensation-seeking crowds as something which belonged to a barbarous age, to a dark age which we have left far behind us—at any rate in opinion, if not always in actual count of years; and with it all its further accompaniment of child labour, transportation, slavery (more or less disguised), and flogging at the cart-tail.

We believe in all sincerity that we belong to an enlightened age, and speak with pride of our enlightenment and our high standard of civilization.

Yet sensationalism of the most vulgar and grossest kind is rampant today . . . and we have been deluged with minute details of 'the most sensational trial of recent years'.

It is possible to ask ourselves what posterity will think of present-day customs, in two hundred years' time, if it chances to find copies of certain newspapers still intact, in the submerged ruins of the British Museum, and reads about our doings, and studies photographs of some of the events that it was confidently supposed would stimulate the public mind.

For it must be remembered that, in these days, no one who steps outside the four sheltering walls of his—or her—house is safe from the camera. People who lived in a camera-free age sometimes complained of their neighbours' prying eyes, but little did they dream that the day would come when the prying eyes would be mechanized, and the records of its prying held fast, and printed in order that millions of other eyes might gloat over the picture of some wretched human being caught by the camera in a moment of intense emotion—whether fear, sorrow, or shame.

Cameras have arisen in our midst like a new race of mechanical ghouls.

Therefore, from a land where a boasted liberty is sometimes indistinguishable from unbridled licence, we receive photographs of a 'man of steel' facing as many cameras as there can be found room for in the inconveniently limited space of a small courthouse, while he listens to sentence of death being passed on him.

As if this were not enough, we are promised—by telephone from one continent to another, so that we may know, without needless and tiresome delay, what a really splendid sensation is awaiting us—that, by kind permission of a highly-placed and responsible official, we shall have the unprecedented pleasure of seeing a flash-light photograph of this same man, taken in his cell when he has his first meeting with his unhappy wife, after his condemnation.

'20th Century Justice Through a Camera Lens',
Sunday Referee, 1935

In the last few years a new kind of bore has arisen in the large cities—a bore who is, if possible, more malignant, more dangerous, more lethal than any private bore—than any retired major, or old lady with domestic worries.

For the noise bore afflicts the community in general, not only the private individual. The noise bore is a person who prides himself on being a nuisance to his neighbours, and who regards the power of being a nuisance as a proof that he is 'as good as' anybody (not realising that it proves merely that he is worse-mannered and more of a bore).

He regards noise rather as the Scotch regard Burns, as a kind of national heritage, and any objection to unnecessary noise is made, at once, the excuse for an avalanche of rudeness.

The worst of all noise bores is the bore possessed of a barking dog —I see the triumph of this particular bore has been reached: an unhappy woman has committed suicide because she could not stand the incessant barking of her neighbours' dogs for another day, and her complaints had been received by nothing but rudeness and further lack of consideration. I hope the owners of the dogs are proud of themselves.

Let it be understood at once that I am exceedingly fond of all animals, but that does not make me able to understand why affection for dogs is shown by shutting the poor animals outside in the cold to bark unceasingly all day and drive the neighbours to madness. But any attempt to stop this cruelty to dog and man is at once treated by all the half-wits all over the country as an attack upon the British Constitution.

When recently I wrote a letter to the Press suggesting that people should not shut their dogs outside their neighbours' windows to bark all day—since this incessant yapping makes both work and rest impossible—I received abusive letters from the whole of our national heritage of half-wits and quarter-wits.

Some of these persons called me a Bolshevik (although why it should be regarded as communistic to suggest that people should be good-mannered I cannot conceive). Others called me a vivisectionist.

Some called me a Roman Catholic; others, again, merely complained about my face, stating that it is uglier than that of any dog (though I was unaware that this simple request laid me open to a beauty competition). One lady, writing from 'Beulah', in the north of England, said that if I would 'stop writing this poetry' and would instead take the little darlings for walks, I might yet earn the gratitude and respect of the nation.

Another person said, 'If you were shut up alone all night, you would howl!' (But, my dear madam, your supposition is quite erroneous. I am shut up alone every night—for I am not one of these modern rovers—yet I do not howl.)

Another letter writer ordered me to get up from my bed in the middle of the night and see if the dog 'wanted anything'. Others, again, said, 'Chain up the owners. Do not persecute the poor dogs.'

I should like nothing better, but would not the police, I suggest with all humility, be a little surprised at the sight of a well-known poet, a maiden lady of austere aspect, chaining up householders in back yards in the middle of the night?

Others, again, accused me of 'enjoying cruelty'. Why, if it is not an indiscreet question, is it 'enjoying cruelty' to want to get on with my work? (Now, take my advice, and do not write silly letters about that, for if you do you will be answered, and you may not enjoy the answer.)

And has it ever struck my correspondents that the little darling in question may not be suffering vivisection, but may merely be barking at cats? And why, if it comes to that, should it be an offence against the British Constitution to wish not to be barked to death by dogs, yet remain perfectly respectable and even laudable not to wish to be howled to death by cats?

Have cats no rights? Are not cats, like everybody else, subject to the immortal passions?

Are these immortal passions to be put out of a cat's life simply because you, selfish creatures that you are, do not like the sound of their expression? Perish the thought! (I suppose I shall now be told that I am advocating free love and the abolition of all home ties, but I do not care.)

A cat has just as much right to his love affairs as you have to yours. And it is your duty to get out of your beds in the middle of the night to inquire if the cat wants anything.

But, seriously, have my kind, but not excessively intelligent, correspondents ever tried to show their love for animals by helping animals?

Would it not be a greater proof of our love for animals if we put the energy taken up by writing these pert letters and being a general nuisance into urging our respective Members of Parliament to insist that the penalties inflicted in the case of cruelty to animals should be made more severe—that in every case of wilful cruelty to animals there should be no option of a fine?

Hardly a week passes without all decent persons being sickened by some case of horrible and bestial cruelty towards a wretched animal or bird. We read of singing birds being blinded by a red-hot needle, of vile cruelties towards some poor dog or cat or horse.

The horrible creatures who inflict these cruelties are either mad, in which case they should be segregated, or the worst kind of criminals, in which case they should also be segregated.

Live and let live—thus one of my most imbecile correspondents ended her letter. Let us give and take. Do not let us regard it as right and proper that artists and other people should be barked to death by dogs.

Yet, on the other hand, let us show, by the penalties inflicted on those guilty of cruelty to animals, that we intend to discourage cruelty.

'Must thé World Be So Noisy?'
Sunday Express, 1928

A suggestion has been made, by certain unkind and cynical persons, that, since Dr Bridges has died, this great nation had better leave the Laureateship unfilled.

Now, why do people make this kill-joy and unkind suggestion? Will you be kind enough to tell me why? Enlighten me as to why we should deprive poets of their little joke, deprive the Great British Public, and the crowd, of its Aunt Sally. (A harmless Aunt Sally, who is prevented, by dignity, from throwing back the coconut.)

Why on earth, or by what unearthly means, Dr Bridges ever became Poet Laureate, nobody will ever know. He was one of the most learned prosodists that our race (the supreme race for producing poets) has ever evolved. His book on Milton's prosody is unsurpassed for learning and sensitiveness. He was a man who lived for his art, who was incapable of letting that art sink to the level of the 'Bright Young People'.

Why was he made Poet Laureate? Perhaps because this strange and, in spite of everything, lovable nation, that produced Shakespeare and did *not* bully him (because artist-baiting was at that time an unknown sport)—that produced Shelley and *did* bully and bait him, because it conceived that his private life was as much its affair as his poetry—that terrified and hunted Keats into his grave—that frightened Tennyson into 'The Charge of the Light Brigade'—that badgered Swinburne—yet felt that poetry *does* count after all!

It is, spiritually speaking, as courageous to be a real poet as to be a polar explorer . . . There are desert wastes, and hungers waiting for the real poet as for the explorer. And as it is a lamentable fact that to the English the universe consists of foreigners this leaves a person like myself, who was born (without my consent) into the Church of England, with the feeling that to get into Heaven is more difficult than to get into the Royal Enclosure at Ascot, and that it is just as amusing, once one has arrived there! And all this is a proof that our footsteps are set in the right path.

This esoteric feeling that the English are 'different' has affected the Laureateship too. England has to be uplifted (and inflated). I wonder whether she should be uplifted, principally, from a maritime point of view, or agriculturally, or merely domestically (otherwise suburbanly)?

Now if I had to choose a Poet Laureate, I should choose him from the last point of view. Mr Alfred Noyes would be *my* choice. I *know* that he did not actually *write* 'Tip-toe through the Too-Lips, Through the Too-Lips, Through the Too-Lips, Through the . . . etc.' (I dare not tell you the effect that song has on me: the description would resemble one of Mr James Joyce's strangest effects, and I should become a best-seller) but he *did* write something like 'The Band of Hope among the Lilacs'. And there we have the domestic life which is the backbone of old England.

Mr Masefield would uphold the maritime point of view. But, on the other hand, he *did* write 'The Widow in the Bye Street' (a poem which makes me behave like Mr Maxton, when praised) and 'The Everlasting Mercy'. So I think he is out of the running.

If we are an agricultural nation (and Lord Beaverbrook gives me the direst forebodings on this subject), there is Miss Sackville West with her poem 'The Land'. Miss Sackville West, had it not been for a flaw in fate, would have been Nature's Gentleman. Nobody is more able to tell you what country life in this English climate is like than she!

'Water alone is quite untouched by snow,' she writes: a brave little line, all by itself, and without a friend.

And if we are troubled by the uneasy movements of sheep: 'Scour the short wool for maggot, tick, or ked.'

Shelley would not have helped you like that; and he was very rightly chucked (or driven) out of England.

The great thing about this poetry, of course, is that the People shall not be made Uncomfortable; and that is where Shelley is such a wash-out. And another great thing about poetry is that it shall discover some moral message, like the moral message of 'If'.

(And I will give sixpence to anyone who can discover the moral message of either Milton's 'Sabrina Fair' or his 'Hymn on the Nativity'. Yes, I know the Hymn is about Christ, but it doesn't mention cricket or playing the game once.)

Oh, yes, there *are* poets I might mention. Mr W. B. Yeats, Mr W. H. Davies, and Mr Walter de la Mare. The younger poets stand up when they come into the room.

But who wants *poets* nowadays?

'Who Wants Poets Now?'
Evening News, 1930

Women's poetry, with the exception of Sappho (I have no Greek and speak with great humility on that subject) and with the exception of 'Goblin Market' and a few deep and concentrated, but fearfully incompetent poems of Emily Dickinson, is *simply awful*—incompetent, floppy, whining, arch, trivial, self-pitying—and any woman learning to write, if she is going to be any good at all, would, until she has made a technique for herself (and one has to forge it for oneself, there is no help to be got) write in as hard and glittering a manner as possible, and with as strange images as possible—strange, but believed in. Anything to avoid that ghastly wallowing . . .

Selected Letters

It is generally believed that poetry springs from the poet's head, as Minerva sprang from the head of Jove. That is an easy explanation of the birth of our goddess, but it is not one which satisfies me. If we were to ask any of the poets of the past, we should without doubt be told that poetry is just as much a matter of physical aptitude as of spiritual. The poet feels, with his poetry, the same certainty yet excitement as a jockey feels with a racehorse. He has sensitive hands that feel the horse's mouth, that understand all the variations of speed; he has a body that is supremely fitted to ride the horse, a body that is light and that seems like part of this polished and victorious speed.

I believe that a poem begins in the poet's head, and then grows in his blood, as a rose grows among its dark leaves.

Alexander Pope

Most of the rules for women poets begin with a 'Don't' or an 'Avoid'. 'Avoid metaphysics.' 'Don't be pompous.' 'Avoid the sonnet form, and, when possible, long lines.' For poetry is largely an affair of muscle. When we ask ourselves why Christina Rossetti's 'Goblin Market' is one of the best poems ever written by a woman, and why Mrs Elizabeth Barrett Browning's 'Aurora Leigh' is not, the answer is this. It is not only a matter of inspiration: Christina Rossetti in her poem found only and made use of a technique and a manner suitable to feminine muscles, whereas Mrs Browning used a technique and a manner which is only suitable to a man. Failure was the inevitable result. Women poets will do best if they realise that male technique is not suitable to them. No woman writing in the English language has ever written a great sonnet, no woman has ever written great blank verse. Then again, speaking generally, as we cannot dispense with our rules, so we find free verse difficult. It is true that the lady writing under the initials H.D. writes admirable and suave free verse which is technically among the best free verse written today; but she is an exception. I like the contents of Amy Lowell's free verse, but I find it for the most part formless and tuneless. Though her poems please me faintly while I am reading them, they leave no impression on my mind, because they are not definite entireties, and for this reason: they have no organic form. Free verse is a form—for it should have organic form—more suitable to men.

There have been men poets with a technique equally suitable to women: Verlaine, for instance, and Skelton to some degree. Verlaine is the most admirable example possible, not in his religious poems, but such poems, at once acrid and supremely elegant, as 'A poor young Shepherd', 'Green', 'Spleen', all the 'Fêtes Galantes', 'Tournez, tournez, bons chevaux de bois', and a hundred others. Certain of George Peele's songs, and Fletcher's appearing in their plays, would be good models for women, if they are kept sharp in form. Théophile Gautier's poems are written in a form suitable to women, but Baudelaire, in spite of his supreme elegance, is essentially a male poet. The French poets are our best models, because of their light and elegant form, for we are never successful, to my knowledge, in lines where the syllables must be heavily weighted. A woman of genius could have written all Verlaine and all Gautier, but a woman could not have written Dryden's 'Alexanders' Feast'; not because of the inspiration, but because technically it does not lie within her muscles.

Women's poetry should, above all things, be elegant as a peacock, and there should be a fantastic element, a certain strangeness in its beauty. But above all, let us avoid sentimentality: do not let us write about Pierrot, or Arcady, or how much good we should like to do in the world! And let us avoid 'a wonderful world is open to us': like the children dressed in mourning of whom Arthur Rimbaud wrote in his 'Après le Déluge', from our great glass house we can look at the marvellous pictures; or we can 'animer le clavecin des prés' with our finger—to quote again from Rimbaud; or we can write of those 'plantations prodigieuses oú les gentilshommes sauvages chassent leur chroniques sous la lumière qu'on a créé'. There is really no need to write 'Aurora Leigh'. The poem in question was meant well, but it is obvious that Mrs Browning, having once begun it, did not know how to stop, and it ended by becoming a kind of nervous tic. Her feeble state of health, no doubt, had much to do with this, and with the general weakness of her poetry. The 'Sonnets from the Portuguese' are, for the most part, beautiful in emotion, so sincere that in this way they are beyond criticism; but they are not beautiful as sonnets. What can one say of a sonnet which begins with such a ridiculous line as

> Yes, call me by my pet-name, let me hear
> The name—etc.

Mrs Browning's inspiration was for the most part earthbound, probably by her physical delicacy, poor lady. But the main trouble is that she and we are for ever haunted by the shade of her horsehair sofa. We cannot get away from it. She is always prostrated, and never in fine fighting trim—the pink of condition for a poet. If she writes of Pan and his rivers and reeds, those rivers turn into a horsehair sofa before our very eyes. She was always capable of this magic, but of this alone. Yet she was the kindest and best of women, and we can love her as a person whilst lamenting her as a poet, and disliking her rare and unexplainable talent for making great things small, and giving small things an importance, out of their focus. Whilst we are reading her, we have the comfortable certainty that the currants in her stillroom were withered stars, that infinity was bounded as the skins of her golden grapes, and that the sound of the sea was, in reality, no more remote than the splashing of water upon her washing-stand. She loved the kitchen fires of this life, and the warm and homely chirrup of human crickets. For always her work reminds me of Monsieur Jean Cocteau's dictum: 'With us there is a house, a lamp, a plate of soup, a fire, wine and pipes at the back of every important work of art . . .' and of that other sentence: 'A holy family is not necessarily a holy family: it may also consist of a pipe, a pint of beer, a pack of cards, and a pouch of tobacco.'

We turn with relief to Christina Rossetti's 'Goblin Market', for how fluent and easy is this poem—easy to all appearance, but not in reality. The rhythm swings like a bird upon a bough, or flows as spontaneously as a summer wind through bunched cool leaves. There is no faltering anywhere; inspiration and form are one and the same. What delicious prettiness, as of all young things in the early summer! Oh, the innocence and sweetness, and the dewy bloom on the fruit! Here, assuredly, is the perfect poem written by a woman. How different is this exquisite technique, the swan-like floating movement of the grave part, and the prettiness and childishness, like a little bird dancing, of the gay lines; how different is this from the clod-hopping, hearty tweed-clad manner of certain modern women verse writers, tumbling over everything they see, in their would-be mannishness! However hard we work in the future, however perfectly we teach our form to fit our inspiration, we cannot hope to write a poem more perfect in its own way than 'Goblin Market'.

'Some Observations on Women's Poetry'
Vogue, 1925

The reason why a great many people dread the very thought of poetry can, I think, be ascribed to two causes: the irritating behaviour of pseudo-intellectuals, and the memory of schooldays martyrised by the boredom of Boys on Burning Decks, Stately Homes of England and Lays of Ancient Rome. Later in life, Mr T. E. Brown's ghastly grot-wot-plot verses about his garden would be enough to set anyone against poetry—if only stuff of this sort came their way, but if they turn against the real poetry they are missing something: indeed they are! They are missing sunlight by which to see the wonders of the world.

I can imagine nothing more wonderful than to discover poetry for oneself when one is very young (or indeed, for that matter, at any age). Speaking personally, the whole world was transformed for me —became a living heavenly thing, of heavenly joys and sorrows.

For the purpose of poetry is to give joy, to wash and freshen the colours of the world, to heal the agonies of the soul, to strengthen and ennoble and invigorate. The following was written in Blake's *Vision of the Last Judgment*. 'What,' it will be questioned, 'when the sun rises, do you not see a round disk of fire, something like a guinea? Oh no, no, I see an innumerable company of the Heavenly Host crying "Holy, Holy, Holy, to the Lord God Almighty".'

The poet, the great artist, sees everything as holy. One of the most important living painters, Picasso, is supposed to have said, 'There are painters who transform the sun to a yellow spot, but there are others who with the help of their art and their intelligence, transform a yellow spot into a sun.' (From an apocryphal letter published originally in *Ogomak*—Moscow—16 May 1926, and quoted by Sergei Eisenstein in *The Film Sense* translated by J. Leyda (Faber and Faber).)

I ask you which is the greater and more important artist, the man who sees a sun as a yellow spot, or the man who sees the yellow spot as the sun? It is not certain that those brought face to face with a great vision will see it for themselves, at first. That comes to the great artist: then it becomes our possession also, and our life is transformed and made happier by it. Happiness—ah, there is the test! 'The poets of the cosmos', said Whitman, 'concentrate in the pleasure of things, they possess the superiority of genuineness over all fiction and romance . . . facts are shower'd over with light—the daylight is lit with more volatile light, the deep between setting and rising sun goes deeper manyfold. Each precise object and condition exhibits its beauty, the multiplication table its, the carpenter's trade its . . .'

In fact, as he says in *A Song of the Rolling Earth,*

> Whoever you are! motion and reflection are
> especially for you,
> The divine ship sails the divine sea for you.

And why does he say this? because 'The known universe has one complete lover, and that is the poet. He consumes an eternal passion,' and 'Poets', he said elsewhere, 'are the friends and homegivers of the whole earth, bracing the earth, and braced with the whole earth.'

That is exactly what the poet does. He gives us our home—the earth made incomparably wonderful, he takes us by the hand and tells us to see things for ourselves. For 'a great poem is no finish to a man or woman, but rather a beginning.'

The poet is our spokesman. He speaks for all of us, he says things for which we, ourselves, cannot find words. And he is not dismayed, although he may see that there is much blackness in the world, for 'from the sunlike centrality and reach of his vision, he has a faith without cloud.' (That was originally said by Emerson, of Plato.)

Do not allow people to put you against poetry.

One reason why you may dislike the thought of modern poetry is because you are confusing us with certain of our predecessors who suffered from over-civilization, stultified sense of sight and hearing. Discriminate, too, between the real poets and the persons who write verse through political piety. For a new form of intolerance has set in. No matter how bad, and how incompetent a verse writer may be, if he has read Marx and walked in a procession, he is accepted by people who know nothing about poetry, as a poet.

To hate the order of the world is not enough. Nothing will make a man a poet if he has not a genius for poetry. But Heaven has many mansions, and reading poetry is one.

'Why Not Like Poetry?'
Woman's Journal, 1944

To do justice to Edith Sitwell either as critic or lecturer would demand a separate volume.

To represent this aspect of her work we have chosen this extract from the lecture incorporated in the anthology Tradition and Experiment *published by Oxford University Press in 1929.*

. . . Not only has he seen with different eyes, but it is impossible that we shall all see alike at the present time, although the crowd would prefer uniformity of sight. The modernist artist gives us the great chance of exerting an individuality in seeing. The older beauty, the beauty of the Old Masters, is in the beauty of species and of mass —the new beauty is highly individualized and separate. The modern artist is not concerned with things in the mass, he is passionately interested in the fulfilling of the destinies of the single individuals that make up the mass—whether these individuals are men, or leaves, or waves of the sea. The great quality of the old masters in all the arts is force, used in the scientific sense of the term—the binding together of the molecules of the world. That is partly what made their sense of design so tremendous. The great quality of the modern masters is an explosive energy—the separating up of the molecules—exploring the possibilities of the atom. This is at once the quality and the danger of pioneer poetry. The aim of the modernist poets—the constant aim—is to reconcile this necessity of exploring the possibilities of the atom, with the necessity for logical design and form. The primary needs in poetry today are a greater expressiveness, a greater formality, and a return to rhetoric (good rhetoric, be it understood). Expressiveness and rhetoric mean almost but not quite the same thing. Bad rhetoric, by which I mean superimposed rhetoric —images which are meaningless and unrelated to the material and shape of the poem—is bad poetry. It was bad rhetoric which produced Stephen Phillips. But, with the exception of Wordsworth, the unceasing enemy of rhetoric, all our greatest poetry has been created, partly, by its rhetoric. Examine Milton for the truth of this. We must fear the debilitated state and lowered vitality which is shown by the outcry for understatement, for quietness, for neutral tints in poetry.

Another need in poetry is a higher sense of balance between the two components of a work of art—the spiritual side and the physical side. As regards form, there is, on the one hand, too much lolling over the borders of freedom into vacancy; on the other hand, too much tight-lacing and revulsion against growth. On this subject Mr Ezra Pound, in an article on Dolmetsch, said: 'Any work of art is a compound of freedom and of order. It is perfectly obvious that art hangs between chaos on the one hand and mechanics on the other. A pedantic insistence upon detail tends to drive out major form. A firm hold on major form makes for a freedom of detail.'

This is true. The proof of originality in a work of art is to produce personality in the bare line. At the same time there has grown up, nowadays, an almost maniacal hatred of beauty in detail—a loathing of imagery. Persons who are incapable of perceiving the relationship between any two objects and who are, consequently, incapable of perceiving the design of the world, refer to images as bric-à-brac. Naturally, the greatest poetry is not that on which the images are encrusted in such a way that they could tumble off without the design being disturbed: but that in which you cannot separate the image from the structure. Flesh and hair make the living form more beautiful, you may have observed, however elegant the structure of the bone may be. But English poetry today is a positive charnel-house of deformed and strengthless skeletons on the one hand, and on the other, a warehouse full of rolls of cheap linoleum—all this because of fear—fear of life, fear of madness, fear of free verse, though, as Mr Eliot has pointed out, 'the term is a loose one . . . any verse is called free by people whose ears are unaccustomed to it'.

Every now and then a great outcry arises from the people and the Press—a complaint that modern art is mad—in other words, irrational. I can only hope that the people are right. All great art contains an element of the irrational. One might almost say that art is the irrational spirit contained in a structure of the purest and most logical form. Without that logical form or architecture the irrational does, of course, become lunacy. The irrational spirit in logical form produced such creators as Shakespeare, Michelangelo, da Vinci, Beethoven. On the other hand, the logical spirit in irrational form produced such creators as Mr Gossip of the *Daily Sketch*, the surrealists, all the little English and American would-be poets living in Paris, Mr Desmond McCarthy, Dr Frank Crane of the 'Tonic Talks'. Art is magic, not logic. This craze for the logical spirit in irrational shape is part of the present harmful mania for uniformity— in an age when women try to abolish the difference between their aspects and aims and those of men, in an age when the edict has gone forth for the abolition of personality, for the abolition of faces— which are practically extinct. It is because of this hatred of personality that the crowd, in its uniformity, dislikes artists endued with an individual vision.

Yet when we come to consider the realm of new poetry, or of newness, and consequently strangeness—in any of the arts—let us remember that the irritation felt by people contemplating this newness has been felt by each generation towards the pioneer artists of their time. It is an irritation which is, however painful to the artist, in some ways natural to mankind. Yet it is obvious that it would not have been useful for Christopher Columbus to discover a potato patch in Spain, nor would it have been useful for Newton to discover the truths found by Galileo; and this applies equally to the arts. What an artist is for is to tell us what we see but do not know that we see. His duty is not to repeat to us, word for word, exactly what we, our fathers, and grandfathers prattled about from the cradle. But a great many people are over-tired when they have passed the age of twenty, and they don't want to be made to travel to Christopher Columbus's discoveries, or to hear the truths that were found by Newton. They are inclined to laugh at the unknown, to mock at its strange fantastic appearance, forgetting that this queer irritating substance when it becomes, as it will become automatically, a classic, will be so known, that future generations will take its beauty for granted without worrying about it. Many people say, as they have always said about contemporary work of any importance: 'These discoveries bring no great message to mankind.' How do they know? Every message is not concerned with sentimental relations between people. That is not the only aspect with which poetry is concerned. And the aspects of modern poetry are very varied. It is absurd to pretend that modernist poets have no love for humanity and are not interested in humanity.

A great many of the poems by the most advanced school—those poems which seem strangest to us—deal with the growth of consciousness—or with consciousness awakening from sleep. Sometimes you find a consciousness that has been like that of a blind person, becoming aware, intensely aware, of the nature of a tree, or of a flower, or of the way in which rain hangs or falls from objects, for the first time, and, seeing that nature, guessing, however dimly, that there is a reason, a design, somewhere outside their present state of consciousness. You find the animal state of consciousness, shaping itself from within, beginning to evolve shape out of its thick black blob of darkness. For with the development of shape out of chaos, with the power to grasp something physically, consciousness begins.

Tradition and Experiment

As biographer, and, for that matter, novelist, she excelled as a painter of portraits. These were often of minor characters, drawn succinctly, sometimes moving, more often satirical.

Portrait of 'Good' Brown

Good Brown had also, *in excelsis,* the pleasing gift of being in a state of overwhelming distress on all melancholy occasions, and the same tendency to tearfulness which the Queen had admired in Lord Melbourne; so that it was not only a kindly condescension, it was a positive pleasure, to break bad news to him. Indeed, he peers at us from the gentle pages of Her Majesty's diary, through a perfect cascade of tears, which were ever in readiness, and which sprouted from his eyes on all suitable occasions, to the admiration of all beholders. We find the phrase 'Good Brown quite overwhelmed' over and over again, and this state of affairs could be brought about as well by the present of a biscuit-box as by the news of a death. For instance, on September the 28th, 1878, poor Sir Thomas Biddulph was very ill, and whilst the Queen was writing letters in the garden-house, at a quarter to one, a fountain of tears broke at her feet, and in the centre of it Good Brown could be plainly discerned, saying, 'It's all over.' The Queen added: 'Good Brown so vexed and so kind and so feeling.' Again, on the 'blessed anniversary', August the

26th, 1878, the Queen, having given Princess Beatrice a mounted enamelled photograph of 'Our dear Mausoleum' and a silver belt of Montenegrin workmanship, sent after breakfast for her faithful Brown, and presented him with 'an oxidized silver biscuit-box and some onyx studs'. He was greatly pleased with the former and the tears came into his eyes and he said, 'It is too much.' But the Queen said, 'God knows it is not, for one so devoted and faithful.'

It is a melancholy truth, and one reflecting no credit on human nature, that cynical and heartless persons, bewildered by Good Brown's ever-ready tears, ascribed these, together with the fact that under the stress of strong emotion he had been known to totter in his walk, to causes other than grief. It is indeed reported of him that on one occasion, bowed down under the weight of some over-whelming sorrow, he fell to the ground, and for some moments remained there, in what seemed to the observers to be a merciful oblivion; but when this phenomenon was reported to Her Majesty she replied, gently, that she herself had distinctly been aware of a slight earthquake shock. For Good Brown's faithfulness was the only comfort amidst her desolation, and his tears seemed but an accompaniment of her sorrow.

Victoria of England

Portrait of Tennyson

On November the 19th, 1850, in a study of a house at Boxley near Maidenhead, a man whose appearance combined in almost equal proportions the grandeur of Homer and the rectitude of Mr Arnold of Rugby, the ruggedness of the Alps and the calm of an English Sabbath (cow-bells intermingling, as one might say, with church-bells), sat reading a letter.

Outside the window, the gold-mosaic'd trees of autumn had the cold splendour of a mausoleum, the grass, thick as a beaver's fur, the Mendelssohnian waterfall, these were at once ordered yet wild, like the appearance of the poet. And Mr Tennyson gazed from the letter to the view with a distinct sense of satisfaction. Not long before this time, his friend Mr Carlyle had described him as a 'Lifeguards-man spoilt by making poetry'; but the letter which had just arrived proved at least that the spoiling had not been complete from a worldly point of view, since it was a notification that Her Majesty had appointed Mr Tennyson as Poet Laureate.

This honour was conferred as a result of the Prince Consort's deep admiration for *In Memoriam*, and was, as well, a kind of prize won by the moral loftiness of the poet. He had, for instance, a truthfulness which could not be diverted under any circumstances, and his son places it on record that he was in the habit of saying: 'I would pluck my hand from a man even if he were my greatest hero or my dearest friend, if he wronged a woman, or told her a lie.' Indeed, it is reported of him that, when hearing, at a garden-party, a faint complaining sound, he turned to the lady next to him and said: 'Young woman, your stays creak.' But such was his love of truth, that five minutes afterwards he made his way to the distant part of the garden to which she had fled, and added: 'Young woman, I was wrong. It was not your stays, it was my braces.'

The same conscientiousness imbued every action, great or small, and was combined, strangely enough, with a sense of fun which came and went, but which was acute to a singular degree.

Mr Tennyson had had no expectation of this rise to power, for his predecessor Wordsworth had been dead for some months; it seemed to him, therefore, a strange coincidence that, only the night before he received the offer of the post, he should have dreamt that the Prince Consort came and kissed him on the cheek, in answer to which proof of affection the poet said in his dream: 'Very kind, but very German.' For some days Mr Tennyson was in doubt as to whether he should accept the Laureateship or not, but in the end he did, ascribing the decision to the fact that during dinner his friend Mr Venables had told him that if he became Poet Laureate he would always, when dining out, be offered the liver wing of a fowl.

Victoria of England

Portrait of a Doctor and his Patient

This led to Sir Charles Hall, that famous physician of the seventeenth century, becoming the centre of a scene as animated as it was remarkable. The windows of every house in the village to which he had been called, the grass-grown streets, and especially the village green outside the house of Mr Thomas Gobsill, 'a lean man, aged about twenty-six or twenty-seven', were swarming with excited yokels, as Sir Charles, calling for a ladder, and setting this against Mr Gobsill's house, bound that gentleman head downwards upon the ladder, and shook it violently.

The reason for this remarkable energy and enterprise, on the part of Sir Charles, was that Mr Gobsill, who suffered from wind, had for some time past been in the habit—on the advice of 'a friend'—of swallowing round white pebbles, in order to quell this disorder. At first, the prescription acted admirably, and Mr Gobsill was, in the due course of nature, delivered of both pebbles and wind; but some time afterwards the wind returned to him, and Mr Gobsill returned to the pebbles, and both wind and pebbles clung to Mr Gobsill and would not be parted from him. Mr Gobsill concluded, very naturally, that the best plan would be to repeat the dose, and this he did, until, instead of the original dose of nine pebbles, he had swallowed two hundred. Mr Gobsill's two hundred pebbles had remained clamped in the inner recesses of his being for the space of two years and a half, when he noticed that his appetite had gone, and that he was suffering from indigestion. He therefore consulted Sir Charles who, on examining the patient, found that if Mr Gobsill were severely shaken, the stones could be heard rattling as if they were in a bag. When the scene which I have described was enacted, the stones made a slight, slow, noisy journey in the direction of Mr Gobsill's mouth, but immediately he was reversed, and placed upon his feet once more, the surrounding multitude were gratified by the sound of the two hundred stones falling, one after another, into their original resting-place.

I do not know what was his eventual fate, or if he went to an early grave, accompanied by these faithful minerals; but his biographer, Mr Kirby, assures us, with an owlish gravity, that 'when he lay in bed, the stones would sometimes get up almost to his heart, and give him great uneasiness: at such times he was obliged to rise upon his knees, or stand upright, when he could hear them drop, and he always reckoned above one hundred.'

The English Eccentrics

Portrait of a Ghost

Sarah Whitehead, aged in this life less than twenty years, gathered up her broken dust, her blood that had turned to stone and, in the space of some hours, those remains of ruin found themselves once more in the home of her friends.

In the days and nights that followed, those wrecked and jagged pieces left by ruin, were drawn together until they formed some kind of despairing prison for a huge world of primitive chaos wherein no form existed, only a period of huge clots of darkness followed by a universe of mad and chattering light that had once been empty waiting sunlight. Then, slowly, her whole being would be invaded by some huge and formless bulk, growing vaster as it loomed out of the blackness and the light, until both blackness and light were blotted out. Then after an aeon that existed not in time, that huge bulk would shrink until it was nothing but a small helpless creature, emitting a terrible broken crying, a hopeless, helpless whimpering as it was torn to pieces. But no sound from that crying reached the world beyond, for the prison that entombed it was too strong, and that prison longed to break, but could not. Yet I have heard that sound raising itself, amid the little tumults of the dust, the lip-clicks of worms that are soon to transform themselves into the speech, and the kiss of mankind; although the busy dusty world is too deafened by the sound of the machines that it has made for the trapping and murdering of time to listen to those sounds that are clear as the songs of angels.

The English Eccentrics

Portrait of an Ornamental Hermit

Whilst these persons of varying respectability were trying, in their several ways, to preserve their lives, others, equally, or more, praiseworthy, were trying to escape the consequences of being alive. And, in aid of this praiseworthy desire, certain noblemen and country squires were advertising for Ornamental Hermits. Nothing, it was felt, could give such delight to the eye, as the spectacle of an aged person with a long grey beard, and a goatish rough robe, doddering about amongst the discomforts and pleasures of Nature.

The Honble Charles Hamilton, whose estate was at Pains' Hall, near Cobham, Surrey, and who lived in the reign of King George the Second, was one of these admirers of singularity and silence, and, having advertised for a hermit, he built a retreat for this ornamental but retiring person on a steep mound in his estate.

This hermitage annoyed Mr Horace Walpole, who announced that it was ridiculous to set aside a quarter of one's garden to be melancholy in: and, indeed, the retreat seems to have been remarkable more for its discomfort than for its beauty, for we learn that there was 'an upper appartment, supported in part by contorted legs and roots of trees, which formed the entrance to the cell'. Still, Mr Hamilton seems to have found no difficulty in procuring the hermit; and in any case, a professional discomfort was only to be expected by the hermit, who, according to the terms of the agreement, must 'continue in the hermitage seven years, where he should be provided with a Bible, optical glasses, a mat for his feet, a hassock for his pillow, an hourglass for his timepiece, water for his beverage, and food from the house. He must wear a camlet robe, and never, under any circumstances, must he cut his hair, beard, or nails, stray beyond the limits of Mr Hamilton's grounds, or exchange one word with the servant.' If he remained without breaking one of these conditions, in the grounds of Mr Hamilton for seven years, he was to receive, as a proof of Mr Hamilton's admiration and satisfaction, the sum of seven hundred pounds. But if, driven to madness by the intolerable tickling of the beard, or the scratching of the camlet robe, he broke any of the conditions laid down, he was not to receive a penny! It is a melancholy fact that the Ornamental Hermit stayed in his retreat for exactly three weeks!

The English Eccentrics

Portrait of an Actor

But there was a fresh scene, and this time of unexampled pathos, when Mr Coates appeared at the Haymarket Theatre in *Romeo and Juliet* on the occasion of a benefit performance in aid of Miss Fitz-Henry, the daughter of an old lady named Lady Perrott, who had invoked Mr Coates' aid on a previous occasion. Miss FitzHenry, as Juliet, became so terrified by the menacing attitude of the audience, that, shrieking, she clung to the scenery and pillars in great agitation; and could not be dislodged. Another time, in the duel scene where Romeo kills Tybalt, all was ruined, and the house was convulsed with laughter at the appearance of a bantam cock, which strutted at the very feet of Romeo, at whom it had been thrown. Mr Coates was in despair, but luckily, at the last and darkest moment, old Capulet seized the cause of the trouble and bore him, crowing loudly, and flapping his wings, off the stage.

His biographers enquire, not without indignation, 'what should we think now if an amateur of good private fortune made his appearance, drawing houses that even Garrick might have envied, and one who combined with dramatic taste that for unique and brilliant equipages —what would the present generation think of such a person being received with cries derisive of his armorial bearing, real or assumed, together with remarks upon his carriage and servants?' What, indeed?

The play continued, though, when Romeo left the stage after killing Tybalt, he stood in the wings and shook his sword at the box from which the cock had been thrown on to the stage, with the result that the occupants of the box yelled that he must apologise for shaking his sword. Mr Coates, very naturally, refused to do so, and the interruptions continued until the occupants of the pit turned on the interrupters and pelted them with orange peel. The play continued, then, without any further interruption until the moment came when Romeo kills Paris. Then the latter, lying dead upon the ground, was raised to life by 'a terrific blow on the nose from an orange'. The corpse rose to his feet and, pointing in a dignified way to the cause of his revival, made his way off the stage. Mr Coates, we are told, was 'considerably annoyed' during the Tomb Scene, by shouts of 'Why don't you die?'

The English Eccentrics

Portrait of Squire Waterton

Life at Walton Hall was full of surprises, and it need hardly be said that the Squire's daily round was planned on lines entirely different to that of anybody else. He never slept in a bed, for instance, but on the floor, wrapped in his cloak, and with a block of beech-wood for a pillow. He rose at 3.30, and after lighting his fire, spent half an hour in the chapel, and then began his day's work. He detested smart young gentlemen, whom he christened 'Miss Nancies' and 'Man milliners', but, beyond these, loved all human creatures.

He cherished a great friendship, for instance, with a young lady chimpanzee, who, in her caged condition, suffered from ill health. The Wanderer visited her daily and, on leaving, invariably imprinted a gallant kiss upon her cheek.

As for owls, the twenty-seventh lord of Walton Hall once journeyed from Italy to England with cages filled with these; and, having succeeded in passing his friends through the not unnaturally astonished Custom House of Genoa, he decided that as a bath was necessary to him it was necessary also to the owls. Alas, the bath was not a success, and many of the owls died . . .

The great naturalist and traveller made four journeys to the New World in search of adventure, and in order to find the woorali poison, which was one of the chief interests of his existence. In 1812, the date of his first journey, he found that the region had undergone but little change since the time of Raleigh. Knowing that the towers of El Dorado were but castles in the air, he wished to know if Lake Panina were a myth.

It was during these wanderings that Mr Waterton took a ride upon a crocodile, and, in his anxiety to study the dental arrangements of the serpent, shared his bedroom for one night with a Coulacanara, 'fourteen feet long, not poisonous, but large enough to have crushed one of us to death. A Coulacanara of fourteen feet in length is as thick as a common boa of twenty-four,' as Mr Waterton remarked drily . . .

As for the woorali poison, that much-cherished, much-sought-for treasure, it is satisfactory to know that Mr Waterton did meet with it at last, and that he bore it home in triumph to England. He claimed that it would cure hydrophobia—I do not know for what reason—and his experiments with the treasured woorali were as fantastic as any of his other exploits. On one occasion, he and his friend Mr Higginbotham, the eminent surgeon of Nottingham, poisoned a donkey, not very charitably, as I think, with the beloved but feared woorali, producing apparent death. Then, with a lancet, they made an incision in the long-suffering quadruped's windpipe, producing artificial respiration. Life returned, the donkey rose, Mr

Waterton rode round the room upon its back, and it was for many years afterwards a pensioner on the estate of Walton Hall.

The English Eccentrics

Portrait of Wyndham Lewis
(Alias Henry Debingham)

Mr Debingham was alone when he received Becky's letter, a sitter having just left the studio. This was situated in a piece of waste ground haunted by pallid hens, squawking desolately and prophetically, and the appearance of Mr Debingham's hair aroused in some observers the conviction that the feathers of these had sought within its shades a safe refuge from the general confusion. Another school of thought, however, ascribed the alien substances by which it appeared to be bestrewn to a different cause, believing them to be a sprinkling of the snows of Time. For the nature of his toilette and his general appearance, undoubtedly aroused attention and gave rise to speculation. His complexion, always dark, was at moments darker than others; and this phenomenon was due to no freak of nature or change in pigmentation, but to habits and chance. His clothes seemed as much a refuge as a covering, and when fully equipped to face the world and the weather, he presented much the same appearance as that which we are privileged to see in photographs taken of certain brave men at the very moment of their rescue after six months spent among the Polar Wastes and the blubber.

Now, giving a savage kick to the warring and varying objects which hid the floor from view, and which seemed to spend the whole time in clamouring for his attention . . . He grinned, and as he grinned, his personality underwent a lightning change. It was as if you had been looking at a lantern slide . . . A click, a fade-out, and another slide . . . had taken its place . . . For this remarkable man, who was a sculptor in those moments which he could spare from thinking about himself, and from making plans to confute his enemies, had a habit of appearing in various roles, partly in disguise (for caution was part of his professional equipment) and partly in order to defy his loneliness . . .

There was the Spanish role, for instance, in which he would assume a gay manner, very masculine and gallant, and deeply impressive to a feminine observer. When appearing in this character he would wear a sombrero, would, from time to time, allow the exclamation Caramba!' to escape him, and would build castles in the air . . . with square blockish movement of his thick meat-coloured hands . . . He would, too, when out of doors, draw his stick along the railings, with what he hoped was a flash of teeth. But always, just as the teeth were about to flash, the sun went in, so that the phenomenon was not discernible, or his bootlaces came undone and he was forced to do them up, so that the people on the top of the passing omnibus, who had been intended to witness and to admire the flash, could not see it. His life was full of little disappointments of this kind.

I Live Under A Black Sun

['Wyndham Lewis figured as Debingham', Edith Sitwell to Pamela Hansford Johnson, *Selected Letters*]

Portrait of Mrs Vanelden

The house in which Mrs Vanelden lived had a double personality. The door and the window-sills were painted a sharp and chattering white, a striped curtain, bright as the summer weather, sheltered the door from the heat, an awning of the same material covered the balcony, and suspended from the latter were baskets of geraniums, and also of large flaunting marguerites that had a hard, boastful innocence and were as shining and glaring as if they had been painted. Everything in the rooms on the ground floor and first and second floors was very bright and happy and summery, it spoke of ease and of optimism; but on the top floor, or, as Mrs Vanelden persisted in calling it, 'the nursery floor' (she had never brought herself to remove the small gate on the landing which had prevented her four children from falling downstairs), where the girls shared a sitting-room, all was dinginess, all was dust and confusion. It was crowded with half-finished occupations, taken up because there was nothing more amusing to do at the moment, and forgotten before they were completed, dog-eared books left open on a table, pieces of soiled embroidery thrown down on a chair, a half-darned stocking, an unfinished letter, a half-filled cup of tea that had gone cold. It was a room in which something was always being lost—a handbag or a heart—and recovered again in a slightly dilapidated condition from under a little drift of dust.

The household, too, seemed to have a double personality, and to be divided into two sections. Mrs Vanelden's section was the ante-chamber to a discreet paradise, to a heaven that made allowances. She was a woman in late middle age, whose clothes bore a close resemblance to an untidy nest, in the midst of which a musty density, a wingless but feathery entity, brooded over nothingness. The nest was covered with mossy velvet, fronds of feather, tinkling bright objects that looked as if they might have been stolen and made use of by a jackdaw, and pieces of dry and withered narrow ribbon that gave the impression of being pieces of straw. In colour and con-sistency, her hair was like sodden autumn leaves, and this, again, added to her nest-like appearance. It was drawn back in such a way that her face wore a look of innocent surprise, and wherever she might be, she gave the impression that she had found herself there inadvertently, and had reached the spot by some unexplainable means. Her eyes, which were round and shaped like those of a goose, were left deliberately vacant of thought, in order that occasionally an expression of great tenderness towards the whole world might spring into them. But this, again, would be quickly withdrawn as soon as it had served its purpose by striking the right note, much as a cuckoo will spring from the clock, strike the hour, and then return to its seclusion. For Mrs Vanelden, who prided herself on the possession of a good heart, was careful not to make much use of this, for fear of ruining it by an overstrain.

She had spent much time in Switzerland, patronising the mountains, praising their stature and grandeur with an amused, light and summery laugh; and into this laugh she had carefully instilled the echo of the mountain bells. It had been trained to move in silvery arpeggios, going first up, then down. At moments, however, when she was tired or was, for one reason or another, intending to show a particular amiability to somebody, a more natural laugh sounded, and this was strangely reminiscent of the sound made by a cuckoo when considering the means by which its offspring might most safely and unobtrusively be placed in another bird's nest. Her voice was deliberately simple, it was designed to show that she was a simpleton, and she was in the habit of retailing stories which showed her in this light, which exhibited her utter unworldliness. She was always, it appeared, being cheated and deceived, and for some reason this seemed to give her a great deal of pleasure. 'You know what I am,' she would say, and would laugh at herself affectionately.

She had little money, but owing to her simplicity and unworldliness, had laid up for herself, as it were, much treasure in heaven. Her most worldly friends—and she had many—prided themselves on the fact that they could set store by such a simple-minded creature. That she should take it for granted that they would appreciate and value at its true worth such simple-mindedness, was an obvious tribute to the often unsuspected goodness of the hearts that lay within them, and it was rewarded by loans of villas on the Riviera, boxes at the opera, motors, and by scores of invitations. Nobody was more surprised than Mrs Vanelden when these blessings were showered upon her. But though, as she explained, she cared little for these things, indeed, they took up much of the time which she would have far preferred to spend in reading quietly ('you know what I am') it would have seemed ungrateful, almost churlish, to refuse them.

She would frequently lament the constant calls on her time made by these invitations and by her hosts of friends, saying, with a little resigned laugh: 'Mais que voulez-vous? I suppose it is a duty like another, to give sympathy, or advice, or the support of one's presence. But people spoil me too much, and I must confess that there are moments when I would like to have a little time for reading, for my own thoughts, for self-development.'

To Mrs Vanelden, self-development meant an increase of cosiness, an added certainty that she was right in every action, every thought. She lived for the comfort of the mind, and the whole of existence seemed so dependent upon her convenience, that you felt she had spun the world out of herself, as a silk-worm spins silk—or a spider her web—to form a cocoon, a place of warmth, a surrounding, a nest for herself, or a trap for others; and this impression was increased by the fact that she spent a great deal of time in knitting, weaving webs of soft wool to protect herself from the blasts from heaven. When you were with her, your inner world died.

The society in which she mixed was very varied. As I have hinted, the nest (and she brooding within it) was situated in the shade of many powerful and protective persons, eminent and accommodating divines, sleek and pouting, filling their coats and their own spiritual needs as compactly and fully as a neatly rounded potato fits its skin, celebrated and acquisitive divorcees who, during the reign of King Edward the Seventh, had cast their hearts about as if they were nice hard tennis balls; and leaders of society, some with voices like the bellowing of the Golden (or Brazen) Calf, others like a tunicate, possessing, to quote the scientific description of this elementary form of life, a preference for dwelling amidst mud, a stomach and a mouth, but neither nerves nor a heart. There were, too, a good many elderly peers and a few clean-shaven American, or pseudo-American, business-women, possessed of large salaries and immense competence, who carried huge and expensive bags, with gold fittings, from which they would produce what appeared to be time-tables, and whose voices, movements and general habits gave the impression that they had portable homes situated on the platforms of Victoria station.

Nor were these all. For in the shadow of these magnificent figureheads of various kinds could be discerned a dim and amorphous undergrowth, persons useful but not powerful, discreet sycophantic and anonymous women, the ghosts of fashionable restaurants, pondering and pandering, waiting and watching, to discover, chronicle and hymn the praise of the newest fashion in behaviour, customs, and persons.

Such was the background against which the simplicity of Mrs Vanelden showed in such admirable relief.

Her woman friends seemed, for the most part, geometrical cyphers, sexless figures of indestructible, highly varnished Birmingham hardware, but with a Metropolitan polish, and turned out according to the latest international taste in hardware. Their faces were like the definition of Zero . . . 'Nothing—nought—duck's egg—goose's egg —cypher—none—nobody . . .' and from these epitomes would issue the new fashionable voice, deliberately colourless and wooden, or tinny and tiny, or rich and artificially hoarse. It might be said of these ladies that Respectability was the only outcast with whom they were not on speaking terms. They could bear neither her nor her votaries, making an exception, however, in favour of Mrs Vanelden and her daughters, for the reason that 'their house is *too* amusing, my dear. You never know who you may find there.' To these were added a crowd of young men, screaming about 'chic' and 'the latest thing, my dear', in voices high and shrill as those of parrots or peacocks. Their costumes were as striking as the feathers of these birds, and they had attained to a certain gossip-column fame because of their schemes of interior decoration, walls covered with boot-buttons or straw, or furniture made of steel. Amongst these sophisticated persons there were, however, a few girls whose youthfulness, even childishness, equalled that of Mrs Vanelden's daughters. And two of these latter examples now rushed into the room, clapping their hands and screaming in high childish voices.

This outbreak occurred at a moment when Mrs Vanelden, her daughters, and a select company of greater and lesser friends were seated round the dining-room table, having nursery tea, as the hostess called it. For Mrs Vanelden had never quite grown up, as she confessed, and nursery tea was one of the simple pleasures to be enjoyed in her house. As the young girls burst into the room, Mrs Vanelden, who was in the habit of taking her guests on a personally conducted tour of her principal characteristics, acting as guide and showman, and pointing out, with a gentle, half-amused, half affectionate laugh, the less easily discerned treasures of the collection, was descanting on her love of flowers, a passion that was amongst her prettiest originalities.

'I *adore* flowers. I can't live without them. It is my way, I suppose; I am like that. And the simpler the flowers are, the more I love them. Primroses are the flowers I really love the best, dear *soft* things. How I should love to wander out into the woods now, yes, at this moment, and pick some.'

'But you couldn't pick them now,' said a young man. 'Primroses in summer!'

'For me,' said Mrs Vanelden quietly, 'there are *always* primroses. I adore them! Lord Sunningdale—dear naughty thing, he is always spoiling me, he knows what I am, and says someone must take care of me, for I never take care of myself—sent me such a huge box of orchids this morning, out of his greenhouses. I suppose they are very magnificent really, people who know tell me they are. Still, I shall always love primroses *best*, though of course I love these flowers too, because they come from my dear old friend.'

A middle-aged man, raising his eyes from his plate, said with a nervous titter: '*I* love pansies! I always talk to them if I can. They say such a lot to me, with those lovely black-fringed eyes of theirs. You have no idea of the things one can say to a pansy.'

I Live Under A Black Sun

Portrait of Miss Linden

In her small bedroom, far away in Ireland, now that all the household noises had ceased and the prying eyes were shut in sleep, Miss Linden, who had passed the last fifteen years of her life in pulling strenuously at frayed ends, without any hope of reconciling them, behind hermetically sealed doors, whilst showing in public a langorous and admired coquetry, with the coquetry increasing as the admiration diminished, finished re-reading the letter. She had read it, not once, but three times, so that she might be certain that nothing had escaped her, and now, putting it away hurriedly and secretively, she sat down again, looking round the familiar room. Once, her eyes caught those of her own reflection in the glass, and she looked at it curiously, as if she were seeing the face of an acquaintance whom she had known in past years, expecting to see traces in it of a long illness and of many adventures of which she was ignorant. It was strange; even a month ago, when she looked in her mirror, it had seemed to her smooth and beautiful—her face and her whole body had looked as if it were carved by some calm and dark wind from the Pyramids. But now—and perhaps it was only because the insufficient light of the one candle, stuttering like an idiot's tongue, told one nothing, the darkness of her face seemed changed; it was no longer smooth, but full of abysses as if she were already very old and her life was over. There were depths of hollow darkness about her, behind the vast black blaring shadow of her eyes, tunnelled harsh and animal as the braying of an ass, in her wide nostrils that opened upon darkness, in the large beast-furred mole near her lips, that belied the tip-toeing life that she had led for so many years. Her body, her face, seemed blackened, charred, and twisted, as if some enormous fire had devoured her life and had then died in the daylight, leaving only this ruin, this empty hulk slumbering behind lidless and wide-open eyes.

I Live Under A Black Sun

1942-1947

Miss Sitwell's poems are loved and reverenced everywhere, as they should be. Their music is superb, like the sweeping and powerful periods of William Blake in his prophetic robes.

Richard Church in John O' London's Weekly

Very few poets of our time have such true eloquence, such supple craftsmanship, or such inner fire.

G. S. Fraser in The Observer

After 1940 is the period of long lines and long odes, comparable with Mr Eliot's 'Four Quartets' or Yeats's post Byzantine manner.

Cyril Connolly, Previous Convictions

Street Songs is having really terrific reviews. Of course the *Undertakers Gazette* and the *East Anglian Advertiser* speak about 'these pleasant pages' and tell me where I get off and a Mr Austin Clarke in some Irish paper says that though it is obvious I feel things, my technique is so bad that I can't express it—or words to that effect. But, on the other hand, *The Times Literary Supplement*, which I can't help feeling is slightly more important, has fairly let itself go, about 'this majestic assurance', 'noble and unassailable simplicity', 'the true greatness of her poetic art'. And Stephen Spender, who never, I think, cared much for my poetry before, now says the poems are extremely beautiful.

Selected Letters

With the publication of Street Songs *in 1942, Edith Sitwell found herself accepted as a major poet. Macmillans, who had replaced Duckworths as her publisher, brought out her* Poet's Notebook; *in 1944 came her second collection,* Green Song, *then, in the last year of the war, her own selection from her work called* The Song of the Cold.

It was a second flowering, considered by most critics to be her best. Her style had changed. She used long lines:

sometimes unrhymed, but with occasional rhymes, assonances and half assonances, used outwardly and inwardly in the lines, to act as ground rhythm.

Preface to *Collected Poems*

Her statement, too, had changed:

I wrote of the summer of the earth and of the heart, and of how the warmth of the heart faded and only a false brotherhood remained. But as yet the sun itself had not been harnessed to a war-machine and used against us. We could still remember the holy life-giving warmth.

What had brought it about? Anguish, of course, at the outbreak of another war, more terrible than the first and, it could be claimed, predicted in her novel I Live Under A Black Sun:

He had been watching the soldiers march by on their way to join the procession. So gay they looked, and their uniforms and muskets were so bright that they seemed like sparkles of the heat—you would never think that darkness could overtake them; yet their shadows under the huge gold sun were haggard and ragged, were all bent and broken, and looked as if they were already old—or as if no hope was left in all the world. These foolish mockeries walked side by side with the strong young men, so full of blood, so full of hope, the promise of the future. And the steady trained march raised up a lot of dust—you would think that the whole world was made of dust, the whole of existence, everything that you touched, that you loved, that you

215

knew. And in the great heat the sound of their footsteps seemed intensified, far louder and more hollow, so that you could not believe you were listening to the sound of only two companies marching. You would have thought that six million men were on the march— yes, six million men.

There was another reason for the second flowering—isolation, brought on by conditions of war. Forced to leave Paris; her father abroad; her mother and Helen Rootham both dead, Edith Sitwell now lived with her brother Osbert at Renishaw.

Once again she had been removed from the pressures of the immediate. The long sight was restored. She was again 'a little outside life'. The 'deep humanist passion' recognized by the critic Jack Lindsay took the place of the more personal passions of the previous decade. The poet's perspective was restored.

The reason for the amount of work she produced was the leisure offered her by life at Renishaw. Wordsworth, a poet she quoted very often, defined poetry as emotion recollected in tranquillity. Edith Sitwell had found the tranquillity necessary to recollect the emotion of the previous decade. Not that leisure meant idleness. She regarded herself as a working woman. Her day began when she woke at five or six in the morning. She went to bed early and, as she told T. S. Eliot when writing to invite him to Renishaw:

Nobody ever comes down to breakfast—people disappear for hours on end if they want to, go out by themselves if they want to, or stop in by themselves. They go away to work, if they feel like it, or for siestas that last for hours. Nobody is ever hurried or badgered.

Selected Letters

This was an atmosphere in which to read, to write, and to contemplate. She wrote about 'the world reduced to the Ape as mother, teacher, protector', and she wrote about the faith which redeemed it:

With poor Christopher Smart, I blessed Jesus Christ with the Rose and his people, which is a nation of living sweetness.

Preface to *Collected Poems*

'Now,' said John Russell in the Sunday Times, *she 'belongs to the greatest tradition of English religious poetry.'*

Still falls the Rain

The Raids, 1940. Night and Dawn

Still falls the Rain—
Dark as the world of man, black as our loss—
Blind as the nineteen hundred and forty nails
Upon the Cross.

Still falls the Rain
With a sound like the pulse of the heart that is changed to the
    hammer-beat
In the Potter's Field, and the sound of the impious feet

On the Tomb:
       Still falls the Rain
In the Field of Blood where the small hopes breed and the human
    brain
Nurtures its greed, that worm with the brow of Cain.

Still falls the Rain
At the feet of the Starved Man hung upon the Cross.
Christ that each day, each night, nails there, have mercy on us—
On Dives and on Lazarus:
Under the Rain the sore and the gold are as one.

Still falls the Rain—
Still falls the Blood from the Starved Man's wounded Side:
He bears in His Heart all wounds,—those of the light that died,
The last faint spark
In the self-murdered heart, the wounds of the sad uncomprehending
    dark,
The wounds of the baited bear,—
The blind and weeping bear whom the keepers beat
On his helpless flesh . . . the tears of the hunted hare.

Still falls the Rain—
Then—O Ile leape up to my God: who pulles me doune—
See, see where Christ's blood streames in the firmament:
It flows from the Brow we nailed upon the tree
Deep to the dying, to the thirsting heart
That holds the fires of the world,—dark-smirched with pain
As Caesar's laurel crown.

Then sounds the voice of One who like the heart of man
Was once a child who among beasts has lain—
'Still do I love, still shed my innocent light, my Blood, for thee.'

Lullaby

Though the world has slipped and gone,
Sounds my loud discordant cry
Like the steel birds' song on high:
'Still one thing is left—the Bone!'
Then out danced the Babioun.

She sat in the hollow of the sea—
A socket whence the eye's put out—
She sang to the child a lullaby
(The steel birds' nest was thereabout).

'Do, do, do, do—
Thy mother's hied to the vaster race:
The Pterodactyl made its nest
And laid a steel egg in her breast—
Under the Judas-coloured sun.
She'll work no more, nor dance, nor moan,
And I am come to take her place.
Do, do.

There's nothing left but earth's low bed—
(The Pterodactyl fouls its nest):
But steel wings fan thee to thy rest,
And wingless truth and larvae lie
And eyeless hope and handless fear—
All these for thee as toys are spread,
Do—do—

Red is the bed of Poland, Spain,
And thy mother's breast, who has grown wise
In that fouled nest. If she could rise,
Give birth again,

218

In wolfish pelt she'd hide thy bones
To shield thee from the world's long cold,
And down on all fours shouldst thou crawl
For thus from no height canst thou fall—
Do, do.

She'd give no hands: there's naught to hold
And naught to make: there's dust to sift,
But no food for the hands to lift.
Do, do.

Heed my ragged lullaby,
Fear not living, fear not chance;
All is equal—blindness, sight,
There is no depth, there is no height:
Do, do.

The Judas-coloured sun is gone,
And with the Ape thou art alone—
Do,
    Do.'

Serenade: Any Man to Any Woman

Dark angel who art clear and straight
As cannon shining in the air,
Your blackness doth invade my mind
And thunderous as the armoured wind
That rained on Europe is your hair;

And so I love you till I die—
(Unfaithful I, the cannon's mate):
Forgive my love of such brief span,
But fickle is the flesh of man,
And death's cold puts the passion out.

I'll woo you with a serenade—
The wolfish howls the starving made;
And lies shall be your canopy
To shield you from the freezing sky.

219

Yet when I clasp you in my arms—
Who are my sleep, the zero hour
That clothes, instead of flesh, my heart,—
You in my heaven have no part,
For you, my mirage broken in flower,

Can never see what dead men know!
Then die with me and be my love:
The grave shall be your shady grove
And in your pleasaunce rivers flow

(To ripen this new Paradise)
From a more universal Flood
Than Noah knew: but yours is blood.

Yet still you will imperfect be
That in my heart like death's chill grows,
—A rainbow shining in the night,
Born of my tears . . . your lips, the bright
Summer-old folly of the rose.

Street Song

'Love my heart for an hour, but my bone for a day—
At least the skeleton smiles, for it has a morrow:
But the hearts of the young are now the dark treasure of Death,
And summer is lonely.

Comfort the lonely light and the sun in its sorrow,
Come like the night, for terrible is the sun
As truth, and the dying light shows only the skeleton's hunger
For peace, under the flesh like the summer rose.

Come through the darkness of death, as once through the branches
Of youth you came, through the shade like the flowering door
That leads into Paradise, far from the street,—you, the unborn
City seen by the homeless, the night of the poor.

You walk in the city ways, where Man's threatening shadow,
Red-edged by the sun like Cain, has a changing shape—

Elegant like the Skeleton, crouched like the Tiger,
With the age-old wisdom and aptness of the Ape.

The pulse that beats in the heart is changed to the hammer
That sounds in the Potter's Field where they build a new world
From our Bone, and the carrion-bird days' foul droppings and
    clamour—
But you are my night, and my peace,—

The holy night of conception, of rest, the consoling
Darkness when all men are equal,—the wrong and the right,
And the rich and the poor are no longer separate nations,—
They are brothers in night.'

This was the song I heard; but the Bone is silent!
Who knows if the sound was that of the dead light calling,—
Of Caesar rolling onward his heart, that stone,
Or the burden of Atlas falling.

O Yet Forgive

O yet forgive my heart in your long night!
I am too poor to be Death's self so I might lie
Upon your heart . . . for my mortality
Too sad and heavy is, would leave a stain
Upon young lips, young eyes . . . You will not come again:
So the weight of Atlas' woe, changed to a stone,
And that stone is my heart, I laid above
Your eyes, till blind as love
You no more see the work of the old wise.

But you in your long night are not deceived:
And so, not heeding the world, you let it roll
Into the long abyss
And say, 'What is that sound? I am alone . . .
Is it my great sunrise?'

Poor Young Simpleton

1. An Old Song Re-sung

'Once my love seemed the Burning Bush,
The Pentecost Rushing of Flames:
Now the Speech has fallen to the chatter of alleys
Where fallen man and the rising ape
And the howling Dark play games.

For she leaned from the light like the Queen of Fairies
Out of the bush of the yellow broom . . .
"I'll take out that heart of yours," she said,
"And put in your breast a stone.
O, I'll leave an empty room," she said,
"A fouled, but an empty room." '

II

'I walked with my dead living love in the city—
The Potter's Field where the race of Man
Constructs a new world with hands thumbless from unuse—
(Pads like a tiger's)—a skeleton plan.

We walked in the city where even the lightning—
The Flag of Blood flying across the world,
The Flag of immeasurable Doom, of God's warning—
Is changed to a spider's universe, furled

For a banner of hunger . . . the world of the thunder
Is dulled till it seems but the idiot drum
Of a universe changed to a circus—the clatter
Where the paralysed dance in the blind man's slum.

But the sun was huge as a mountain of diamonds
That starved men see on a plain far away:
It will never buy food, but its red fires glittered
On the Heart of Quietness, my Eden day.

For she was the cool of the evening, bringing
The dead child home to the mother's breast,
The wanderer homeward, far from the hammer
That beats in the Potter's Field: she was my rest,

And the Burning Bush, and the worker's Sunday,
The neighbour of Silence, speech to the still,
And her kiss was the Fiery Chariot, low swinging
To take me over the diamond hill.

Where the crowds sweep onward, mountaineers, nomads
From cities and continents man has not seen,
With beachcombers drifted from shores that no wave has known,
Pilgrims to shrines where no God-head has been,

We watched the somnambulists, rope-walkers, argonauts,
Avatars, tamers of steel-birds and fugitives
From dream and reality, emigrants, mourners,
And each with his Shadow, to prove that Man lives!

And with them come gaps into listening Darkness:
The gun-men, the molochs, the matadors, man-eaters,
Hiding in islands of loneliness, each one
Infections of hatred and greed-plague and fear.

For the season of red pyromaniacs, the dog-days
Are here, and now even the sun of a kiss
Sets a city on fire, and the innocent roses
Are the fever of foolish world-summers; and this

Beloved of my skeleton laughed, and said, "Tell me—
Why give me your heart like an eagle that flies,
Or a sun?—You should give me a crow for my dinner,
Or a flat dirty penny to lay on my eyes."

And how can I save the heart of my Eden
That is only the hammering heart of the town,
When the only world left is my skeleton's city
Where the sun of the desert will never go down?

She has hearkened the Spider's prudence, the wisdom
That, spinning a foul architecture, unfurled
From his belly a city he made out of Hunger—
Constructed for Hunger's need: his is the world.

So what can I give to her? Civilisation's
Disease, a delirium flushed like the rose
And noisy as summer? Hands thumbless from unuse—
(From pads like a tiger's what bright claw grows?)

Though faithless the rose and the flesh, yet the city,
That eternal landscape, the skeleton's plan,
Has hope for its worm . . . I will give her the pity
For the fallen Ape, of the Tiger, Man.

For my Eden is withered. I, damned by the Rainbow,
Near that fouled trodden alley, the bed where she lies,
Can wake no false dawn,—where, for want of a penny,
She lies with the sins of the world on her eyes.'

Song

Once my heart was a summer rose
That cares not for right or wrong,
And the sun was another rose, that year,
They shone, the sun and the rose, my dear—
Over the long and the light summer land
All the bright summer long.

As I walked in the long and the light summer land,
All that I knew of shade
Was the cloud, my ombrelle of rustling grey
Sharp silk, it had spokes of grey steel rain—
Hiding my rose away, my dear,
Hiding my rose away.

And my laughter shone like a flight of birds
All in the summer gay,—
Tumbling pigeons and chattering starlings
And other pretty darlings, my dear,
And other pretty darlings.

To my heart like a rose, a rain of tears
(All the bright summer long)
Was only the sheen on a wood-dove's breast,
And sorrow only her song, my love—
And sorrow only my rest.

I passed a while in Feather Town—
(All the bright summer long)—

The idle wind puffed that town up
In air, then blew it down.

I walk alone now in Lead Town
(All in the summer gay . . .)
Where the steady people walk like the Dead—
And will not look my way.

For withering my heart, that summer rose,
Came another heart like a sun,—
And it drank all the dew from the rose, my love,
And the birds have forgotten their song
That sounded all summer long, my dear—
All the bright summer long.

Green Flows the River of Lethe—O

Green flows the river of Lethe—O
Long Lethe river
Where the fire was in the veins—and grass is growing
Over the fever—
The green grass growing . . .

I stood near the Cities of the Plains;
And the young girls were chasing their hearts like the gay butterflies
Over the fields of summer—
O evanescent velvets fluttering your wings
Like winds and butterflies on the Road from Nothing to Nowhere!

But in the summer drought
I fled, for I was a Pillar of Fire, I was Destruction
Unquenched, incarnate and incarnadine.

I was Annihilation
Yet white as the Dead Sea, white as the Cities of the Plains.
For I listened to the noontide and my veins
That threatened thunder and the heart of roses.

I went the way I would—
But long is the terrible Street of the Blood
That had once seemed only part of the summer redness:

225

It stretches for ever, and there is no turning
But only fire, annihilation, burning.

I thought the way of the Blood would never tire.
But now only the red clover
Lies over the breath of the lion and the mouth of the lover—

And green flows Lethe river—O
Long Lethe river
Over Gomorrah's city and the fire . . .

Tears

My tears were Orion's splendour with sextuple suns and the million
Flowers in the fields of the heaven, where solar systems are setting—
The rocks of great diamonds in the midst of the clear wave
By May dews and early light ripened, more diamonds begetting.
I wept for the glories of air, for the millions of dawns
And the splendours within Man's heart with the darkness warring,
I wept for the beautiful queens of the world, like a flower-bed
    shining,—
Now gathered, some at six, some at seven, but all in Eternity's
    morning.
But now my tears have shrunk and like hours are falling:
I weep for Venus whose body has changed to a metaphysical city
Whose heart-beat is now the sound of the revolutions—for love
    changed
To the hospital mercy, the scientists' hope for the future,
And for darkened Man, that complex multiplicity
Of air and water, plant and animal,
Hard diamond, infinite sun.

The Song of the Cold

Huge is the sun of amethysts and rubies,
And in the purple perfumes of the polar sun
And homeless cold they wander.

But winter is the time for comfort and for friendship,
For warmth and food—
And a talk beside a fire like the Midnight Sun—
A glowing heart of amber and of musk. Time to forget
The falling night of the world and heart, the polar chaos
That separates us each from each. It is no time to roam
Along the pavements wide and cold as Hell's huge polar street,
Drifting along the city like the wind
Blowing aimlessly, and with no home
To rest in, only famine for a heart—
While Time means nothing to one, as to the wind
Who only cares for ending and beginning.

Here in the fashionable quarters of the city,
Cold as the universal blackness of Hell's day,
The two opposing brotherhoods are swept
Down the black marble pavements, Lethe's river.
First come the worlds of Misery, the small and tall Rag-Castles,
Shut off from every other. These have no name,
Nor friend to utter it . . . these of the extinct faces
Are a lost civilisation, and have no possession
But the night and day, those centuries of cold.
Even their tears are changed now to the old
Eternal nights of ice round the loveless head
Of these who are lone and sexless as the Dead.

Dives of the Paleocrystic heart, behold
These who were once your brothers! Hear their voices
Hoarsened by want to the rusty voice of the tiger, no more crying
The death of the soul, but lamenting their destitution.
What life, what solar system of the heart
Could bring a restitution
To these who die of the cold?
                    Some keep their youthful graces,
Yet in their winding-sheets of rags seem early
Made ready for the grave . . . Worn to the bone by their famine,
As if by the lusts that the poor Dead have known
Who now are cold for ever . . . Those who are old
Seem humbler, lean their mouths to the earth as if to crop
The kind earth's growth—for this is the Cainozoic period

When we must learn to walk with the gait of the Ape and Tiger:
The warmth of the heart is dead, or has changed to the world's
    fever—
And love is but masked murder, the lust for possession,
The hunger of the Ape, or the confession
Of the last fear, the wish to multiply
Their image, of a race on Oblivion's brink.

Lazarus, weep for those who have known the lesser deaths, O think
How we should pity the High Priests of the god of this world, the
    saints of Mammon,
The cult of gold! For see how these, too, ache with the cold
From the polar wastes of the heart . . . See all they have given
Their god! Are not their veins grown ivy-old,
And have they not eaten their own hearts and live in their famine?

Their huge Arithmetic is but the endless
Repetition of Zero—the unlimited,
Eternal.—Even the beat of the heart and the pulse is changed to this:
The counting of small deaths, the repetition
Of nothing, endless positing and suppression of
              Nothing . . . So they live
And die of inanition . . .

              The miser Foscue,
Weaving his own death and sinking like a spider
To vaults and depths that held his gold, that sun,
Was walled in that grave by the rotting hand of the dust, by a trap-
    door falling.
Do the enormous rays of that Sun now warm his blood, the appalling
Empty gulf of his veins—or fertilise
His flesh, that continent of dryness? . . . Yellow, cold,
And crumbling as his gold,
Deserted by the god of this world, a Gold Man like a terrible Sun,
A Mummy with a Lion's mane,
He sits in this desert where no sound of wave shall come,
And Time's sands are of gold, filling his ears and eyes;
And he who has grown the talons of the Lion
Has devoured the flesh of his own hands and heart in his pain.

Pity these hopeless acolytes . . . the vain
Prudence that emulates the wisdom of the Spider
Who spins but for herself—a world of Hunger
Constructed for the needs of Hunger . . . Soon
Their blankets will be thinner than her thread:
When comes the Night when they have only gold
For flesh, for warmth, for sheet—
O who would not pity these,
Grown fleshless too as those who starve and freeze!

Now falls the Night on Lazarus and Dives—
Those who were brothers, those who shared the pain
Of birth, and lusts, and the daily lesser deaths,
The beat of the dying heart, the careful breaths:
'You are so worn to the bone, I thought you were
    Death, my brother—
Death who will warm my heart.' 'Have you too known the cold?
Give me your hand to warm me. I am no more alone.
There was a sun that shone
On all alike, but the cold in the heart of Man
Has slain it. Where is it gone?'

So in the great Night that comes like love, so small they lie
As when they lay close to their mother's breast,
Naked and bare in their mortality.

Soon comes the Night when those who were never loved
Shall know the small immortal serpent's kiss
And turn to dust as lover turns to lover . . .
Than all shall know the cold's equality . . .
Young Beauty, bright as the tips of the budding vine,
You with the gold Appearances from Nothing rise
In the spring wind, and but for a moment shine.

Dust are the temples that were bright as heat . . .
And, perfumed nosegay brought for noseless Death,
Your brightest myrrh can not perfume his breath!

That old rag-picker blown along the street
Was once great Venus. But now Age unkind
Has shrunken her so feeble and so small—

Weak as a babe. And she who gave the Lion's kiss
Has now all Time's gap for her piteous mouth.
What lullaby will Death sing, seeing this
Small babe? And she of the golden feet,
To what love does she haste? After these centuries
The sun will be her only kiss—now she is blackened, shrunken, old
As the small worm—her kiss, like his, grown cold.

In the nights of spring, the inner leaf of the heart
Feels warm, and we will pray for the eternal cold
Of those who are only warmed by the sins of the world—
And those whose nights were violent like the buds
And roots of spring, but like the spring, grew old.
Their hearts are tombs on the heroic shore,
That were of iris, diamond, hyacinth,
And now are patterned only by Time's wave . . . The glittering plinth
Is crumbling . . . But the great sins and fires break out of me
Like the terrible leaves from the bough in the violent spring . . .
I am a walking fire, I am all leaves—
I will cry to the Spring to give me the birds' and the serpents' speech
That I may weep for those who die of the cold—
The ultimate cold within the heart of Man.

An Old Woman

I

I, an old woman in the light of the sun,
Wait for my Wanderer, and my upturned face
Has all the glory of the remembering Day,
The hallowed grandeur of the primeval clay
That knew the Flood, and suffered all the dryness
Of the uncaring heaven, the sun its lover.

For the sun is the first lover of the world,
Blessing all humble creatures, all life-giving,
Blessing the end of life and the work done,
The clean and the unclean, ores in earth, and splendours

Within the heart of man, that second sun.
For when the first founts and deep waterways
Of the young light flow down and lie like peace
Upon the upturned faces of the blind
From life, it comes to bless
Eternity in its poor mortal dress—
Shining upon young lovers and old lechers
Rising from their beds, and laying gold
Alike in the unhopeful path of beggars
And in the darkness of the miser's heart.
The crookèd has a shadow light made straight,
The shallow places gain their strength again—
And desert hearts, waste heavens, the barren height
Forget that they are cold.
The man-made chasms between man and man
Of creeds and tongues are filled, the guiltless light
Remakes all men and things in holiness.

And he who blessed the fox with a golden fleece,
And covered earth with ears of corn like the planets
Bearded with thick ripe gold,
For the holy bread of mankind, blessed my clay:
For the sun cares not that I am a simple woman,
To him, laughing, the veins in my arms and the wrinkles
From work on my nursing hands are sacred as branches
And furrows of harvest . . . to him, the heat of the earth
And beat of the heart are one,—
Born from the energy of the world, the love
That keeps the Golden Ones in their place above,
And hearts and blood of beasts ever in motion,—
Without which comets, sun, plants, and all living beings
And warmth in the inward parts of the earth would freeze.
And the sun does not care if I live in holiness:
To him, my mortal dress
Is sacred, part of the earth, a lump of the world
With my splendours, ores, impurities, and harvest,
Over which shines my heart, that ripening sun.

Though the dust, the shining racer, overtake me,
I too was a golden woman like those that walk

In the fields of the heavens:—but am now grown old
And must sit by the fire and watch the fire grow cold,—
A country Fate whose spool is the household task.
Yet still I am loved by the sun, and still am part
Of earth. In the evenings bringing home the workers,
Bringing the wanderer home and the dead child,
The child unborn and never to be conceived,
Home to the mother's breast, I sit by the fire
Where the seed of gold drops dead and the kettle simmers
With a sweet sound like that of a hive of bees;
And I wait for my Wanderer to come home to rest—
Covered with earth as if he had been working
Among the happy gardens, the holy fields
Where the bread of mankind ripens in the stillness.
Unchanged to me by death, I shall hold to my breast
My little child in his sleep, I shall seem the consoling
Earth, the mother of corn, nurse of the unreturning.

Wise is the earth, consoling grief and glory,
The golden heroes proud as pomp of waves,—
Great is the earth embracing them, their graves,
And great is the earth's story.
For though the soundless wrinkles fall like snow
On many a golden cheek, and creeds grow old
And change,—man's heart, that sun,
Outlives all terrors shaking the old night:
The world's huge fevers burn and shine, turn cold,
Yet the heavenly bodies and young lovers burn and shine,
The golden lovers walk in the holy fields
Where the Abraham-bearded sun, the father of all things,
Is shouting of ripeness, and the whole world of dews and
        splendours are singing
To the cradles of earth, of men, beasts, harvests, swinging
In the peace of God's heart. And I, the primeval clay
That has known earth's grief and harvest's happiness,
Seeing mankind's dark seed-time, come to bless,
Forgive and bless all men like the holy light.

II *Harvest*

I, an old woman whose heart is like the Sun
That has seen too much, looked on too many sorrows,
Yet is not weary of shining, fulfilment, and harvest,
Heard the priests that howled for rain and the universal darkness,
Saw the golden princes sacrificed to the Rain-god,
The cloud that came and was small as the hand of Man.
And now in the time of the swallow, the bright one, the chatterer,
The young women wait like the mother of corn for the lost one—
Their golden eyelids are darkened like the great rain-clouds.
But in bud and branch the nature of Fate begins
—And love with the Lion's claws and the Lion's hunger
Hides in the brakes in the nihilistic Spring.—
Old men feel their scolding heart
Reproach the veins that for fire have only anger.
And Christ has forgiven all men—the thunder-browed Caesar,
That stone-veined Tantalus howling with thirst in the plain
Where for innocent water flows only the blood of the slain,
Falling for ever from veins that held in their noonday
The foolish companion of summer, the weeping rose.
We asked for a sign that we have not been forsaken—
And for answer the Abraham-bearded Sun, the father of all things,
Is shouting of ripeness over our harvest for ever.
And with the sound of growth, lion-strong, and the laughing Sun,
Whose great flames stretch like branches in the heat
Across the firmament, we almost see
The great gold planets spangling the wide air
And earth—
          O sons of men, the firmament's belovèd,
The Golden Ones of heaven have us in care—
With planetary wisdom, changeless laws,
Ripening our lives and ruling hearts and rhythms,
Immortal hungers in the veins and heart
Born from the primal Cause
That keeps the hearts and blood of men and beasts ever in motion,
The amber blood of the smooth-weeping tree
Rising toward the life-giving heat of the Sun . . .
For is not the blood,—the divine, the animal heat

That is not fire,—derived from the solar ray?
And does not the Beast surpass all elements
In power, through the heat and wisdom of the blood
Creating other Beasts—the Lion a Lion, the Bull a Bull,
The Bear a Bear—some like great stars in the rough
And uncreated dark—or unshaped universes
With manes of fire and a raging sun for heart.
Gestation, generation, and duration—
The cycles of all lives upon the earth—
Plants, beasts, and men, must follow those of heaven;
The rhythms of our lives
Are those of the ripening, dying of the seasons,
Our sowing and reaping in the holy fields,
Our love and giving birth—then growing old
And sinking into sleep in the maternal
Earth, mother of corn, the wrinkled darkness.
So we, ruled by those laws, see their fulfilment.
And I who stood in the grave-clothes of my flesh
Unutterably spotted with the world's woes
Cry, 'I am Fire. See, I am the bright gold
That shines like a flaming fire in the night—the gold-trained planet,
The laughing heat of the Sun that was born from darkness—
Returning to darkness—I am fecundity, harvest.'
For on each country road,
Grown from the needs of men as boughs from trees,
The reapers walk like the harvesters of heaven—
Jupiter and his great train, and the corn-goddess,
And Saturn marching in the Dorian mode.
We heard in the dawn the first ripe-bearded fire
Of wheat (so flames that are men's spirits break from their thick
    earth);
Then came the Pentecostal Rushing of Flames, God in the wind that
    comes to the wheat,
Returned from the Dead for the guilty hands of Caesar
Like the rose at morning shouting of red joys
And redder sorrows fallen from young veins and heart-springs,
Come back for the wrong and the right, the wise and the foolish,
Who like the rose care not for our philosophies
Of life and death, knowing the earth's forgiveness

And the great dews that come to the sick rose:
For those who build great mornings for the world
From Edens of lost light seen in each other's eyes,
Yet soon must wear no more the light of the Sun
But say farewell among the morning sorrows.
The universal language of the Bread—
(O Thou who art not broken, or divided—
Thou who art eaten, but like the Burning Bush
Art not consumed—Thou Bread of Men and Angels)—
The Seraphim rank on rank of the ripe wheat—
Gold-bearded thunders and hierarchies of heaven
Roar from the earth: 'Our Christ is arisen, He comes to give a sign
    from the Dead.'

Eurydice

Fires on the hearth! Fires in the heavens! Fires in the hearts of Men!
I who was welded into bright gold in the earth by Death
Salute you! All the weight of Death in all the world
Yet does not equal Love—the great compassion
For the fallen dust and all fallen creatures, quickening
As is the Sun in the void firmament.
It shines like fire. O bright gold of the heat of the Sun
Of Love across dark fields—burning away rough husks of Death
Till all is fire, and bringing all to harvest!

See then! I stand in the centre of my earth
That was my Death, under the zenith of my Sun,
Bringing a word from Darkness
That Death too has compassion for all fallen Nature.
For as the Sun buries his hot days and rays
To ripen in earth, so the great rays of the heart
Are ripened to wisdom by Death, and great is our forgiveness.

When through the darkness Orpheus came with his Sun-like singing
Like the movements in the heavens that in our blindness
Could we but emulate, would set right our lives—
I came to the mouth of the Tomb, I did not know our meeting would
    be this:—

Only like the return at evening
Of the weary worker in the holy fields—
The cry of welcome, the remembered kiss!

In the lateness of the season, I with the golden feet
That had walked in the fields of Death, now walk again
The dark fields where the sowers scatter grain
Like tears, or the constellations that weep for the lateness of the
     season—
Where the women walk like mourners, like the Afternoon ripened,
     with their bent heads;
Their golden eyelids, like the drifts of the narcissus
In spring, are wet with their tears. They mourn for a young wife who
     had walked these fields—
So young, not yet had Proserpina tied up her golden hair
In a knot like the branchèd corn . . . So good was she—
With a voice like the sweet swallow. She lies in the silent Tomb,

And they walk in the fields alone. Then one of the Dead who lay
Beneath the earth, like the water-dark, the water-thin
Effigy of Osiris, with a face green as a moon,—
He who was lying in darkness with the wheat
Like a flame springing from his heart, or a gold sound,
Said to me, 'We have been blind and stripped God naked of things
To see the light which shines in the dark, and we have learned
That the gold flame of the wheat may spring from a barren heart.'

When I came down from the Metropolis of the Corn,
Then said the ferine dust that reared about me,
'I have the famine of the lion, all things devour,
Or make them mine . . . Venus was powerful as me—
Now is she but a handful of dry amber dust;
And my tooth cracked the husk, the dry amber wall
That held the fire of the wheat. That fire is gone—
And remember this, that Love, or I, have ground
Your heart between the stones of the years, like wheat.'

But as I left the mouth of the Tomb, far off, like the noise of the dark
     wild bees,
I heard the sounds arise from the dwellings of Men, and I thought of
     their building,

Their wars, their honey-making, and of the gold roofs built against
    Darkness.

And I had learned beneath the earth that all gold nature
Changes to wheat or gold in the sweet darkness.
Why do they weep for those in the silent Tomb,
Dropping their tears like grain? Her heart, that honeycomb,
Thick Darkness like a bear devours . . . See, all the gold is gone!
The cell of the honeycomb is six-sided . . . But there, in the five cells
    of the senses,
Is stored all their gold . . . Where is it now? Only the wind of the
    Tomb can know.
But I feared not that stilled and chilling breath
Among the dust . . . Love is not changed by Death,
And nothing is lost and all in the end is harvest.

As the earth is heavy with the lion-strong Sun
When he has fallen, with his hot days and rays,
We are heavy with Death, as a woman is heavy with child,
As the corn-husk holds its ripeness, the gold comb
Its weight of summer . . . But as if a lump of gold had changed to
    corn,
So did my Life rise from my Death. I cast the grandeur of Death away
And homeward came to the small things of Love, the building of the
    hearth, the kneading of daily bread,
The cries of birth, and all the weight of light
Shaping our bodies and our souls. Came home to youth,
And the noise of summer growing in the veins,
And to old age, a serene afternoon,
An element beyond time, or a new climate.

I with the other young who were born from darkness,
Returning to darkness, stood at the mouth of the Tomb
With one who had come glittering like the wind
To meet me—Orpheus with the golden mouth,
You—like Adonis born from the young myrrh-tree, you, the vine-
    branch
Broken by the wind of Love . . . I turned to greet you—
And when I touched your mouth, it was the Sun.

Song

We are the darkness in the heat of the day,
The rootless flowers in the air, the coolness: we are the water
Lying upon the leaves before Death, our sun,
And its vast heat has drunken us . . . Beauty's daughter,
The heart of the rose, and we are one.

We are the summer's children, the breath of evening, the days
When all may be hoped for,—we are the unreturning
Smile of the lost one, seen through the summer leaves—
That sun and its false light scorning.

Green Song

After the long and portentous eclipse of the patient sun
The sudden spring began
With the bird-sounds of Doom in the egg, and Fate in the bud that is
    flushed with the world's fever—
But those bird-songs have trivial voices and sound not like thunder,
And the sound when the bud bursts is no more the sound of the
    worlds that are breaking.—
But the youth of the world, the lovers, said, 'It is Spring!
And we who were black with the winter's shade, and old,
See the emeralds are awake upon the branches
And grasses, bird-blood leaps within our veins
And is changed to emeralds like the sap in the grasses.
The beast-philosopher hiding in the orchards,
Who had grown silent from the world's long cold,
Will tell us the secret of how Spring began
In the young world before the Fall of Man.
For you are the young spring earth
And I, O Love, your dark and lowering heaven.'

But an envious ghost in the spring world
Sang to them a shrunken song
Of the world's right and wrong—
Whispered to them through the leaves, 'I wear
The world's cold for a coat of mail

Over my body bare—
I have no heart to shield my bone
But with the world's cold am alone—
And soon your heart, too, will be gone—
My day's darling.'

The naked Knight in the coat of mail
Shrieked like a bird that flies through the leaves—
The dark bird proud as the Prince of the Air—
'I am the world's last love . . . Beware—

Young girl, you press your lips to lips
That are already cold—
For even the bright earthly dress
Shall prove, at last, unfaithfulness.

His country's love will steal his heart—
To you it will turn cold
When foreign earth lies on the breast
Where your young heart was wont to rest
Like leaves upon young leaves, when warm was the green spray,
And warm was the heart of youth, my day's darling.

And if that ghost return to you—
(The dead disguised as a living man)
Then I will come like Poverty
And wear your face, and give your kiss,
And shrink the world and that sun, the heart,
Down to a penny's span:

For there is a sound you heard in youth,
A flower whose light is lost—
There is a faith and a delight—
They lie at last beneath my frost
When I am come like Time that all men, faiths, loves, suns defeat,
My frosts despoils the day's young darling.

For the young heart like the spring wind grows cold
And the dust, the shining racer, is overtaking
The laughing young people who are running like fillies,
The golden ladies and the ragpickers,
And the foolish companions of spring, the wild wood lilies.'

But the youth of the world said, 'Give me your golden hand
That is but earth, yet it holds the lands of heaven;
And you are the sound of the growth of spring in the heart's deep
    core,
The hawthorn-blossoming boughs of the stars and the young
    orchards' emerald lore.'

And hearing that, the poor ghost fled like the winter rain—
Sank into greenish dust like the fallen moon
Or the sweet green dust of the lime-flowers that will be blossoming
    soon.
And spring grew warm again—

No more the accusing light, revealing the rankness of Nature,
All motives and desires and lack of desire
In the human heart; but loving all life, it comes to bless
Immortal things in their poor earthly dress—
The blind of life beneath the frost of their great winter,
And those for whom the winter breaks in flower
And summer grows from a long-shadowed kiss.
And Love is the vernal equinox in the veins
When the sun crosses the marrow and pith of the heart
Among the viridian smells, the green rejoicing.
All names, sounds, faiths, delights, and duties lost
Return to the hearts of men, those households of high heaven.
And voices speak in the woods as from a nest
Of leaves—they sing of rest,
And love, and toil, the rhythms of their lives,
Singing how winter's dark was overcome,
And making plans for tomorrow as though yesterday
Had never been, nor the lonely ghost's old sorrow,
And Time seemed but the beat of heart to heart,
And Death the pain of earth turning to spring again
When lovers meet after the winter rain.
And when we are gone, they will see in the great mornings
Born of our lives, some memory of us, the golden stalk
Of the young, long-petalled flower of the sun in the pale air
Among the dew . . . Are we not all of the same substance,
Men, planets, and earth, born from the heart of darkness,
Returning to darkness, the consoling mother,

For the short winter sleep—O my calyx of the flower of the world,
you the spirit
Moving upon the waters, the light on the breast of the dove.

The Youth with the Red-Gold Hair

The gold-armoured ghost from the Roman road
Sighed over the wheat,
'Fear not the sound and the glamour
Of my gold armour—
(The sound of the wind and the wheat)
Fear not its clamour . . .
Fear only the red-gold sun with the fleece of a fox
Who will steal the fluttering bird you hide in your breast.
Fear only the red-gold rain
That will dim your brightness, O my tall tower of the corn,
You,—my blonde girl . . .'
But the wind sighed 'Rest.' . . .
The wind in his grey knight's armour—
The wind in his grey night armour—
Sighed over the fields of the wheat, 'He is gone . . .
Forlorn.'

You, the Young Rainbow

You, the young Rainbow of my tears, the gentle Halcyon
Over the troubled waters of my heart:
Lead now, as long ago, my grief, your flock, over the hollow
Hills to the far pastures of lost heaven.
But they are withered, the meadows and the horizon
Of the gentle Halcyon, hyacinthine sun;
Cold are the boughs, the constellations falling
From the spring branches; and your heart is far
And cold as Arcturus, the distance of all light-years
From the flowering earth and darkness of my heart.

The Poet Laments the Coming of Old Age

I see the children running out of school;
They are taught that Goodness means a blinding hood
Or is heaped by Time like the hump on an agèd back,
And that Evil can be cast like an old rag
And Wisdom caught like a hare and held in the golden sack
Of the heart . . . But I am one who must bring back sight to the blind.

Yet there was a planet dancing in my mind
With a gold seed of Folly . . . long ago . . .
And where is that grain of Folly? . . . with the hare-wild wind
Of my spring it has gone from one who must bring back sight to the
    blind.

For I, the fool, was once like the philosopher
Sun who laughs at evil and at good:
I saw great things mirrored in littleness,
Who now see only that great Venus wears Time's filthy dress—
A toothless crone who once had the Lion's mouth.

The Gold Appearances from Nothing rise
In sleep, by day . . . two thousand years ago
There was a man who had the Lion's leap,
Like the Sun's, to take the worlds and loves he would,
But (laughed the philosopher Sun, and I, the fool)

Great golden Alexander and his thunder-store
Are now no more
Than the armoured knight who buzzed on the windowpane
And the first drops of rain.

He lies in sleep . . . But still beneath a thatch
Of hair like sunburnt grass, the thieving sweet thoughts move
Towards the honey-hive . . . And another sweet-tooth Alexander runs
Out of the giant shade that is his school,
To take the dark knight's world, the honeycomb.

The Sun's simulacrum, the gold-sinewed man
Lies under a hump of grass, as once I thought to wear
With patience, Goodness like a hump on my agèd back
. . . But Goodness grew not with age, although my heart must bear
The weight of all Time's filth, and Wisdom is not a hare in the
    golden sack

Of the heart . . . It can never be caught. Though I bring back sight to
the blind,
My seed of Folly has gone, that could teach me to bear
That the gold-sinewed body that had the blood of all the earth in its
veins
Has changed to an old rag of the outworn world
And the great heart that the first Morning made
Should wear all Time's destruction for a dress.

Most Lovely Shade

Most lovely Dark, my Æthiopia born
Of the shade's richest splendour, leave not me
Where in the pomp and splendour of the shade
The dark air's leafy plumes no more a lulling music made.

Dark is your fleece, and dark the airs that grew
Amid those weeping leaves.
Plantations of the East drop precious dew
That, ripened by the light, rich leaves perspire.
Such are the drops that from the dark airs' feathers flew.

Most lovely Shade . . . Syrinx and Dryope
And that smooth nymph that changed into a tree
Are dead . . . the shade, that Æthiopia, sees
Their beauty make more bright its treasuries—
Their amber blood in porphyry veins still grows
Deep in the dark secret of the rose
And the smooth stem of many a weeping tree,
And in your beauty grows.

Come then, my pomp and splendour of the shade,
Most lovely cloud that the hot sun made black
As dark-leaved airs,—
                              Come then, O precious cloud,
Lean to my heart: no shade of a rich tree
Shall pour such splendour as your heart to me.

The Swans

In the green light of water, like the day
Under green boughs, the spray
And air-pale petals of the foam seem flowers,—
Dark-leaved arbutus blooms with wax-pale bells
And their faint honey-smells,
The velvety syringa with smooth leaves,
Gloxinia with a green shade in the snow,
Jasmine and moon-clear orange-blossoms and green blooms
Of the wild strawberries from the shade of woods.
Their showers
Pelt the white women under the green trees,
Venusia, Cosmopolita, Pistillarine—
White solar statues, white rose-trees in snow
Flowering for ever, child-women, half stars
Half flowers, waves of the sea, born of a dream.

Their laughter flying through the trees like doves,
These angels come to watch their whiter ghosts
In the air-pale water, archipelagos
Of stars and young thin moons from great wings falling
As ripples widen.
These are their ghosts, their own white angels these!
O great wings spreading—
Your bones are made of amber, smooth and thin
Grown from the amber dust that was a rose
Or nymph in swan-smooth waters.
                              But Time's winter falls
With snows as soft, as soundless . . . Then, who knows
Rose-footed swan from snow, or girl from rose?

The Two Loves

I

The dead woman black as thunder, upright in the Spring's great
    shroud
Of flowers and lightnings, snows and sins and sorrows, cried like the
    loud

Noise of Spring that breaks in heart and bud . . .
'Oh should you pass—
Come not to this ground with your living lass:
For I have a light to see you by!
Is it the Burning Bush—
Is it Damnation's Fire . . .
Or the old aching heart with its desire?
I only know I tried to bless
But felt that terrible fire burn to the bone—
Beneath Time's filthy dress.'

II

But where are the seeds of the Universal Fire
To burn the roots of Death in the world's cold heart?
The earth of my heart was broken and gaped low
As the fires beneath the equator of my veins.
And I thought the seeds of Fire should be let loose
Like the solar rains—
The light that lies deep in the heart of the rose;
And that the bloom from the fallen spring of the world
Would come again to the cheek grown famine-white
As winter frost—
Would come again to the heart whose courage is lost
From hunger. When in this world
Will the cold heart take fire? In the hour when the sapphire of the
      bone—
That hard and precious fire wrung from the earth—
And the sapphire tears the heavens weep shall be made one.

But, in the summer, great should be the sun of the heart
And great is the heat of the fires from elementary and terrestrial
      nature—
Ripening the kernel of amethysts in the sun of the peach—
The dancing seas in the heart of the apricot.
The earth, the sun, the heart, have so many fires
It is a great wonder
That the whole world is not consumed. In such a heat of the earth,
      under
The red bough, the Colossus of rubies, the first husbandman and
      grave-digger, the red Adam,

Dug from the earth of his own nature, the corn effigy
Of a long-buried country god, encrusted with earth-virtues,
And brought to a new birth
The ancient wisdom hiding behind heat and laughter,
Deep-rooted in Death's earth.

Gone is that heat. But this is the hour of brotherhood, the warmth
    that comes
To the rejected by Life—the shadow with no eyes—
Young Icarus with the broken alar bones
And the sapped and ageing Atlas of the slums
Devoured by the days until all days are done—
To the Croesus of the breadline, gold from the sun,
And the lover seeing in Woman the rankness of Nature,—
A monstrous Life-force, the need of procreation
Devouring all other life . . . or Gravity's force
Drawing him down to the centre of his earth.
These sprawl together in the sunlight—the negation
Of Life, fag-ends of Ambition, wrecks of the heart,
Lumps of the world, and bones left by the Lion.
Amid the assembly of young laughing roses
They wait for a rebirth
Under the democratic sun, enriching all, rejecting no one . . .
But the smile of youth, the red mouth of the flower
Seem the open wounds of a hunger that is voiceless—
And on their lips lies the dust of Babel's city;
And the sound of the heart is changed to the noise of revolutions—
The hammer of Chaos destroying and rebuilding
Small wingless hopes and fears in the light of the Sun.
Who dreamed when Nature should be heightened to a fever—
The ebullition of her juices and humours—
The war of creed and creed, of starved and starver—
The light would return to the cheek, and a new Word
Would take the place of the heart?
                        We might tell the blind
The hue of the flower, or the philosopher
What distance is, in the essence of its being—
But not the distance between the hearts of Men.

I see Christ's wounds weep in the Rose on the wall.
Then I who nursed in my earth the dark red seeds of Fire—
The pomegranate grandeur, the dark seeds of Death,
Felt them change to the light and fire in the heart of the rose . . .
And I thought of the umbilical cords that bind us to strange suns
And causes . . . of Smart the madman who was born
To bless Christ with the Rose and his people, a nation
Of living sweetness . . . of Harvey who blessed Christ with the solar
    fire in the veins,
And Linnaeus praising Him with the wingèd seed!—
Men born for the Sun's need—
Yet theirs are the hymns to God who walks in darkness.
And thinking of the age-long sleep, then brought to the light's birth
Of terrestrial nature generated far
From heaven . . . the argillaceous clays, the zircon and sapphire
Bright as the tears of heaven, but deep in earth—
And of the child of the four elements,
The plant—organic water polarised to the earth's centre,
And to the light:—the stem and root, the water-plant and earth-plant;
The leaf, the child of air; the flower, the plant of fire—
And of One who contracted His Immensity
And shut Himself in the scope of a small flower
Whose root is clasped in darkness . . . God in the span
Of the root and light-seeking corolla . . . with the voice of Fire I
    cry—
Will He disdain that flower of the world, the heart of Man?

Of the Wise and the Foolish

A fool sat by the roadside
Upon a lonely stone.
His hair was grey as ass-fur.
He sang 'Alone—alone—'
To the ass-grey dust singing,
'Brother, to thee I come.
The ass that prophesied to Augustus
The victory of Actium.'

Sailor, What of the Isles?

'Sailor, what of the isles—
The green worlds grown
From a little seed? What of the islands known and those unknown?'

'I have returned over the long and lonely sea;
And only human need
For the world of men is mine; I have forgot Immensity.

The rustling sea was a green world of leaves;
The isle of Hispaniola in its form
Was like the leaf of a chestnut-tree in June.
And there is the gold region—the gold falls like rain with a long and
    leafy tune.

An old man bore us lumps of gold . . . the small,
Like walnuts husked with earth; the great,
As large as oranges, and leafy earth
Still clung to them. And when you thought that fireflies lit the night,
These were but nuggets, lying on the dark earth, burning bright.'

'Sailor, what of the maps of the known world?' 'The old Chinese,
Whose talk was like the sound of June leaves drinking rain,
Constructed maps of the known world—the few
Islands and two countries that they knew.

They thought the heavens were round,
The earth square, and their empire at the earth's centre . . .
        just as you
And I believe we are the world's centre and the stars
Are grown from us as the bright seas in a rind of gold
Are grown from the smooth stem of the orange-tree.

Those maps of the Yellow Empire then were drawn,
As we think, upside down;
Tongking was placed
Where usually the North stands, and Mongolia graced
The South. The names, too, were writ upside down.
For how is it possible, in this flat world, to know
Why South should be below, the North above—
Why man should hold creeds high one moment, the next moment
    low?'

'Sailor, what of the maps of skies? Is that Orion?'

                                                        'No, the sight
Is of a far island. What you see
Is where they are gathering carbuncles, garnets, diamonds bright
As fireflies with a gardener's rake under the spice-trees and the
    orange-trees.'

'Sailor, what do you know of this world, my Self . . . a child
Standing before you?—Or an isle
To which no sail has crossed over the long and lonely sea?
What do you know of this island, of the soil
In which all sainthood or insanity, murder or mockery grows—a
    leafy tree?'

'No more than the gardeners and astronomers who make
Their catalogues of stars for heavens and seeds for garden beds
Know of their green worlds; or the soil, of the great beasts
Whose skin shines like gold fire or fireflies, and whose nostrils snort
    great stars—
The beasts—huge flowers grown from the stem of the green dark-
    ness; each beast holds
The entire world of plants,
All elements and all the planetary system in
Itself (while the flower holds only the plant-world)
And freed from its stem by light, like the flowers in air—

No more than the father knows of the child, or the sailor of chartless
    isles.'

Gardeners and Astronomers

Where the green airs seem fanning palms and the green psalms
Of greater waters, where the orange hangs huge as Orion, and day-
    long great gauds and lauds of light

Pierce their gold through the seeds, behold their secrets,
And the weight of the warm air
Shapes the exquisite corolla to a world of gold rain
Closed in thick gold armour like a King's,

Old men, dark-gold with earth and toil,
Praise their green heavens. 'Who would look dangerously high in air
At planets, who may safely watch the earth
For the lesser solar system of the plants,
And for the spring's rebirth?

Then why are we less than the astronomers?
Than Hipparchus, who saw a comet that foretold
The birth of Mithridates and began
To form his catalogue of stars that are no more
Than the long-leaved plants in our garden-shed?

And men of emeralds walking through the night
Of early Chinese annals, Emperor Hwan-Té
Whose pleasure-dome was an observatory, Chien-Ké
Who shook a branch and all the stars together glittered bright:
Now are they but the dust of lilies on our garden-bed.

And why are we less than these?
Does not each dark root hold a world of gold?
And was not Aristophanes,
Who gave the world green laughter, son of the garden-goddess?'

So said the old men, gold with toil and ripeness
As their great fathering Sun.
                              But in the cities,
New criminals and sages, pariah Suns in heavens of evil,
Ripen new forms of life from primeval mud.

And Man, the planet-bacillus, acts new virtues
(The eunuch's chastity, the gentleness of the untoothed tiger,
More insolent than youth, more cruel than spring),

And longs for the night when each has his own world.
                                        Some dream that all are equal,
As in the gardener's world of growth: the plant and planet,
                              King and beggar;
And Fallen Man dreams he is falling upward. And the eyeless
Horizontal Man, the Black Man, who in the Day's blazing diamond-
     mine, follows the footsteps
Of Vertical Man, is ever cast by him
Across all growth, all stone—he, great as Man's ambition,

And like to Man's ambition, with no body
To act ambition—he, the sole horizon,
Epitome of our age, now rules the world.

Their faces stained by the cool night like wine
Under the violet planets of night-dew, Night-roamers, Magians,
And the Bacchantes of the suburbs with their hair like the torn vines
That are lifted by the night-wind, know all things are equal:
Hades and Dionysus, Being, Not-Being.

And those who see the virtues hidden in the compass
Of the green mantles, see the lamentable planets of those lives
As no more than the planets in green heavens of the gardens.

And in the gardens the airs sing of growth:
The orange-tree still sighs,
'I am the Dark that changed to water and to air,
The water and the air that changed to gold—
The gold that turned into a plant. From the cool wave of the air
    grows a smooth
Stem, and from this the gold, cold orange-tree.'

And happy as the Sun, the gardeners
See all miasmas from the human filth but as the dung
In which to sow great flowers,
Tall moons and mornings, seeds, and sires, and suns.

The Queen of Scotland's Reply to a Reproof from John Knox

Said the bitter Man of Thorns to me, the White Rose-Tree:
'That wonted love of yours is but an ass's bray—
The beast who called to beast
And kicked the world away!'
(All the wisdom of great Solomon
Held in an ass's bray.)

When body to body, soul to soul
Were bare in the fire of night
As body to grave, as spirit to Heaven or Hell,
What did we say?

'Ah, too soon we shall be air—
No pleasure, anguish, will be possible.
Hold back the day!'
For in this moment of the ass-furred night
You called the hour of the Beast, was born
All the wisdom of great Solomon
From the despisèd clay!
All the wisdom of Solomon
Held in an ass's bray.

Song

You said, 'This is the time of the wild spring and the mating of the
    tigers,
This is the first vintage of the heat like the budding of wild vines—
The budding of emeralds and the emerald climate,

When flowers change into rainbows and young insects
Are happy, the people have heart-strings like the music
Of the great suns, oh never to be quenched by darkness.'

But I am the water-carrier to the Damned, and dark as water.
Only those nights, my eyes, have no more rain,
And dead are the merciful fountains
Since the world changed into a stone again.

I am the grave of the unpitied Sisyphus,
My heart, that rolled the universe, a stone
Changed to me, like your heart, up endless mountains.

A Hymn to Venus

An old woman speaks:
'Lady, beside the great green wall of Sea
I kneel to make my plea

To you, great Rose of the world . . . Beyond the seeds of petrifaction,
    Gorgon of itself,

Behind the face bright as the Rose—I pray
To the seeds of fire in the veins that should
Hold diamonds, iris, beryls for their blood,—

Since you are grown old too, and should be cold,
Although the heat of the air
Has the motion of fire
And light bears in its heart
A cloud of colour . . . where

The great heap ripens in the mine
Of the body's earth, ruby, garnet, and almandine,

And in the dark cloud of the blood still grows
The rainbow, with the ruby and the rose.

Pity me then—a poor old woman who must wear a rag
Of Time's filth for a dress . . .
O who would care to hold
That miserly rag now!

So I, whose nights were violent as the buds
And roots of Spring, was taken by the Cold,

Have only the Cold for lover. Speak then to my dust!
Tell me that nothing dies
But only suffers change,—
And Folly may grow wise.

So we shall be transmuted—you who have grown chill, and I
Unto whose heart
My love preferred a heart like a winding-sheet of clay—
Fearing my fires would burn his body away!

Gone are your temples that were bright with heat.
But still I kneel at the feet
Of you who were built through aeons by a million lives,
Whispers, and instincts, under the coralline light
That seems the great zone of sea-depths . . .

                                    Through your grief
In my blood grows
Like chlorophyll in the veins of the deep rose,

253

Our beauty's earthly dress
(Shrunk now to dust)—shall move through all degrees
Of Life, from mineral to plant, and from still rock to the green
    laughing seas;

From life's first trance, the mineral consciousness
That is deep blankness inside an invisible
And rigid box—defined, divisible

And separate from the sheath—(breathe not too deep
If you would know the mineral's trancèd sleep . . .
So measure Time that you, too, are apart
And are not conscious of the living heart)—

To the plant that seeks the light that is its lover
And knows not separation between cover
And sentience . . . The Sun's heat and the dew's chill
It knows in sleep with an undreaming thrill;

And colour breathes that is reflected light.
The ray and perfume of the Sun is white:
But when these intermingle as in love
With earth-bound things, the dream begins to move,

And colour that sleeps as in a dreamless cloud
Deep in the mineral trance within that shroud
Then to a fluid changes, grows
Deep in the stem and leaves of the dark rose.

So could the ruby, almandine and garnet move
From this great trance into a dreaming sleep,
They might become the rose whose perfume deep
Grows in Eternity, yet is
Still unawakened for its ephemeral hour
Beneath the great light's kiss;

The rose might seek the untamed rainbow through
The remembering Eden of a drop of dew;
Until at last in heavenly friendship grows
The ruby and the rainbow and the rose.
Nor will the one more precious than the other be—
Or make more rich the Shadow's treasury.

So, Lady, you and I,
And the other wrecks of the heart, left by the Lion
Of love, shall know all transmutations, each degree!
Our apeish skeletons, clothed with rubies by the light,
Are not less bright
In the Sun's eye than is the Rose . . . and youth, and we,
Are but waves of Time's sea.

Folly and wisdom have dust equal-sweet,
And in the porphyry shade
Of this world's noon
The Poor seem Dives, burning in his robes bright as the rose—
Such transmutations even the brief moment made!'

Song

The Queen Bee sighed, 'How heavy is my sweet gold!'
To the wind in the honey-hive.
And sighed the old King, 'The weight of my crown is cold—
And laden is life!'
'How heavy,' sighed the gold heart of the day, 'is the heat!'
Ah, not so laden sweet
As my heart with its infinite gold and its weight of love.

Elegy for Dylan Thomas

Black Venus of the Dead, what Sun of Night
Lies twined in your embrace, cold as the vine?
O heart, great Sun of Darkness, do you shine

For her, to whom alone
All men are faithful—faithless as the wave
To all but her to whom they come after long wandering . . .

Black giantess who is calm as palm-trees, vast
As Africa! In the shade of the giantess
He lies in that eternal faithfulness.

He, made of the pith and sap of the singing world—
Green kernel of a forgotten paradise
Where grass-hued, grass-soft suns brought the first spring
(Green fervours, singing, saps, fertilities)
And heat and moist lay on unseeing eyes
Till shapeless lumps of clay grew into men, now lies
Far from the Babel clamour. In his rest
He holds the rays of the universe to his stilled breast.

Before our Death in Birth, our Birth in Death,
Teaching us holy living, holy dying, we who cry
At the first light and the first dark, must learn

The oneness of the world, and know all change
Through the plant, the kingly worm (within whose shape all Kings
     begin,
To whom all Kings must come) through beast, to Man.

The fraternal world of beast and plant lies on his eyes:
The beast that holds all elements in itself—
The earth, the plant, the solar system: for each beast
Is an infinity of plants, a planet, or a moon,
A flower in the green dark, freed from its stem in earth,
Shrouded with black veils like the mourning Spring,
Under the vines of Grief (the first plantation since the Flood)
The mourners weep for the solary iris that God showed to Noah—

Our hope in this universe of tears. But he is gone—
He sleeps, a buried sun
That sank into the underworld to spread
A gold mask on the faces of the Dead—

Young country god, red as the laughing grapes
When Sirius parches country skins to gold and fire.

And he, who compressed the honey-red fire into holy shapes,
Stole frozen fire from gilded Parnassian hives,

Was Abraham-haired as fleeces of wild stars
That all night rage like foxes in the festival
Of wheat, with fire-brands tied to their tails under the wheat-ears

To avert the wrath of the Sun, gold as the fleeces
Of honey-red foxes. Now he is one with Adam, the first gardener.
   He sang

Of the beginning of created things, the secret
Rays of the universe, and sang green hymns
Of the great waters to the tearless deserts. Under
The fertilisation of his singing breath
Even the greyness and the dust of Death
Seemed the grey pollen of the long September heat

On earth where Kings lie wearing the whole world as their crown,
Where all are equal in the innocent sleep
That lulls the lion like a child, and is the clime
Of our forgiveness. Death, like the holy Night
Makes all men brothers. There, in the maternal

Earth, the wise and humbling Dark, he lies—
The emigrant from a forgotten paradise—
The somnambulist
Who held rough ape-dust and a planet in his fist—

Far from the empires of the human filth
Where the Gorgons suckle us with maternal milk
Black as the Furies', and the human breast
Can yield not even the waters of the Styx. But rest

For these he brought; to the Minotaur in the city office
Crying to the dunghill in the soul 'See, it is morning!'

And seeing all glory hidden in small forms,
The planetary system in the atom, the great suns
Hid in a speck of dust.
        So, for his sake,
More proudly will that Sisyphus, the heart of Man,
Roll the Sun up the steep of heaven, and in the street
Two old blind men seem Homer and Galileo, blind
Old men that tap their way through worlds of dust
To find Man's path near the Sun.

257

Song

Where is all the bright company gone—
The Trojan Elaine and the Knight Sir Gawaine?
Why have they glided out of the rain?
The Queens were bright as the waters' sheen,
Beautiful, bountiful as the grain;
The Knights were brighter than stars in the sky
(The moons thick as roses in hot July)—
As bright as the raindrops and roses in June,
And many and merry as notes in a tune.
Alas, they are gone and I am alone,
For all they glided out of the rain.
And now I sit under the bright apple-tree
And weep that ever the speech was spoken
That the false angel said unto me.
For had I never the apple-branch broken,
Death had not fallen on mankind and me.

Street Acrobat

Upon the shore of noon, the wide azoic
Shore of diamonds where no wave comes, sprawled the nation
Of Life's rejected, with the vegetation
Of wounds that Life has made

Breaking from heart and veins. Why do they tend
With pride this flora of a new world? To what end?

But wearing the slime of Lethe's river for a dress—
Peninsulas of Misery in the Sea of Nothingness

With waves of dead rags lapping islands of the Shade,
They seem. With these for audience—
From whom you could not hope even for pence

To lay upon your eyes—
Street-corner Atlas, you support a world
Whose solar system dies in a slum room.
And what is the world you balance on your shoulder?

What fag-ends of ambition, wrecks of the heart, miasmas
From all Time's leprosies, lie there? The diamonds of the heat

Clothe you, the being diseased by Civilisation—
(With a void within the soul that has attracted
The congestion or intoxication
Of Astral Light—a gulf of diamonds—
Gyrations, revolutions, vortices
Of blinding light timed by the new pulsation!)

You work false miracles of anarchies
And new moralities
Designed for Bird-Men, grown with the growth of wings
From needs of Fear—
And balance high above an immeasurable abyss
Of blinding emptiness and azure vast profundities.

To the sound of ragged Madness beating his drum
Of Death in the heart, you, the atavistic, the Ape-Man,
The World-Eater, call to Darkness your last Mate
To come from her world, the phantom of yours. Then, Strong Man,
      shake
The pillars of this known world, the Palace, and Slum.

Or bear this breaking world—turn acrobat
And execute dizzy somersaults from Real
To the Ideal—swing from desolate heavens
Of angels who seem Pharisees and Tartuffes,
Januses, gulls, and money-lenders, mediums,
In those false heavens of cloud—down to a comfortable hell—
And swing this easy world and watch it heel
Over before it fell,

To the admiration of the Lost Men nursing their wounds
And the children old in the dog's scale of years—
With only this sight for bread . . . (Oh, seeing these,
I thought the eyes of Men
Held all the suns of the world for tears, and these were shed—
Are fallen and gone!
So dark are the inexpiable years.)

But I, whose heart broke down to its central earth
And spilled its fire, its rubies, garnets, like the heat
And light from the heart of the rose,
Still lie immortal in the arms of Fire
Amid the ruins. The Acrobat on his tight-rope, stretched from beast
To God, over a vast abyss

Advances, then recedes. Or, on his ladder of false light,
Swings from mock heaven to real hell. And Galileo, blind,
Stares with his empty eyes on the crowds of planets and young roses
Beyond the arithmeticians'

Counting! O, the grandeur of the instinct! The young people and
    young flowers,
Who, careless, come out in green dark,
Are numberless as the true heavens; still, in this world
We measure by means of the old mathematicians'
Rods, or by rays of light, by the beat of Time, or the sound of the
    heart,
And vibrating atoms that soon will be Man or Flower.

Dirge for the New Sunrise

(Fifteen minutes past eight o'clock on the morning of
Monday the 6th of August 1945)

Bound to my heart as Ixion to the wheel,
Nailed to my heart as the Thief upon the Cross,
I hang between our Christ and the gap where the world was lost

And watch the phantom Sun in Famine Street—
The ghost of the heart of Man . . . red Cain
And the more murderous brain
Of Man, still redder Nero that conceived the death
Of his mother Earth, and tore
Her womb, to know the place where he was conceived.

But no eyes grieved—
For none were left for tears:
They were blinded as the years

Since Christ was born. Mother or Murderer, you have given or
    taken life—
Now all is one!

There was a morning when the holy Light
Was young . . . The beautiful First Creature came
To our water-springs, and thought us without blame.

Our hearts seemed safe in our breasts and sang to the Light—
The marrow of the bone
We dreamed was safe . . . the blood in the veins, the sap in the tree
Were springs of Deity.

But I saw the little Ant-men as they ran
Carrying the world's weight of the world's filth
And the filth in the heart of Man—
Compressed till those lusts and greeds had a greater heat than that
    of the Sun.

And the ray from that heat came soundless, shook the sky
As if in search of food, and squeezed the stems
Of all that grows on the earth till they were dry—
And drank the marrow of the bone:
The eyes that saw, the lips that kissed, are gone
Or black as thunder lie and grin at the murdered Sun.

The living blind and seeing Dead together lie
As if in love . . . There was no more hating then,
And no more love: Gone is the heart of Man.

The Canticle of the Rose

The Rose upon the wall
Cries—'I am the voice of Fire:
And in me grows
The pomegranate splendour of Death, the ruby garnet almandine
Dews: Christ's Wounds in me shine.

I rise upon my stem,
The Flower, the whole Plant-being, produced by Light
With all Plant-systems and formations . . . As in Fire

All elements dissolve, so in one bright
Ineffable essence all Plant-being dissolves to make the Flower.

My stem rises bright—
Organic water polarised to the dark
Earth-centre, and to Light.'

Below that wall, in Famine Street,
There is nothing left but the heart to eat

And the Shade of Man . . . Buyers and sellers cry:
'Speak not the name of Light—
Her name is Madness now . . . Though we are black beneath her kiss,
As if she were the Sun, her name is Night:
She has condemned us, and decreed that Man must die.'

There was a woman combing her long hair
To the rhythm of the river flowing . . .
She sang 'All things will end—
Like the sound of Time in my veins growing:
The hump on the dwarf, the mountain on the plain,
The fixed red of the rose and the rainbow's red,
The fires of the heart, the wandering planet's pain—
All loss, all gain—
Yet will the world remain!'

The song died in the Ray . . . Where is she now?
Dissolved, and gone—
And only her red shadow stains the unremembering stone.

And in Famine Street the sellers cry,
'What will you buy?

A dress for the Bride?'
(But all the moulds of generation died
Beneath that Ray.)
                    'Or a winding-sheet?'
(Outworn . . . The Dead have nothing left to hide.)

'Then buy' said the Fate arisen from Hell—
That thing of rags and patches—
'A box of matches!

For the machine that generated warmth
Beneath your breast is dead . . . You need a fire
To warm what lies upon your bone . . .
Not all the ashes of your brother Men
Will kindle that again—
Nor all the world's incendiaries!
Who buys—Who buys—?
Come, give me pence to lay upon my staring lidless eyes!'

But high upon the wall
The Rose where the Wounds of Christ are red
Cries to the Light—
'See how I rise upon my stem, ineffable bright
Effluence of bright essence . . . From my little span
I cry of Christ, Who is the ultimate Fire
Who will burn away the cold in the heart of Man . . .'
Springs come, springs go . . .
'I was reddere on Rode than the Rose in the rayne . . .'
'This smel is Crist, clepid the plantynge of the Rose in Jerico.'

The Shadow of Cain is about the fission of the world into warring particles, destroying and self destructive. It is about the gradual migration of mankind after that Second Fall of Man that took the form of the separation of brother and brother, of Cain and Abel, of nation and nation, of the rich and the poor—the spiritual migration of these into the desert of the Cold, towards the final disaster, the first symbol of which fell on Hiroshima.

The poem came into being thus.

On the 10th of September, 1945, nearly five weeks after the fall of the first atom bomb, my brother Sir Osbert Sitwell and I were in the train going to Brighton, where we were to give a reading. He pointed out to me a paragraph in *The Times*, a description by an eye-witness of the immediate effect of the atomic bomb upon Hiroshima. That witness saw a totem pole of dust arise to the sun as a witness against the murder of mankind . . . A totem pole, the symbol of creation, the symbol of generation.

Preface to *Collected Poems*

A major poet had written a major work. It was an event which asked for, and received, comment from the critics. The most enlightened, in Edith Sitwell's eyes, came from Jack Lindsay, who reviewed the poem after its publication in 1948 by John Lehmann:

'To see Edith Sitwell's poems in anything like their true proportion we must detach ourselves a moment from the confined situation of contemporary criticism in England and from the failing aspects of our culture that it represents. We must think of ourselves and the poems in an enlarged and more secure focus where words like Poetry, Life, Man have regained something of their full humanistic vigour and scope. We must ask, "Who are the poets who will be read till the last blink of time as holding the secret of our cruel and crucial age, its death and renewal? Who are the poets going to the heart of this terrific moment of change and holding to a loving faith in life, not because of superficial reconciliations, but because they look to the depth of the pang and its possibilities?" When we ask anything so simple as that, we shake off the spell of belittling mediocrity that hangs over our culture today, and feel ourselves human again, feel the nature and function of poetry, and see Edith Sitwell's work, beyond all over-simplifications and pseudo complications, in its correct dimensions: large as the bones of a dead universe and delicately close as "branches where the first peach-blossom trembles".

'Since 1945 she has gone on expressing the crossroads at which man stands, with power over the transformation process for death or life, for a golden age or the supreme murder . . . From the gaunt ribs of space emerges the world of evolutionary shapes, and at last man in the immensities, with his fertility hope and his death power becomes gigantic in the bomb, confronting the ultimate choice.'

The Shadow of Cain

Under great yellow flags and banners of the ancient Cold
Began the huge migrations
From some primeval disaster in the heart of Man.

There were great oscillations
Of temperature . . . You knew there had once been warmth;

But the Cold is the highest mathematical Idea . . . the Cold is Zero—
The Nothing from which arose
All Being and all variation . . . It is the sound too high for our
    hearing, the Point that flows

Till it becomes the line of Time . . . an endless positing
Of Nothing, or the Ideal that tries to burgeon
Into Reality through multiplying. Then Time froze

To immobility and changed to Space.
Black flags among the ice, blue rays
And the purple perfumes of the polar Sun
Freezing the bone to sapphire and to zircon—
These were our days.

And now, in memory of great oscillations
Of temperature in that epoch of the Cold,
We found a continent of turquoise, vast as Asia
In the yellowing airs of the Cold: the tooth of a mammoth;
And there, in a gulf, a dark pine-sword

To show there had once been warmth and the gulf stream in our veins
Where only the Chaos of the Antarctic Pole
Or the peace of its atonic coldness reigns.

And sometimes we found the trace
Of a bird's claw in the immensity of the Cold:
The trace of the first letters we could not read:
Some message of Man's need

And of the slow subsidence of a Race;
And of great heats in which the Pampean mud was formed,
In which the Megatherium Mylodon
Lies buried under Mastodon-trumpetings of leprous Suns.

The Earth had cloven in two in that primal disaster.
But when the glacial period began
There was still some method of communication
Between Man and his brother Man—
Although their speech
Was alien, each from each,
As the Bird's from the Tiger's, born from the needs of our opposing
    famines.

Each said 'This is the Race of the Dead . . . their blood is cold . . .
For the heat of those more recent on the Earth
Is higher . . . the blood-beat of the Bird more high
Than that of the ancient race of the primeval Tiger:
The Earth had lived without the Bird

In that Spring when there were no flowers like thunders in the air.
And now the Earth lies flat beneath the shade of an iron wing.
And of what does the Pterodactyl sing—
Of what red buds in what tremendous Spring?'

The thunders of the Spring began . . . We came again
After that long migration
To the city built before the Flood by our brother Cain.

And when we reached an open door
The Fate said 'My feet ache.'
The Wanderers said 'Our hearts ache.'

There was great lightning
In flashes coming to us over the floor:
The Whiteness of the Bread
The Whiteness of the Dead
The Whiteness of the Claw—
All this coming to us in flashes through the open door.

There were great emerald thunders in the air
In the violent Spring, the thunders of the sap and the blood in the
        heart—
The Spiritual Light, the physical Revelation.

In the streets of the City of Cain there were great Rainbows
Of emeralds: the young people, crossing and meeting.

And everywhere
The great voice of the Sun in sap and bud
Fed from the heart of Being, the panic Power,
The sacred Fury, shouts of Eternity
To the blind eyes, the heat in the wingèd seed, the fire in the blood,

And through the works of Death,
The dust's aridity, is heard the sound
Of mounting saps like monstrous bull-voices of unseen fearful mimes:

And the great rolling world-wide thunders of that drumming
    underground

Proclaim our Christ, and roar 'Let there be harvest!
Let there be no more Poor—
For the Son of God is sowed in every furrow!'

We did not heed the Cloud in the Heavens shaped like the hand
Of Man . . . But there came a roar as if the Sun and Earth had come
    together—
The Sun descending and the Earth ascending
To take its place above . . . the Primal Matter
Was broken, the womb from which all life began,
Then to the murdered Sun a totem pole of dust arose in memory
    of Man.

The cataclysm of the Sun down-pouring
Seemed the roar
Of those vermilion Suns the drops of the blood
That, bellowing like Mastodons at war,
Rush down the length of the world—away—away—

The violence of torrents, cataracts, maelstroms, rains
That went before the Flood—
These covered the earth from the freshets of our brothers' veins.

And with them, the forked lightnings of the gold
From the split mountains,
Blasting their rivals, the young foolish wheat-ears
Amid those terrible rains.

The gulf that was torn across the world seemed as if the beds of all
    the Oceans
Were emptied . . . Naked, and gaping at what once had been the Sun,
Like the mouth of the Universal Famine
It stretched its jaws from one end of the Earth to the other.

And in that hollow lay the body of our brother
Lazarus, upheaved from the world's tomb.
He lay in that great Death like the gold in the husk
Of the world . . . and round him, like spent lightnings, lay the Ore—
The balm for the world's sore.

And the gold lay in its husk of rough earth like the core
In the furred almond, the chestnut in its prickly
Bark, the walnut in a husk green and bitter.

And to that hollow sea
The civilisation of the Maimed, and, too, Life's lepers, came
As once to Christ near the Sea of Galilee.

They brought the Aeons of Blindness and the Night
Of the World, crying to him, 'Lazarus, give us sight!
O you whose sores are of gold, who are the new Light
Of the World!'

        They brought to the Tomb
The Condemned of Man, who wear as stigmata from the womb
The depression of the skull as in the lesser
Beasts of Prey, the marks of Ape and Dog,
The canine and lemurine muscle . . . the pitiable, the terrible,
The loveless, whose deformities arose
Before their birth, or from a betrayal by the gold wheat-ear.
'Lazarus, for all love we knew the great Sun's kiss

On the loveless cheek. He came to the dog-fang and the lion-claw
That Famine gave the empty mouth, the workless hands.
He came to the inner leaf of the forsaken heart—
He spoke of our Christ and of a golden love . . .
But our Sun is gone . . . will your gold bring warmth to the loveless
    lips, and harvest to barren lands?'

Then Dives was brought . . . He lay like a leprous Sun
That is covered with the sores of the world . . . the leprosy
Of gold encrusts the world that was his heart.

Like a great ear of wheat that is swoln with grain,
Then ruined by white rain,
He lay . . . His hollow face, dust white, was cowled with a hood of
    gold;
But you saw there was no beat or pulse of blood—
You would not know him now from Lazarus!

He did not look at us.
He said, 'What was spilt still surges like the Flood.

But Gold shall be the Blood
Of the world . . . Brute gold condensed to the primal essence
Has the texture, smell, warmth, colour of Blood. We must take

A quintessence of the disease for remedy. Once hold
The primal matter of all gold—
From which it grows
(That Rose of the World) as the sharp clear tree from the seed of the
    great rose,

Then give of this, condemned to the transparency
Of the beryl, the weight of twenty barley grains:
And the leper's face will be full as the rose's face
After great rains.

It will shape again the Shadow of Man. Or at least will take
From all roots of life the symptoms of the leper—
And make the body sharp as the honeycomb,
The roots of life that are left like the red roots of the rose-branches.'

But near him a gold sound—
The voice of an unborn wheat-ear accusing Dives—
Said, 'Soon I shall be more rare, more precious than gold.'

There are no thunders, there are no fires, no suns, no earthquakes
Left in our blood . . . But yet, like the rolling thunders of all the fires
    in the world, we cry
To Dives: 'You are the shadow of Cain. Your shade is the primal
    Hunger.'
'I lie under what condemnation?'
'The same as Adam, the same as Cain, the same as Sodom, the same
    as Judas.

And the fires of your Hell shall not be quenched by the rain
From those torn and parti-coloured garments of Christ, those rags
That once were Men. Each wound, each stripe,
Cries out more loudly than the voice of Cain—
Saying "Am I my brother's keeper?" ' Think! When the last clamour
    of the Bought and Sold,
The agony of Gold,
Is hushed . . . When the last Judas-kiss

269

Has died upon the cheek of the Starved Man Christ, those ashes that
    were men
Will rise again
To be our Fires upon the Judgment Day!
And yet—who dreamed that Christ has died in vain?
He walks again on the Seas of Blood, He comes in the terrible Rain.

Not even the most enthusiastic admirers of Miss Sitwell's earlier poetry—and the present writer has loved it since his school days—can have foreseen the development of her work during the last six or seven years. With the appearance of *Street Songs* and *Green Song*, those who care for poetry recognized a true poetic and prophetic cry which had not been heard in English since the death of Yeats. This was not merely exquisite poetry: it was great poetry; we felt once more the excitement of having amongst us a poet who could give us back our sight and our belief in the human heart, a poet on Shelley's definition. And, naturally, we are anxious to know by what steps this new eminence has been achieved . . .

In her last published work *The Shadow of Cain* Christian symbols have gained ascendancy. This craggy, mysterious, philosophic poem, in which the poet looks down from a great eminence of time, is at the furthest remove from the lyrics of the *hortus conclusus*. The world without love, the world of absolute zero, is split in two by some such disastrous convulsion of matter as now hangs over our heads, and there are left two protagonists of humanity, Dives and Lazarus. The dialogue between them with which the poem ends, is her deepest and most passionate statement of her concern with original sin. This is the true cry of our time, the cry of all those whose imaginations are still awake and whose hearts are still uncalcined. Miss Sitwell is a religious poet because only thus could she continue to write for this generation without being overcome by despair. She is growing in power and confidence, so that we wait thirstily for each new poem, which, by its beauty, its compassion and its belief in the eternal processes of recreation, can help us to endure the world's fever.

Kenneth Clark, 'On the Developments of
Miss Sitwell's Later Style', *Horizon*

1948–1957

When we come to compare the collected poems of Dame Edith Sitwell with those of Yeats or Mr Eliot or Professor Auden, it will be found that hers have the purest intention of any; the honey may sometimes fail, but it is never adulterated.

Previous Convictions by Cyril Connolly

The visits of Edith Sitwell to America began in the year after the publication of The Shadow of Cain, *1948. She and her brother Osbert Sitwell were invited on the first of their lecture tours, an event which called for a letter of welcome from Frances Steloff, New York's equivalent of Sylvia Beach, and the founder of* The Gotham Book Mart.

The party given for them, on the day after the first of their readings, took pride of place in Bennett Cerf's column in The Saturday Review of Literature, *dated 11 December 1948.*

'The Gotham Book Mart's do for Sir Osbert and Dr Edith Sitwell brought out the darndest assortment of celebrities, freaks, refugees from Park Lane, and the lifted-pinkie set since the famous part for Joan "Cradle-of-the-Deep" Lowell aboard the *Ile de France* in 1929. Wystan Auden, Tennessee Williams, William Saroyan, Jim Farrell, Carl Van Vechten, Marianne Moore, Stephen Spender, William Carlos Williams, Lincoln Kirstein, and Bill Bénet were ogled and fought over like movie stars in front of the Hampshire House. One bearded gent wore a red velvet smoking jacket and looked disdainful. Another sported a Navajo Indian robe and looked dirty. The inevitable *Life* photographers knocked glasses out of the hands of distinguished guests and blandly shooed Hostess Frances Steloff out of her own back office. That I managed to reach the side of Dr Edith myself was a tribute to the all-American interference provided by Mary McGrory of the *Washington Star* who neatly took out the last apparition with a swivel-hipped feint and an astonished "My God, I think that was Oscar Wilde!"'

'Dr Edith was taking the commotion in stride. "As I say in my lectures, I don't like talent," she was telling one poet. "I prefer power and conviction." "I hear you were very funny once in Liverpool," I shouted above the din. "Would you tell me the details?" Dr Edith beamed . . . and said, "Sit down here with me. The incident to which you refer occurred when I was discussing the poetry of D. H. Lawrence. I said it was 'soft, woolly, and hot like a Jaeger sweater'. I thought Lawrence would have a fit but he didn't. The

273

Jaegers, however, did. They informed me indignantly that their sweaters were indeed soft and woolly, but never hot, due to their 'special system of slow conductivity'." '

She was invited again and again, travelling first with Sir Osbert and later with Dylan Thomas. In 1951 'Queen Edith' (as she was nick-named after the publication of Fanfare for Elizabeth, *the first of her two studies of the reign of Elizabeth the First) found herself in Hollywood. Her appearance there could not have been more dramatic as she read the sleep walking scene from* Macbeth, *dressed in a brocade dress of more than usual opulence and wearing a crown.*

I was just announcing that Hell is murky [she wrote to John Lehmann] when a poor gentleman in the audience uttered the most piercing shrieks and was carried out by four men, foaming at the mouth. As one of the spectators said to me, 'You ought to be awfully pleased. It was one of the most flattering things I have ever seen.'

She reported 'A Laocoon entanglement with Miss Mary Pickford' and a meeting with Miss Ethel Barrymore 'which was delightful, although Osbert ascribes my bronchitis to her, as she was breathing heavily'.

Her comment about America was that 'she could not have enjoyed it more'. Anyone who did not like Americans 'must be mad'.

America responded in the form of an invitation from Columbia Pictures to write a film script based on Fanfare for Elizabeth. *This second visit brought her a new friend, George Cukor, but, as might have been foreseen, the film did not come about.*

The company took the precaution of presenting her with a collaborator and though, she reported, she was 'working like a cannibal head hunting', the collaboration was doomed from the start. She told John Lehmann that 'Anne Boleyn eats chocs behind a pillar and pinches Jane Seymour's bottom behind Cardinal Wolseley's back' (Selected Letters).

The film now opens with what would seem to be a sort of pillow fight in the 'dorm' of the 6th form at St Winifred's. When the atmosphere isn't that of Young Bess or The Tudor Wench, it is that of Forever Amber or Sweet Nell of Old Drury. George Boleyn comes into Anne's room when she is in a bath-towel! Henry is always either rolling drunk on the floor, or roaming about in his night clothes, or snoring in bed. The King and Anne (have been) endowed with napkin rings! Marked H.R. and A.B. (after she is Queen) and Elizabeth's governess says 'Give the girl some cookies'. Oh Heaven's above!!

Letter to Alberto de Lacerda,
Selected Letters

Any resemblance to Fanfare for Elizabeth *was entirely accidental, as this extract, from the opening paragraphs of Chapter Four, makes apparent:*

The beings of this Sophoclean tragedy of passions, faiths, lusts, and ambition that had the fever of lust, poured out their blood and spirit in a world of giant spiritual upheavals. Henry the King, once beautiful for all his monstrousness, half a bestial bulk of physical matter, half a kingly being of enlightened greatness and primitive intellect, Catherine, the deserted Queen, a dark and sombre Niobe weeping for her children, and Anne, the summer lightning—these, their forms, their actions, were lit by the enormous flares of fires in which the martyrs perished, kindled in vindication of Henry's regency under God, and in homage to Elizabeth, the new-born offspring of that almost supreme being. Those flares show a face of kingly power, marred by passions and self-will, the face of a darkened and burnt-out Queen-nun, and a face of unutterable terror; a laughing mouth and tears falling like comets down a face that held all the summer's beauty. We think that a voice is about to speak—then a thunderous darkness falls again, and a faint sound arises—the whispering of plots, like the crepitating sound that comes before an earthquake.

The scene, the events, and the beings of the tragedy were bound together in such a manner as to be indivisible. The tragedy had grown slowly and inevitably from the character of the time, and of the actors, from the change in the minds of mankind, from an imaginary incest, superstitious fear, the King's overwhelming infatuation, his lust for power, his need for a son who would save his kingdom from the danger of civil war.

Fanfare for Elizabeth

In April 1954 Edith Sitwell returned to London. To the award of the honorary doctorates received from Leeds, Durham, Sheffield *and* Oxford

Universities she could now add the royal accolade. Dame Edith Sitwell discovered that she had become a national institution, considered by many to be in the tradition of eccentricity hallowed by herself. To some she remained the high priestess of English poetry, especially after the publication of her Collected Poems. *But her fame distorted the image. Those who accepted her as an eccentric tended to disapprove of her poetry. Those who admired her poetry tended to disapprove of her eccentricity.*

Never had she received so much publicity and never had she disliked it more. Her personal life was not happy. The death of Dylan Thomas, that 'poor dear and most wonderful poet', had been followed by the news that Osbert Sitwell had contracted Parkinson's disease. Fame had not brought her security. She had an overdraft at her bank and, although she kept up the outward structure of her life, the fact left her with no peace.

It was at this stage of her life that she met Father Martin D'Arcy S.J. whose book The Nature of Belief *bridged the gap for her between belief and commitment.*

When I was a very small child, I began to see the patterns of the world, the images of wonder. And I asked myself why those patterns should be repeated—the feather and the fern and rose and acorn in the patterns of frost on the window—pattern after pattern repeated again and again. And even then I knew that this was telling us something. I founded my poetry upon it.

Letter to Fr Philip Caraman,
Selected Letters

In 1955 Edith Sitwell was received into the Roman Catholic Church, and, she wrote:

I believe, and trust with all my heart that I am on the threshold of a new life.
But, I will have to be born again. And I have a whole world to see, as it were for the first time, and to understand as far as my capacities will let me.

Ibid

How Many Heavens

The emeralds are singing on the grasses,
And in the trees the bells of the long cold are ringing,—

My blood seems changed to emeralds like the spears
Of grass beneath the earth piercing and singing.

The flame of the first blade
Is an angel piercing through the earth to sing
'God is everything!
The grass within the grass, the angel in the angel, flame
Within the flame, and He is the green shade that came
To be the heart of shade.'

The grey-beard angel of the stone,
Who has grown wise with age, cried 'Not alone
Am I within my silence,—God is the stone in the still stone, the
    silence laid
In the heart of silence' . . . then, above the glade,

The yellow straws of light,
Whereof the sun has built his nest, cry, 'Bright
Is the world, the yellow straw
My brother,—God is the straw within the straw:—
    All things are Light.'

He is the sea of ripeness and the sweet apple's emerald lore.
So you, my flame of grass, my root of the world from which all
    Spring shall grow,
O you, my hawthorn bough of the stars, now leaning low
Through the day, for your flowers to kiss my lips, shall know
He is the core of the heart of love, and He, beyond labouring seas,
    our ultimate shore.

1957–1964

It has been an inspiration to be living and better still, to be writing in her flowering shade.

Sacheverell Sitwell:
'A tribute from her younger brother',
from the programme for her
75th birthday concert, 9 October 1962

'The day I met [Edith Sitwell] was a day of high summer. The setting was the Aldeburgh Festival of 1957 at which she read Blake in the parish church and she wore dark glasses throughout. The most formidable of their kind, they had mirror rims that slanted diabolically towards the temples. They were gold and black beneath a Tudor hat that was studded with gold and framed by two lengths of black chiffon. Her dress was of black satin and worn to the ground; her Chinese coat was gold flecked by green. Hands of great beauty, very long and delicately boned, were weighted by aquamarines that flashed fire in the light slanting through the stained glass windows. I sat in the back pew with the friend who was to introduce me, filled with foreboding. What kind of contact could there be between my prosaic self and so extraordinary a being? What communication would be possible between an expatriate detective novelist with one book to her credit and the grande dame of English literature, who looked like an incarnation of Elizabeth the First, who intoned Blake's mystical lines with the austerity of a Roman Catholic cardinal, who was, in fact, the embodiment of her legend?'

The Last Years of a Rebel,
by Elizabeth Salter

If we repeat Elizabeth Salter's description of her introduction to Edith Sitwell, it is to emphasize the impact of her presence in this, the last decade of her life. Her stylized appearance, her deliberate cultivation of personality, had surrounded her with the aura of a twentieth-century myth. Elizabeth Salter discovered that myth and reality were one. Her vision, so seldom disturbed by the compromises demanded by ordinary living, had retained the perspective of the poet. Her withdrawals had affected her health and her happiness, but her truth remained untainted.

If the second flowering was reaching its end, a third was on its way. In the last eight years of her life Macmillans published her second book on the reign of Elizabeth, The Queens and the Hive, *she compiled two more anthologies, one of Swinburne and the other a personal selection, commissioned by the American publishers Little Brown and published in*

281

England by Victor Gollancz, and she produced her last volume of poetry. It was a slim little book, but in it is some of her best work. Her awareness of death as a personal reality cut away the superstructure of rhetoric and left the 'pure poetic intention' unadorned. La Bella Bona Roba *won for her the Guinness poetry award. To the surprise of her critics and the joy of her admirers, Dame Edith Sitwell was showing the world that she was more than a beloved eccentric and more than a projection of her own publicity. She was a poet.*

She was also a letter writer. In this the last decade of her life, when ill health very often confined her to bed, letters were her chief method of communication with her friends. A letter from Edith Sitwell was worth receiving. It combined wit with elegance. It was invariably interesting and usually extremely funny. If that fun was at the expense of those benighted admirers who formed the legion known as her 'pests' this should not be interpreted as a sign of cruelty. The 'pest' was anonymous. He or she represented the insensitive, the uncomprehending. She had suffered at their hands. Invective was a safety valve, deflecting criticism from those who were close to her. Her loyalty to her brothers, condemned as nepotism by her critics, was extended to those who served her.

Here are a sample few of her later letters, introduced by the stories which led up to them, outlined in Elizabeth Salter's The Last Years of a Rebel.

'Two of the younger and more notorious of her visitors at Oxford were Corso and Ginsberg, the "Beat" poets. Edith had read and liked Ginsberg's poem "Howl" and invited them to luncheon with her at her club. As this encounter was written up in a leading American magazine with rather more colour than accuracy, it might be as well to set the record straight.

'She had chosen the inner dining-room of the Sesame Club "so that the old ducks would not have so much to quack about", but even so we had to file past the tables of diners in their best tweeds and town hats. The procession was headed by Edith, leaning on her ebony stick, her tall cone-shaped hat worn above the long satin dress and inevitable fur coat. She was escorted by Quentin Stevenson, the young poet who had introduced the Americans, and was followed by myself and Corso and Ginsberg in their roll-necked sweaters, jeans and sandals. Ginsberg, with the "look of a starving wolf" as Edith described him, and Corso, blue-eyed and seraphic, the stamp of innocence surviving his history of poverty and notoriety, were contrasts in themselves.

'With Ginsberg on her right and Corso on her left, Edith proceeded to charm them into enjoyment. According to the magazine the conversation was devoted to the use of marijuana cigarettes and the menu consisted of cress sandwiches and tea. In fact it was a meal that had been especially ordered, beginning with smoked salmon and lobster thermidor and ending with the club's speciality, an ice-cream "bombe à l'Américain".

'The subject of drug-taking arose from a discussion about Aldous Huxley's experiments with mescalin. All three young poets admitted to the general use of marijuana amongst their contemporaries and defended it on the grounds of "heightened sensibility". Edith's answer, in no sense of judgement, was simply that "no poet should need a drug to produce extreme sensibility, which must be, if he is any good, a part of his equipment".

'At this point she was not, as reported, offered a marijuana cigarette which she refused on the grounds that marijuana brought her out in spots. It would have taken a great deal more courage than any of the three young men possessed to have offered Edith a "reefer". Characteristically, when she read this account to me later on, it was not the imputation that she smoked marijuana that upset her as much as the doubts cast on her complexion.

' "I am hardly the spot queen," she complained.'

. . . I have been dragged ceaselessly from pillar to post. I've had the oddest adventures. In one, Quentin was involved. Two very young men,[1] Americans, and one having a great sweetness of expression, both poets—you probably have read about them in the *New York Times*—were introduced to me and came to lunch, accompanied by Quentin, who was looking *terrified*! (I may say at this point, that the episode was just as I was beginning the migraine attacks, and was not, as you might say, *curative* in its effects.) They behaved with great courtesy. The poor boy with the sweet expression had, he told me, been sent to prison *at the age of 17 for three years* for organising a

[1] Gregory Corso and Allen Ginsberg

bank robbery! If ever, in my life, I saw anyone who had obviously been sweetened and in a way re-formed, by such a terrible experience, it was that boy. I am sure he is a kind of haunted saint—a saint who has lost his way. For he *has* lost it. The other looked like a famished wolf. The trouble is, I understand, that they are both addicted to a habit the result of which is that nobody can *ever* tell *what* they will do next. (But they can be relied on to do it!) In an interview given to the N.Y.T. the poor boy who had been in prison said that at a recital he gave of his poems in Paris, he had removed all his clothes, and recited as he was when he was born.

Next day I received a letter from a friend of mine, a Don at Oxford, giving me such really terrifying information, that I took to my bed, and lay there with my mouth open, pondering!

However, the luncheon party went off all right, with no untoward incidents. The young man did not recite, and the old ladies whose only experiences are going to dim churches and dimmer lectures, remained wrapped in their mental cotton wool! The young men returned to Paris, so I haven't seen them again.

Letter to James Purdy,
Selected Letters

'Her discovery of James Purdy, the last of a line which began with Wilfred Owen and included Denton Welch, Tom Driberg and Dylan Thomas, represented a minor mystery never solved. She had gone to sleep one afternoon at Montegufoni with windows shuttered and doors closed against draughts and intruders as was her custom, and when she woke up there was a book lying on her bed which had not been there when she went to sleep. It was called *Don't Call Me by my Right Name*. The first story she read concerned two Negro mothers in Chicago, and, convinced that she had stumbled on a great Negro writer, she read the remainder only to discover that the author was a white American of Scottish-Irish ancestry, living in New York. As always, when impressed by new talent, she wrote to the author, and through her recommendation *63 Dream Palace* was published in England by Victor Gollancz. The result was a new and lasting friendship with another young writer, who wrote to tell her that she had become his "patron saint".

'Although in general reviews of *63 Dream Palace* were not quite what she had hoped for, her own review in *The Times Literary Supplement* brought this response from Purdy:

' "I was quite annihilated by your wonderful review of my work . . . I feel like a man who has come out of Plato's cave and looked at the sun! I do want to be worthy of your tribute, Dame Edith, and I will spend the rest of my life writing in the hope that I may."

'The one factor guaranteed to take Edith out of herself was a friend who could interest her. This qualification is necessary as, although her circle continued to widen, not all her friends had the power to do so.

'Among those who had were Pamela Hansford Johnson and her husband, C. P. Snow. Edith had read their work and admired it, and there was an additional link through Pamela's close association with the youthful Dylan Thomas.

'A letter arrived one day from Sir Charles Snow (as he then was). His reason for writing, he said, was a novel which his wife had just finished and which had been suggested by the closing years of Frederick Rolfe's life.

' "In the course of her book," he wrote, "the 'hero', whose name is Skipton, runs across a literary group who are visiting Bruges. The centre of this group is a woman of forty called Dorothy Merlin. This woman is not an amiable character, either seen objectively or through Skipton's paranoiac vision. She is an Australian with seven children: she writes verse-dramas (bad) mainly about having seven children: she gives lectures for the British Council: and the only work of art she knows about, except her own, is *Kristin Lavransdatter*.

' "To our horror, it has just been suggested to us that some readers might think my wife was intending a malicious parody of yourself. I don't think any suggestion I have ever heard has ever surprised me quite so much. I have tried to forget the true origin of this character, and have searched point by point for facts that (a) she is a strong personality (b) she inspires some hero-worship, but I can see not one. She is a bad playwright while you are a major poet; she is an Australian housewife, and you are an aristocrat. She doesn't admit the existence of any other writer, while we have all seen the proofs of your generosity. And so on, in every psychological and physical detail.

' "But both my wife—who is ill at the moment or she would have

285

written to you herself—and myself are distressed even by the suggestion. The literary life is full enough of pinpricks without causing more, however innocently, to those one respects; if there were anything in the book you didn't like my wife would wish to cut it out. Have you time to cast your eye over the typescript? I know it is an infliction to put extra work on to you and we wouldn't think of asking you if we were not bewildered."

'After a few days of enjoying the joke and, no doubt, thinking out an answer—I know, from studying her manuscript books, how carefully she prepared letters which she regarded as important, sometimes copying them out in full before deciding on a final draft— Edith replied as follows:

'Dear Lady Snow,

How much I laughed when I received Sir Charles' letter.

I am, at the same time, alarmed, for I am at the moment finishing a book called *The Queens and the Hive* which is about Queen Elizabeth I and Mary Queen of Scots and contains a rousing account of Catherine de Medici planning the massacre of St Bartholomew's Eve. I am now terrified that this may be supposed, by any readers I may have, to be a lascivious portrait of you. After all, you are not Italian, do not persecute Protestants, and are not the mother-in-law of Mary Queen of Scots, so the likeness springs to the eyes!

What do you suppose I have done with my seven offspring? Eaten them?'

The manuscript The Unspeakable Skipton *was duly read by Edith and pronounced Pamela's finest work. The friendship developed and, in January 1959, from the Castello di Montegufoni where Edith Sitwell now spent her winters, came this letter:*

What great pleasure your delightful, charming letter gave me. I got it just before we were incarcerated for the near-week of non-stop Sundays inflicted by the Italians at this time of year: religious festas, and national festas, during which no post goes out, and church bells ring from 5.30 a.m. till 6 p.m.

I am so distressed, though, to hear about your poor little boy's bad bronchitis. How very worrying for you. I do *hope* he is better.

To amuse him, I am having my book *Façade* sent him, because children usually like some of the poems—'Madame Mouse Trots', for instance. I will sign it for him when I get back to London. I am so sorry to think how anxious you must have been.

I *long* for *Skipton*. You are an angel to say you will send it to me. I am so grateful. I have been longing for it since I read the manuscript. It is, I think and know, an amazing book. The extraordinary insight into that poor, dreadful, pitiable creature's character is astounding.

I knew one person of more or less the same kind, the late Wyndham Lewis. He would, I think, have been before your time. I knew him very well, because I sat to him every day excepting Sundays, for ten months. It was impossible to like him, and in the end, his attitude became so threatening that I ceased to sit for him, so that the portrait of me by him in the Tate has no hands, and I figured as Lady Harriet in his *The Apes of God*. (And he figured as Mr Henry Debingham in the only novel I have ever written, *I Live Under a Black Sun*. It is out of print, but I will see if I can get a copy for you.)

When one sat to him, in his enormous studio, mice emerged from their holes, and lolled against the furniture, staring in the most insolent manner at the sitter. At last, when Tom Eliot was sitting to him, their behaviour became intolerable. They climbed on to his knee, and would sit staring up at his face. So Lewis bought a large gong which he placed near the mouse-hole, and, when matters reached a certain limit, he would strike this loudly, and the mice would retreat.

My mother—a very rude woman—persecuted him unremittingly, and addressed him by a variety of names, the most usual being 'Mr Wilks'.

I think you have second sight. How on earth did you know Fuseli's giant women were in my mind when I wrote 'La Bella Bona Roba'? Also I am founding my recitation of the sleep-walking scene in *Macbeth* (I am going to recite it in June or July) on them.

We lunched in Florence on Christmas Day. We are fond of our hostess and her son, but seemed to find no means of communication with our fellow-guests. One man asked me if I liked writing poetry. At last I felt like the Duke of Gloucester, who was taken, while in Cairo, to a night-club, where a hostess, blue from her eyelids to her cheek-bones, was presented to him. He is reported to have stared at her, silently, for ten minutes, and then to have said: 'I say! Do you know Tidworth? . . .'

Letter to Lady Snow,
Selected Letters

Her letters are Edith Sitwell's most clearly stated proof of her attitude towards the composers who set her work to music. To Humphrey Searle, after the performance of Gold Coast Customs, *she wrote:*

Are you beginning to recover?—For four days I lay like a crocodile on the bank of a river, one hand upraised (as is their habit) in the hope of food being put into it; but otherwise making no sign of life.

You have caused a fearful disturbance here, with that Work to amuse the Kiddies.[1] Robins (Osbert's old soldier servant, who has been with us for thirty years, and is now the butler) kept on waking his wife up, on the night of the performance, by shouting 'Miss Edith is dead'. And his wife, when she saw me (she is the cook) said 'Oh—*Miss*', and tittered nervously, 'Ooh—er'. We *did* have nightmares! The young housemaid creeps in and out of my room, sideways, like a crab, and looks at me as if I were going to bite, and the whole of Sheffield is in a turmoil.

I have just written to the Vice-President of the Columbia Records, in New York, to say what a great work it is. And I think that presently we must get started on Mr Stokowski. I should think he would be mad about it.

I do hope it is going to be done again.

. . . There cannot be the slightest doubt that you have produced a work of genius. I am more excited about it than I can possibly say. Am, indeed, completely overwhelmed by it. It is terrible, awe-inspiring, and noble, even in its horror. And it has produced the dreadful *loneliness* and broken-heartedness of it in a way I could not have believed possible. By that, I mean, that there should have been such an *exact identity* of feeling.

It must have been terrible to do. It is terrible to feel that, let alone bring it out of oneself. I think you are capable of anything.

Letter to Humphrey Searle,
Selected Letters

---

[1] Humphrey Searle's setting of *Gold Coast Customs*

In 1959 Benjamin Britten asked her to write a poem to be included in his celebration of the tercentenary of Purcell, and, in May of the year, she sent it to him with the following letter:

Here is your poem, which I *hope* you will allow me to dedicate to you.[1]

I write it as a recitation poem—right, I trust, for the voice—as a song without music, not as a poem for the page. I think, and hope, the timing, the length, is right. If I had made it longer, it would have been monotonous, owing to it shouting the one theme.

Would it, or would it not, be a good idea to have it heralded by a Fanfare?

I long to see you and Peter. I imagine we have a rehearsal in the morning of the performance, don't we? (or the day before). (Incidentally, I don't know where the performance will be.) If it won't exhaust and bother you both too much, would you lunch with me? I do hope so.

For the last few months, I have been undergoing an agonising, not a lovely sleepy, hibernation. Unable to work, owing to nervous exhaustion and noise, and almost pestered out of my wits by lunatics and persons with grievances. (I am also afflicted by fibrositis in my right shoulder, which makes my handwriting worse than usual.)

I am involved in a Laocoon correspondence with the step-mother of an English leper (poor man). I was so fascinated by this rather unusual occurrence that the grip tightened round me before I knew what was happening, and she now writes to me *every* day (literally). She is obviously a very saintly woman—so I am in the grip for life. In addition, all my other unknown correspondents tell me the full histories of their lives—lives that seem to have been longer, and more full of incident, than any other lives of which I have ever heard . . .

Best love to you and Peter, Edith.

I have, in the poem, drawn on past poems of mine, because, obviously, if one can write *at all*, one can only choose the most suitable medium for what one has to say, and cannot put it into other, weaker words.

Letter to Benjamin Britten,
Selected Letters

[1] 'Praise We Great Men'

Edith Sitwell's The Queens and the Hive *was published in* 1961 *and dedicated to George Cukor, director of her abortive film on* Fanfare for Elizabeth. *Early in* 1962 *George Cukor came to London and, in the course of a visit, told her that it had been Noël Coward who had first pointed out the dedication to him. Through George Cukor, Noël Coward made his first move towards a reconciliation, writing a letter addressed to Greenhill, the flat in Hampstead in which she now lived.*

Edith answered that she had been pleased and touched by his charming letter, which she had answered by telegram as she had been suffering from acute writer's cramp. She added:

How I wish that unprofessional writers would suffer, sometimes, from this disease.

The 9th should be a day for all present to remember. Never before, I think, has anyone attended their own Memorial Service. (The press is madly excited at my being 75 and is looking forward avidly to my funeral.)

I do hope you will find time to come and have a sherry or a cocktail with me when you come to London. Do please ring me up.

In November Noël Coward took up the offer, choosing teatime.

'Both Edith and I waited for his ring at the door with some trepidation; Edith because she was to receive a man whom she had regarded as her enemy for forty years; I because I had admired Mr Coward since I had first discovered his work at the age of seventeen. Mr Coward admitted later that he also felt some trepidation. Because of the feud, neither of them had had the slightest idea of what to expect of the other. Their reaction was one of astonishment as well as delight.

'They sat opposite each other in Edith's small sitting-room, Mr Coward wearing dark glasses because of a complaint that he described, cheerfully, as "pink-eye", Edith in her latest hat, her inevitable fur coat and slippers. Mr Coward sipped his tea and refused sandwiches. Edith went through the motions of lifting her cup to her lips and put it down again untouched. I ate the sandwiches, drank my tea and listened.

'Mr Coward set the ball rolling by apologising for having hurt her feelings, pleading youth. Edith accepted his apology with a warmth that proved past resentments had not only been banished but forgotten. They then went on to discuss "Willie" Maugham and his legal battle with his daughter. Although they were on different sides in the controversy—Mr Coward explaining that he had been very fond of Willie's wife and considered her to have been badly treated, and Edith confessing to a dislike of the lady—she admitted having found Somerset Maugham something of a strain. In fact, she had once tried to avoid meeting him at Bumpus by picking up an imaginary book under a table.

' "Poor Willie," she said, "he simply followed me under the table so that we encountered each other on all fours. 'E-e-edith,' he said to me, 'wh-what are you doing down here?' "

'But it was the discovery of a shared enemy that brought them into triumphant accord. Edith, still full of her grievance against the American lady columnist with the syndicated newspapers, found that Mr Coward knew her personally.

' "Do tell me," Edith asked him, "what is she like?"

'Mr Coward's reply was instantaneous. "My dear Dame Edith, she is one brisk stampede from nose to navel."

'By the time he left they were both regretting the wasted years. As I helped Mr Coward into his coat I told him that I felt I had been present at an historic occasion.

'Mr Coward did not indulge in false modesty. "You have been," he agreed genially.'

The Last Years Of A Rebel,
by Elizabeth Salter

In October 1962, the concert which Edith Sitwell called her Memorial Service was given in her honour in the Festival Hall. Irene Worth and Sebastian Shaw recited Façade, *for which Sir William Walton conducted the orchestra, but the first item on the programme was a reading by Edith Sitwell. By this time she was confined to a wheelchair but the clothes she wore defied this concession to debility. Her dress was red velvet, hat, collar and shoes were gold.*

To feel the full impact of the moment when she began to read, one would have had to see it against the background of the months that had preceded it; to recall the figure, white-faced and supine, sometimes in tears of fatigue because every movement was an effort, the fragile bone protruding from the flannel nightdress, and the transparent, delicate skin that had remained as vulnerable as it must have been in childhood.

291

Her voice was deeper, more slurred, rather softer than of old, but on this night there was nobody to say they could not hear.

The silence in the auditorium conveyed much more than just the quality of listening. It was the hush of respect. The grand old lady who made a throne out of her wheelchair and intoned her opulent images was crowned that night by her achievements.

The audience numbered three thousand, and the supper party after the concert was a roll call of the famous. Noël Coward, who was unable to come, sent a telegram to which Edith Sitwell replied:

How very charming of you to send me that telegram. I appreciated it very much.

Osbert and I were so very sorry you couldn't come, so was Sachie. And we were so sorry for the cause. I do hope the wretched thing is over and done with, and that you weren't in great pain.

The concert and supper party were fun, in a way. But it was all rather like something macabre out of Proust.

The papers excelled themselves—the *Sketch* particularly. I had never met the nice well-meaning reporter who 'covered' the event, but according to him he sat beside me as my weary head sank into my pillow, and just as I was dropping asleep, I uttered these

Famous Last Words
'Be *kind* to me! Not many people are!'
Very moving, I think, don't you? . . .

Letter to Noël Coward,
Selected Letters

After her death on 9 December 1964 came the posthumous publication of her autobiography Taken Care Of. *It is full of gems, some of which have been quoted in this anthology. But these are gems set in a framework of bitterness. In the last months of a life redeemed from disappointment by the force of creative energy, the long sight of the poet was again focused on the immediate. Debilitated by her failing powers, her concentration, previously devoted to her art, turned in on herself. From time to time, released from anxiety about financial affairs, the old energy asserted itself. Her long crusade on behalf of animals flared into letters to the press. Her rejection of vulgarity manifested itself in protests against the obscenities in a literature devoted, she considered, to the destruction rather than to the revivifying of an art form.*

The true autobiography of Edith Sitwell is her Collected Poems, *described by herself as 'hymns of praise to the Glory of life'.*

'Thus [wrote Cyril Connolly], Dame Edith takes up her position with Whitman and Dylan Thomas and the mystics, with Blake and Rimbaud. "To produce a poetry that is the light of the Great Morning, wherein all beings whom we see passing in the common street are transformed into the epitome of all beauty, or of all joy, or of all sorrow." This is her aim.'

The War Orphans

(Written after seeing a photograph of Korean children
asleep in the snow)

The snow is the blood of these poor Dead . . . they have no other—
These children, old in the dog's scale of years, too old
For the hopeless breast—ghosts for whom there is none to care,
Grown fleshless as the skeleton
Of Adam, they have known
More aeons of the cold than he endured
In the first grave of the world. They have, for bed,
The paving stones, the spider spins their blankets, and their bread
Is the shred and crumb of dead Chance. In this epoch of the cold,
In which new worlds are formed, new glaciations
To overcast the world that was the heart,
There is only that architecture of the winter, the huge plan
Of the lasting skeleton, built from the hunger of Man,
Constructed for hunger—piteous in its griefs, the humiliation
Of outworn flesh, the Ape-cerement, O the foolish tattered clothing,
Rags stained with the filth of humanity, stink of its toiling,
But never the smell of the heart, with its warmth, its fevers,
Rapacity, and grandeur. For the cold is zero
In infinite intensity, brother to democratic
Death, our one equality, who holds
Alike the maelstrom of the blood, the world's incendiarism,
The summer redness and the hope of the rose,
The beast, and man's superiority o'er the beast
That is but this:

Man bites with his smile and poisons with his kiss.
When, in each dawn,
The light on my brow is changed to the mark of Cain,
And my blood cries, 'Am I my brother's keeper?' seeing these ghosts
Of Man's forgetfulness of Man, I feel again
The pitiless but healing rain—who thought I only
Had the lonely Lethe flood for tears.

Choric Song

The Red Woman, like the glittering
Dark red cedar tree
Or the sun when its fires are low—
The Esquimau, black as the ancient cold with her hair like the long
    dull ropes of snow
Let down from the creaking cloud—
The White Woman, the huge lightning in the dark of the great
    world—
The Negress black as thunder, the dead woman upright in the
    Spring's shroud—
They shout to their loves across the ocean, the glittering seas of
    delight—
'Mine is the only love in the world, the first beginning of sight!
Of you, the hour when the work of the world, the hunt for our food,
    is done—
Love me, my ultimate Darkness, kiss me, my infinite Sun!'

'His Blood colours my Cheek'
A saying of St Agnes

His Blood colours my cheek.
Ah! Were but those Flames the tongue wherewith I speak
Of the small ambitions I have seen
Rise in the common street
Where the bell that tolls in Bedlam tolls the hour.
Yet still great flowers like violet thunders break

In air, and still the flower of the five-petalled senses
Is surely ours.
I, an old dying woman, tied
To the winter's hopelessness
And to a wisp of bone
Clothed in the old world's outworn foolishness
—A poor Ape-cerement
With all its rags of songs, loves, rages, lusts, and flags of death,
Say this to you,
My father Pithecanthropus Erectus, your head once filled with
    primal night,
You who stood at last after the long centuries
Of the anguish of the bone
Reaching upward towards the loving, the all-understanding sun—
To you, who no more walk on all fours like the first
Gardener and grave-digger, yet are listening
Where, born from zero, little childish leaves and lives begin!
I hear from the dust the small ambitions rise.
The White Ant whispers: 'Could I be Man's size,

My cylinders would stretch three hundred feet
In air, and Man would look at me with different eyes!'

And there the Brazilian insect all day long
Challenges the heat with its heavy noise:
'Were I as great as Man, my puny voice
Would stretch from Pole to Pole, no other sound
Be audible. By this dictatorship the round
World would be challenged—from my uproar would a new
Civilisation of the dust be born, the old world die like dew.'
I watch the new world of rulers, the snub-nosed, the vain and the
    four-handed,
Building a new Babel for the weak
Who walk with the certainty of the somnambulist
Upon the tight-rope stretched over nothingness—
Holding a comet and the small Ape-dust in their fist
Over the grave where the heart of Man is laid.
I hear the empty straw whine to the street
Of the ghost that has no bread, the lonely ghost
That lacks prosperity: 'I am your wheat:

Come and be fed!'
But I see the sun, large as the journeying foot of Man, see the great
    traveller
Fearing no setting, going straight to his destination,
So am I not dismayed.

His Blood colours my cheek;—
No more eroded by the seas of the world's passions and greeds, I rise
As if I never had been Ape, to look in the compassionate, the all-
    seeing Eyes.

La Bella Bona Roba

I cannot tell who loves the skeleton
Of a poor marmoset, nought but boan, boan,
Give me a nakednesse with her cloaths on.

    Richard Lovelace

Alas, lass, lost—
Alas, lost.

Where is my white velvet dress
Of flesh that some called heaven, some sin—
Not pitying the grave that is
Not slaked, that is not satisfied,
For all its triumph? Ah, lass, lost!
Alas, lost.

My arms were mighty as the seas
That gird the great young seeding lands
To make them theirs, and in my hands
Men's fortunes were as Time's sands in
The glass . . . I gave them at the last
The small red worm for paramour.
Where is that might now? Ah, lass, lost!
Alas, all lost.

Once my love had the lion's mouth,
My breasts were the pillars of the South.
Now my mouth has the desert's drouth,
And all that comes

To my breast is the wind and rain—
Alas, lass, lost,
Alas, lost.

The tigerish Spring was in each vein;
The glittering wind of Spring, my mane.
Now am I no more to Spring
Than the violet mist from vine-branches.
Alas, lass, lost.
All, lass, lost.

Now is my body only this:
The infinite geometry
That is the cold. How could I know
Winter would take me, I grow old?
Alas, lass, lost!
Alas, lost.

Young girl, you stare at me as if
I were that Medusa Time
That will change you, too, to stone:
So you, grown old, must lie alone.
Alas, lass, lost!
Alas . . .

A Girl's Song in Winter

That lovely dying white swan, the singing sun,
Will soon be gone. But seeing the snow falling, who could tell one
From the other? The snow, that swan-plumaged circling creature,
    said,
'Young girl, soon the tracing of Time's bird-feet and the bird-feet
    of snow
Will be seen upon your smooth cheek. Oh, soon you will be
Colder, my sweet, than me!'

Outside my house there is still a little flurry of dust, the chatter of
the people who still hope to intrude on me and rot my brain, as they
have tried to do throughout my life.

But all is more silent now, a shrunken world of no horizons. Yet sometimes I see a giant lion-paw on my window-sill, and my three Visitors still come—Her with the one tooth—(but what a grinding wolf's tooth that would be were there something to bite upon instead of just emptiness!)—Her with the one eye, looking into the bleak future, with the blind fumes from the Bomb enclosing it—Her with the one ear, waiting for some message from the Beyond.

These, the three Norns, still visit me. But soon, they will cease to do so.

Then all will be over, bar the shouting and the worms.

Taken Care Of

Heart and Mind

Said the Lion to the Lioness—'When you are amber dust—
No more a raging fire like the heat of the Sun
(No liking but all lust)—
Remember still the flowering of the amber blood and bone,
The rippling of bright muscles like a sea,
Remember the rose-prickles of bright paws,
Though we shall mate no more
Till the fire of that sun the heart and the moon-cold bone are one.'

Said the Skeleton lying upon the sands of Time—
'The great gold planet that is the mourning heat of the Sun
Is greater than all gold, more powerful
Than the tawny body of a Lion that fire consumes
Like all that grows or leaps . . . so is the heart
More powerful than all dust. Once I was Hercules
Or Samson, strong as the pillars of the seas:
But the flames of the heart consumed me, and the mind
Is but a foolish wind.'

Said the Sun to the Moon—'When you are but a lonely white crone,
And I, a dead King in my golden armour somewhere in a dark wood,
Remember only this of our hopeless love:
That never till Time is done
Will the fire of the heart and the fire of the mind be one.'

BIBLIOGRAPHY

ORIGINAL WORKS

The Mother Blackwell, Oxford 1915

Twentieth Century Harlequinade (with Osbert Sitwell) Blackwell, Oxford 1916

Clowns' Houses Blackwell, Oxford 1918

The Wooden Pegasus Blackwell, Oxford 1920

Children's Tales from the Russian Ballet Leonard Parsons, London 1920; re-issued by Duckworth, London 1928

Façade The Favil Press, London 1922

Bucolic Comedies Duckworth, London 1923

The Sleeping Beauty Duckworth, London 1924
     Alfred A. Knopf, New York 1924

Troy Park Duckworth, London 1925
     Alfred A. Knopf, New York 1925

Poor Young People (with Osbert and Sacheverell Sitwell) The Fleuron, London 1925

Poetry and Criticism The Hogarth Press, London 1925
     Henry Holt and Company, New York 1926

Augustan Books of Modern Poetry Ernest Benn Ltd, London 1926

Elegy on Dead Fashion Duckworth, London 1926

Poem for a Christmas Card The Fleuron, London 1926

Rustic Elegies Duckworth, London 1927
     Alfred A. Knopf, New York 1927

Popular Song Faber and Gwyer, London 1928

Five Poems Duckworth, London 1928

Gold Coast Customs Duckworth, London 1929
     Houghton Mifflin, Boston and New York 1929

Alexander Pope Faber & Faber, London 1930
     Cosmopolitan Book Corporation, New York 1930

Collected Poems Duckworth, London 1930

In Spring privately printed, London 1931
Jane Barston Faber & Faber, London 1931
Epithalamium Duckworth, London 1931
Bath Faber & Faber, London 1932
      Harrison Smith, New York 1932
The English Eccentrics Faber & Faber, London 1933
                Houghton Mifflin, Boston and New York 1933
                (revised and enlarged) Vanguard Press, New York 1957
                (revised and enlarged) Dennis Dobson, London 1958
Five Variations on a Theme Duckworth, London 1933
Aspects of Modern Poetry Duckworth, London 1934
Victoria of England Faber & Faber, London 1936
                Houghton Mifflin, Boston 1936
Selected Poems Duckworth, London 1936
                Houghton Mifflin, Boston 1937
I Live under a Black Sun Gollancz, London 1937
                Doubleday, New York 1938
Trio (with Osbert and Sacheverell Sitwell) Macmillan, London 1938
Poems New and Old Faber & Faber, London 1940
Street Songs Macmillan, London 1942
English Women Collins, London 1942
A Poet's Notebook Macmillan, London 1943
Green Song Macmillan, London 1944
                The Vanguard Press, New York 1946
The Weeping Babe Schott & Co. Ltd, London 1945
The Song of the Cold Macmillan, London 1945
                The Vanguard Press, New York 1948
Fanfare for Elizabeth Macmillan, New York 1946
                Macmillan, London 1946
The Shadow of Cain John Lehmann, London 1947
A Notebook on William Shakespeare Macmillan, London 1948
The Canticle of the Rose Macmillan, London 1949
                The Vanguard Press, New York 1949
Poor Men's Music Fore Publications, London 1950
                Alan Swallow, Denver 1950
Façade and Other Poems Duckworth, London 1950

A Poet's Notebook Little, Brown, Boston 1950
Selected Poems Penguin, Harmondsworth 1952
Gardeners and Astronomers Macmillan, London 1953
> The Vanguard Press, New York 1953
Collected Poems The Vanguard Press, New York 1954
> Macmillan, London 1957
The Pocket Poets Vista Books, London 1960
The Outcasts Macmillan, London 1962
The Queens and the Hive Macmillan, London 1962
> Atlantic Monthly Press, Boston 1962

BOOKS EDITED BY OR WITH CONTRIBUTIONS
BY EDITH SITWELL

Wheels (First Cycle) Blackwell, Oxford 1916
Wheels (Second Cycle) Blackwell, Oxford 1917
New Paths 1917–1918 C. W. Beaumont, London 1918
Wheels (Third Cycle) Blackwell, Oxford 1919
Wheels (Fourth Cycle) Blackwell, Oxford 1919
A Miscellany of Poetry 1919 Cecil Palmer and Hayward, 1919
Wheels (Fifth Cycle) Leonard Parsons, London 1920
Wheels (Sixth Cycle) C. W. Daniel, London 1921
Job le Pauvre Bodley Head, London 1922
Yea and Nay Brentano's, London 1923
Meddlesome Matty Bodley Head, London 1925
> Viking Press, 1926
Joy Street Poems Blackwell, Oxford 1927
The Legion Book privately printed, London 1929
Tradition and Experiment O.U.P., London 1929
Lifar Exhibition Catalogue Arthur Tooth & Sons, London 1930
The Pleasures of Poetry Duckworth, London 1930–2
> W. W. Norton, New York 1934
Prose Poems from 'Les Illuminations' Faber & Faber, London 1932
Ten Contemporaries Ernest Benn Ltd, London 1932
Sacheverell Sitwell: Collected Poems Duckworth, London 1926
Twelve Modern Plays Duckworth, London 1938
Edith Sitwell's Anthology Gollancz, London 1940
Look! The Sun Gollancz, London 1941

Maiden Voyage Routledge, London 1943
              L. B. Fischer (of America), 1945
Planet and Glow-worm Macmillan, London 1944
Ronald Bottrall: Selected Poems Editions Poetry, London 1946
Demetrios Capetanakis John Lehmann, London 1947
              The Devin-Adair Co. (of America), 1949
T. S. Eliot, a Symposium Editions Poetry, London 1948
Sleep in a Nest of Flames New Directions, New York 1949
A Book of the Winter Macmillan, London 1950
              The Vanguard Press, New York 1951
The American Genius John Lehmann, London 1951
William Walton: Façade O.U.P., London 1951
Society for Twentieth Century Music: Programme London 1952
A Book of Flowers Macmillan, London 1952
Poetry and Children Edmund Arnold, Leeds 1952
So Late into the Night Peter Russell, London 1952
Cassell's Encyclopaedia of Literature Cassell, London 1953
Cassell's Encyclopaedia of World Literature Funk & Wagnalls, New
    York 1954
English Morning Hutchinson, London 1953
The Fourteenth of October Collins, London 1954
Ezra Pound at Seventy New Directions, New York 1956
Dylan Thomas J. M. Dent, London 1956
              New Directions, New York 1956
American Writing Today New York University Press, New York 1957
Union Street Rupert Hart-Davis, London 1957
Coming to London Phoenix House, London 1957
Selected Poems and New McDowell, Obolensky, New York 1958
The Atlantic Book of British and American Poetry
    Little, Brown, Boston 1958
    Gollancz, London 1959
Hommage à Roy Campbell Société Cevenole du Mercou, 1958
Poems of our Time J. M. Dent, London 1959
              Dutton, New York 1959
Adventures of the Mind Alfred A. Knopf, New York 1959
              Gollancz, London 1960
Collected Poems of Roy Campbell, Volume 3 Bodley Head, London 1960
Swinburne: A Selection Weidenfeld and Nicolson, London 1960
              Harcourt, Brace, New York 1960

Dylan Thomas Heinemann, London 1960
Color of Darkness J. B. Lippincott, Philadelphia and New York 1961
The Collected Poems of Ronald Bottrall Sidgwick and Jackson, London 1961

PERIODICAL CONTRIBUTIONS BY EDITH SITWELL

'Drowned Suns,' *Daily Mirror*, no. 2928, p. 9, 13 March 1913
'Song: Tell me, Where is Sorrow Laid,' *Daily Mirror*, no. 3007, p. 7, 13 June 1913
'Love in Autumn,' *Daily Mirror*, no. 3093, p. 9, 22 September 1913
'In Remembrance,' *Daily Mirror*, no. 3095, p. 7, 24 September 1913
'Serenade,' *Daily Mirror*, no. 3146, p. 9, 22 November 1913
'From an Attic Window,' *Daily Mirror*, no. 3184, p. 7, 7 January 1914
'Song: When Daisies White and Celandine,' *Daily Mirror*, no. 3191, p. 7, 15 January 1914
'Lullaby,' *Daily Mirror*, no. 3563, p. 7, 26 March 1915
'Selene,' *Daily Mirror*, no. 3584, p. 7, 20 April 1915
'Beggarman Blind,' *Daily Mirror*, no. 3616, p. 7, 27 May 1915
'Water Music,' *Daily Mirror*, no. 3788, p. 7, 14 December 1915
'The Blackamoor Goes to Hell,' *Saturday Westminster Gazette*, v. 52, no. 7946, p. 12, 7 December 1918
'Miss Nettybun and the Satyr's Child,' *Saturday Westminster Gazette*, v. 52, no. 7974, p. 13, 11 January 1919
'The Lady with the Sewing Machine,' *Art and Letters*, v. 1, no. 1, p. 8, [February 1919]. [There are two states of this issue, the earlier bearing 'Winter 1918–19' on front cover]
'Solo for Ear-Trumpet,' *Saturday Westminster Gazette*, v. 53, no. 8046, p. 5, 5 April 1919
'Portrait of a Barmaid,' *Cambridge Magazine*, v. 8, no. 27, p. 584, 12 April 1919
'Hymns of Hate,' *Daily Herald*, no. 1049, p. 8, 4 June 1919. [Review of *Any Soldier to his Son* by George Willis]
'Interlude,' *The Monthly Chapbook*, no. 1, p. 23, July 1919. [There were two printings of this issue, the earlier having advertisements printed on orange—not yellow—paper]
'Queen Venus and the Choir-Boy,' *Saturday Westminster Gazette*, v. 54, no. 8121, p. 14, 5 July 1919
'The Girl with the Lint-White Locks,' *Saturday Westminster Gazette*, v. 54, no. 8167, p. 9, 30 August 1919
'What the Goose-Girl Said about the Dean,' 'Tournez, Tournez, bons Chevaux de Bois,' 'By Candlelight,' *Coterie*, no. 2, pp. 38–40, September 1919
'Mandoline,' *Art and Letters*, v. 2, no. 4, pp. 145-146, Autumn 1919

'At the Fair: the Ape sees the Fat Woman,' *Saturday Westminster Gazette*, v. 54, no. 8215, p. 13, 25 October 1919

'At the Fair; I: Springing Jack, II: The Ape watches "Aunt Sally," ' *Coterie*, no. 3, pp. 40–41, December 1919

'Mandoline,' *The Living Age*, v. 303, no. 3935, p. 630, 6 December 1919

'Among the Dark and Brilliant Leaves,' *The Living Age*, v. 304, no. 3942, p. 247, 24 January 1920.

'Two Country Suck-a-Thumbs,' 'Pedagogues & Flower Shows,' *Art and Letters*, v. 3, no. 2, pp. 3–5, Spring 1920

'Sir Rotherham's Ride,' *Saturday Westminster Gazette*, v. 55, no. 8355, p. 11, 10 April 1920

'The Higher Sensualism,' *Athenaeum*, 14 May 1920

'Bank Holiday, I & II,' 'Small Talk, I,' 'Dansons la Gigue,' *Oxford and Cambridge Miscellany*, pp. 9–11, [6] June 1920

'En Famille,' *The Chapbook*, no. 13, pp. 18–19, July 1920

'King Cophetua and the Beggar-Maid,' *Saturday Westminster Gazette*, v. 56, no. 8450, p. 11, 31 July 1920

'Aubade,' *Saturday Westminster Gazette*, v. 56, no. 8503, p. 12, 2 October 1920

'Fleecing Time,' *Saturday Westminster Gazette*, v. 56, n. 8557, p. 13, 4 December 1920

'On the Vanity of Human Aspirations,' *Athenaeum*, no. 4734, pp. 63–64, 21 January 1921

'On the Vanity of Human Aspirations,' *Literary Digest*, v. 68, no. 8, p. 36, 19 February 1921

'Herodiade,' *Saturday Westminster Gazette*, v. 58, no. 6, p. 10, 20 August 1921

'Serenade for Two Cats and a Trombone,' *Saturday Westminster Gazette*, v. 58, no. 8, p. 11, 3 September 1921

'The Doll,' *Form*, v. 1, no. 1, pp. 30–31, October 1921. [Issued in limited and ordinary editions]

'Recent Poetry,' *The Sackbut*, v. 2, no. 4, p. 38, October 1921. [Reviews of *The Farmer's Bride* by Charlotte Mew; *The Chapbook*, no. 10; and *Cranks*]

'Reviews,' *The Sackbut*, v. 2, no. 6, p. 38, December 1921. [Review of *Poems* by Marianne Moore]

'Poems for Music, chosen by Edith Sitwell,' *The Sackbut*, v. 2, no. 6, December 1921. [Two poems chosen by Edith Sitwell]

'Poor Martha,' *Spectator*, v. 128, p. 495, 22 April 1922

'New Publications,' *The Sackbut*, v. 2, no. 11, p. 35, June 1922. [Review of *The Eton Candle* edited by Brian Howard]

'Readers and Writers,' *The New Age*, new series, v. 31, no. 10, pp. 119–120, 6 July 1922. [First of a series of 11 general literary essays]

'Readers and Writers,' *The New Age*, new series, v. 31, no. 11, pp. 133–134, 13 July 1922

'Readers and Writers,' *The New Age*, new series, v. 31, no. 12, pp. 148–149, 20 July 1922

'Readers and Writers,' *The New Age*, new series, v. 31, no. 13, p. 161, 27 July 1922

'New Publications,' *The Sackbut*, v. 3, no. 1, pp. 31–32, August 1922. [Review of *The Chapbook*, May 1922, and *Public School Verse, 1920–21*]

'Readers and Writers,' *The New Age*, new series, v. 31, no. 14, pp. 171–172, 3 August 1922

'Readers and Writers,' *The New Age*, new series, v. 31, no. 15, pp. 184–185, 10 August 1922

'Readers and Writers,' *The New Age*, new series, v. 31, no. 16, p. 196, 17 August 1922

'Readers and Writers,' *The New Age*, new series, v. 31, no. 17, pp. 210–211, 24 August 1922

'Readers and Writers,' *The New Age*, new series, v. 31, no. 18, p. 222, 31 August 1922

'Readers and Writers,' *The New Age*, new series, v. 31, no. 19, p. 236, 7 September 1922

'Readers and Writers,' *The New Age*, new series, v. 31, no. 21, p. 261, 21 September 1922

'Rain,' *Weekly Westminster Gazette*, v. 1, no. 33, p. 20, 30 September 1922

'Braga's Serenata,' *Weekly Westminster Gazette*, v. 1, no. 40, p. 16, 18 November 1922

'Promenade Sentimentale,' *Spectator*, v. 129, p. 727, 18 November 1922

'Winter,' 'Spring,' *English Review*, v. 36, no. 3, pp. 201–204, March 1923

'Winter,' *Rhythmus*, v. 1, no. 3, pp. 48–51, March 1923

'Rain,' *The Living Age*, v. 316, no. 4105, p. 610, 10 March 1923

'Cacophony for Clarinet,' 'By the Lake,' *The Chapbook*, no. 37, pp. 13–14, May 1923

'Daphne,' *Spectator*, v. 130, p. 799, 12 May 1923

'Advice to Young Poets,' *Weekly Westminster Gazette*, v. 2, no. 65, pp. 16–17, 12 May 1923

'Miss Stein's Stories,' *The Nation and Athenaeum*, v. 33, no. 15, p. 492, 14 July 1923. [Review of *Geography and Plays*]

'Some Books of Verse,' *Weekly Westminster Gazette*, v. 2, no. 75, pp. 18–19, 21 July 1923. [Reviews]

'The Gardener, from "The Princess in the Sleeping Wood," ' *The Nation and Athenaeum*, v. 34, no. 4, p. 154, 27 October 1923

'La Rousse, from The Sleeping Princess,' *Oxford Outlook*, v. 5, no. 24, pp. 110–111, November 1923

'March for a Toy Soldier,' 'Dirge for a Gollywog,' 'The Little Musical Box,' *No. 1 Joy Street*, pp. 96–100, [9 November] 1923

'Aubade,' *Spectator*, v. 131, p. 993, 22 December 1923

'Undergrowth,' *The Golden Hind*, v. 2, no. 6, pp. 5–7, 10–16, January 1924. [Standard edition, and Edition-de-Luxe of 75 signed copies]

'Song from "The Sleeping Beauty," ' *The Nation and Athenaeum*, v. 34, no. 22, p. 765, 1 March 1924

'Mademoiselle Richarde,' *Spectator*, v. 132, p. 504, 29 March 1924

'Chanson Gris,' *Vogue* [London], v. 63, no. 8, p. 46, late April 1924

'Yesterday,' *The Nation and Athenaeum*, v. 35, p. 177, 10 May 1924

'Colonel Fantock,' *Spectator*, v. 132, p. 880, 31 May 1924

'Yesterday,' *The Literary Digest*, v. 81, no. 10. p. 40, 7 June 1924

'The Country Cousin,' *Vogue* [London], v. 64, no. 4, p. 32, late August 1924

'Jane Austen and George Eliot,' *Vogue* [London], v. 64, no. 4, pp. 32, 72, late August 1924

'Song from "The Sleeping Beauty," ' *The Literary Digest*, v. 82, no. 6, p. 34, 9 August 1924

'Funny Loo,' *No. 2 Joy Street*, p. 134, [1 September] 1924

'Three Women Writers,' *Vogue* [London], v. 64, no. 7, pp. 81, 114, October 1924. [Katherine Mansfield, Gertrude Stein, Dorothy Richardson]

'On an Autumn Evening spent in reading Cowper,' *The Fortnightly Review*, new series, v. 116, pp. 558–559, October 1924

'Pleasure Gardens,' *The Nation and Athenaeum*, v. 36, no. 8, p. 297, 22 November 1924

'Four in the Morning,' *Vogue* [London], v. 64, no. 12, p. 33, late December 1924

'Three Poor Witches,' *Spectator*, v. 133, p. 1022, 27 December 1924

'The Man with the Green Patch,' *The Criterion*, v. 3, no. 10, pp. 244–248, January 1925

'Some Observations on Women's Poetry,' *Vogue* [London], v. 65, no. 5, pp. 59, 86, early March 1925

'Cendrillon and the Cat,' *Vogue* [London], v. 66, no. 2, p. 29, late July 1925

'The Criticism of Poetry,' *Saturday Review of Literature*, v. 2, no. 7, pp. 117–118, 12 September 1925

'The Work of Gertrude Stein,' *Vogue* [London], v. 66, no. 7, pp. 73, 98, early October 1925

'The Scandal,' *The Nation and Athenaeum*, v. 38, no. 12, p. 437, 19 December 1925

'Valse Maigre, 1843,' *Vogue* [London], v. 66, no. 12, p. 42, late December 1925

[Review], *The New Criterion*, v. 4, no. 2, pp. 390–392, April 1926. [Review of *The Making of Americans* by Gertrude Stein]

'Poème: An Interview with Mars' (from 'The Childhood of Cendrillon'), *Commerce*, Cahiers Trimestriels, cahier VII, pp. 113–123, Printemps 1926. [With a French translation by M. V. Larbaud]

'My Brother's Book,' *Weekly Dispatch*, 10 October 1926. [Review of *Before the Bombardment* by Osbert Sitwell]

'Who are the Sitwells—and why do they do it?,' *Weekly Dispatch*, 14 November 1926

'A New Poet,' *The Nation and Athenaeum*, v. 40, no. 14, pp. 514–515, 8 January 1927. [Review of *Poems* by Peter Quennell]

'Our Family Ghost,' *Weekly Dispatch*, 15 May 1927

'My Awkward Moments,' *Daily Mail*, 15 October 1927

'The Dog,' *The Nation and Athenaeum*, v. 42, no. 2, p. 117, 22 October 1927

'How Fame Looks to a Poetess,' *Literary Digest*, v. 95, no. 5, p. 29, 29 October 1927

'Panope,' *The New Republic*, v. 54, no. 690, p. 16, 22 February 1928

'The Peach Tree,' *Saturday Review of Literature*, v. 4, p. 775, 21 April 1928

'Must the World be so Noisy?,' *Sunday Express*, p. 9, 24 June 1928

'People I Annoy,' *Daily Mail*, 25 June 1928

'A Poet of Fiery Simplicity,' *T.P.'s Weekly*, p. 598, 8 September 1928. [Review of *The Heart's Journey* by Siegfried Sassoon]

'Modern Poetry, I, II,' *Time & Tide*, v. 9, pp. 308–309 and 332–333, 1928

'Are there still Bohemians?,' *Daily Chronicle*, 31 October 1928

'Modern Values,' *Spectator*, v. 141, no. 5243, pp. 950–1, 22 December 1928

'The Bat,' *Time & Tide*, v. 10, p. 7, 4 January 1929

'The Cherry Tree,' *Time & Tide*, v. 10, p. 34, 11 January 1929

'The Poems of Charlotte Mew,' *Time & Tide*, v. 10, p. 755, 21 June 1929

'Men who Interest Me,' *Daily Express*, 14 August 1929

'Oh, to be in Scarborough, now that August's here,' *Daily Express*, 17 August 1929

[Review], *The Criterion*, v. 9, no. 34, pp. 130–134, October 1929. [Review of Charlotte Mew's *The Farmer's Bride* and *The Rambling Sailor*]

'Charwoman,' *Time & Tide*, 18 October 1929

'The Ghost Whose Lips Were Warm', 'The Peach Tree'. Translated into French by Pierre d'Exidenil and Felix Crosse. *Echanges*, no. 1, December 1929

'Who wants Bets now?,' *Evening News*, 25 April 1930

'Modernist Poets,' *Echanges*, no. 2, June 1930

'Life's Tyrannies—and my gospel of happiness,' *Evening News*, p. 8, 16 July 1931

'Stories of Beau Nash,' *Evening News*, p. 11, 13 May 1932

'Don't Become a Standard Person,' *Yorkshire Weekly Post*, 4 June 1932

'Why Worry about your Age?,' *Yorkshire Weekly Post*, 23 July 1932

'Miss Sitwell presents a Genius,' *The Graphic*, v. 121, no. 3059, p. 133, 28 July 1933. [On Pavel Tchelitchew]

'Is our Civilization a Benefit?,' *Time & Tide*, v. 14, no. 37, p. 1086, 16 September 1933

'Poets wise—and otherwise,' *Morning Post*, 6 March 1934

'The Truth about Blood Sports,' *Sunday Referee*, no. 2999, p. 10, 24 February 1935

'Some Notes on my Own Poetry,' *London Mercury*, v. 31, no. 185, pp. 448–454, March 1935

'Twentieth Century Justice through a Camera Lens,' *Sunday Referee*, no. 3001, p. 13, 10 March 1935

'Here is a Dickens of our Time,' *Sunday Referee*, no. 3003, p. 12, 24 March 1935. [On the novels of Walter Greenwood]

'It is fear that breeds War,' *Sunday Referee*, no. 3005, p. 12, 7 April 1935

'People I Meet in the Train,' *Sunday Referee*, no. 3007, p. 10, 21 April 1935

'What do we Mean by Liberty?,' *Sunday Referee*, no. 3009, 5 May 1935

'What is Slavery?,' *Sunday Referee*, no. 3011, p. 12, 19 May 1935

'Prelude,' *London Mercury*, v. 32, no. 188, pp. 108–110, June 1935

'Let's scrap Parliament,' *Sunday Referee*, no. 3013, p. 12, 2 June 1935

'Testament of a Young Man,' *Time & Tide*, v. 16, pp. 1548–1549, 26 October 1935. [Review of *World Without Faith* by John Beevers]

'A Correspondence on the Young English Poets, between Edith Sitwell and Robert Herring,' *Life and Letters To-Day*, v. 13, no. 2, pp. 16–24, December 1935

'Gangsters, Fraudulent Financiers, War-Mongers, Sneak-Motorists . . .,' *Sunday Referee*, p. 12, 26 January 1936

'Of Calamancoes, Shalloons, Garlets, Tabbeys & a hundred others,' *Harper's Bazaar* [London], v. 13, no. 5, pp. 60, 90, February 1936

'Four New Poets,' *London Mercury*, v. 33, no. 196, pp. 383–390, February 1936. [Reviews of William Empson, Ronald Bottrall, Dylan Thomas and Archibald MacLeish]

'Making Faces at the World,' *Sunday Referee*, p. 12, 23 February 1936

'Two Songs: Come, my Arabia . . .; My desert has a noble sun for heart,' *Caravel* [Majorca], no. 5, p. [8], March 1936

'Mustard and Cress,' *Sunday Referee*, p. 2, 19 April 1936

'(Dis)pleasures of Bickering,' *Good Housekeeping*, v. 29, no. 3, pp. 24–25, 131, May 1936

'The Late Miss Sitwell (Auto-obituary III),' *The Listener*, 29 July 1936

'A Head of Feather and a Heart of Lead,' *Harper's Bazaar* [London], v. 14, no. 5, pp. 56, 70, August 1936

'Quintessence,' *Harper's Bazaar* [London], v. 15, no. 3, pp. 52–53, 112–113, December 1936

'A New Poet: achievement of Mr. Dylan Thomas,' *Sunday Times*, no. 5927, p. 9, 15 November 1936. [Review of *Twenty-Five Poems*]

'H. G. Wells,' *Sunday Referee*, p. 12, 27 December 1936

'That English Eccentric, Edith Sitwell,' *Sunday Referee*, p. 14, 3 January 1937

'On Dramatic Clothes,' *Daily Express*, 8 November 1937

'Precious Stones and Metals,' *Harper's Bazaar* [London], v. 19, no. 5, pp. 68–69, 82, February 1939

[Review], *Life and Letters To-Day*, v. 23, no. 27, pp. 239–241, November 1939. [Review of *The Turning Path* by Ronald Bottrall]

'On a Night of Full Moon,' *Harper's Bazaar* [New York], no. 2734, pp. 84, 139, 1 March 1940

'Lullaby,' *Times Literary Supplement*, Spring books supplement, p. i, 16 March 1940

'Any Man to Any Woman,' *Life and Letters To-Day*, v. 25, no. 32, pp. 35–36, April 1940

[Review], *Life and Letters To-Day*, v. 27, no. 38, pp. 57–59, October 1940. [Review of *A.B.C.'s* by Charles Henri Ford]

'Song: We are the rootless flowers in the air,' *Life and Letters To-Day*, v. 27, no. 39, p. 128, November 1940

'Street Song,' 'The Youth with the Red-Gold Hair,' 'Ragged Serenade: Beggar to Shadow,' *Life and Letters To-Day*, v. 28, no. 41, pp. 48–51, January 1941

'Poor Young Simpleton,' 'Song: Once my heart was a summer rose,' *Life and Letters To-Day*, v. 30, no. 49, pp. 198–202, September 1941

'Still Falls the Rain,' *Times Literary Supplement*, p. 427, 6 September 1941

'Any Man to Any Woman,' *Vice Versa*, v. 1, nos. 3–5, p. 41, January 1942

'Bread of Angels,' *Times Literary Supplement*, p. 177, 4 April 1942

'The Poet's Sister,' *Spectator*, v. 168, p. 455, 8 May 1942. [Review of *Journals* of Dorothy Wordsworth]

'Some Notes on Poetry,' *Tribune*, no. 303, p. 18, 16 October 1942

'A Mother to her Dead Child,' *Times Literary Supplement*, p. 526, 24 October 1942

'Green Song,' *Life and Letters To-Day*, v. 35, no. 64, pp. 132–135, December 1942

'Notes on Shakespeare,' *View*, 3rd series, no. 1, pp. 16–18, 36, April 1943

'Anne Boleyn's Song,' *Times Literary Supplement*, p. 200, 24 April 1943

'A Sleepy Tune,' *Adam*, year XVI, no. 182, pp. 1–2, May 1943

'Heart and Mind,' *Times Literary Supplement*, p. 298, 19 June 1943

'Lecture on Poetry since 1920,' *Life and Letters To-Day*, v. 39, no. 75, pp. 70–97, November 1943

'Invocation,' *New Writing and Daylight*, pp. 7–9, Winter 1943–44

'O Bitter Love, O Death,' *Times Literary Supplement*, p. 32, 15 January 1944

'Lo, this is she that was the world's desire,' *Life and Letters To-Day*, v. 40, no. 79, pp. 133–135, March 1944

'Holiday,' *Times Literary Supplement*, p. 176, 8 April 1944

'Why not Like Poetry?,' *Woman's Journal*, v. 34, no. 200, pp. 10–11, 56, June 1944

'Heart and Mind,' *Atlantic Monthly*, v. 174, no. 1, p. 61, July 1944

'The Poetry of Demetrios Capetanakis,' *New Writing and Daylight*, pp. 44–50, Autumn 1944

'Girl and Butterfly,' *Penguin New Writing* 20, pp. 93–96, 1944

'A Song at Morning,' *Horizon*, v. 10, no. 60, p. 372, December 1944

[Review], *Horizon*, v. 11, no. 61, pp. 70–73, January 1945. [Review of *Noblesse Oblige* by James Agate]

'Fanfare for Elizabeth', *Harper's Bazaar* [New York], no. 2803, p. 30, July 1945

'From "Fanfare for Elizabeth," ' *Life and Letters To-Day*, v. 46, pp. 13–27, 98–107, 152–166; v. 47, pp. 6–17; July, August, September, October 1945

'Eurydice,' *Horizon*, v. 12, no. 68, pp. 77–80, August 1945

'The Two Loves,' *New Writing and Daylight*, pp. 15–17, 1945

'Some Notes on "King Lear," ' *New Writing and Daylight*, pp. 77–89, 1945

'The Poet Laments the Coming of Old Age,' *Orion* [I], pp. 28–29, 1945

'A Song of the Cold,' *Penguin New Writing*, 23, pp. 52–56, 1945

'A Sleepy Tune,' *View*, series V, no. 6, pp. 4–5, January 1946

'Some Notes on Shakespeare,' *View*, series V, no. 6, pp. 8–9, January 1946

'Some Notes on Shakespeare,' *View*, v. 6, no. 3, pp. 15, 25, May 1946

'Mary Stuart to James Bothwell: casket letter no. 2,' *Penguin New Writing* 27, pp. 22–23, Spring 1946

'A Note on "Measure for Measure," ' *The Nineteenth Century*, v. 140, no. 835, pp. 131–135, September 1946

'Notes from a Poet's Notebook,' *View* [v. 6, no. 6], pp. 24–26, Fall [October] 1946

' "Iago," ' *New Writing and Daylight*, pp. 141–151, 1946

'Early Spring,' *Orion III*, pp. 59–61, 1946

'A Simpleton,' *Horizon*, v. 16, no. 90, p. 6, July 1947

'Hymn to Venus (from "A Canticle of the Rose"),' *Poetry London*, v. 3, no. 11, pp. 31–34, September–October 1947

'Comment on Dylan Thomas,' *The Critic*, v. 1, no. 2, pp. 17–18, Autumn 1947

'William Blake,' *Spectator*, p. 466, 10 October 1947. [Review of *Fearful Symmetry* by Northrop Frye and *Selected Poems* edited by Denis Saurat]

'Dirge for the New Sunrise,' *Orion IV*, pp. 26–27, 1947

'The Bee-Keeper,' *Penguin New Writing*, 32, pp. 25–27, 1947

'The Coat of Fire,' *Horizon*, v. 17, no. 100, pp. 236–238, April 1948

'Of the Clowns and Fools of Shakespeare,' *Life and Letters To-Day*, v. 57, no. 129, pp. 102–109, May 1948

'Chain-Gang: penal settlement,' *Sunday Times*, 4 July 1948

'A Note on Hamlet,' *Tribune*, pp. 23–24, 24 September 1948

'A Simpleton,' *Harper's Bazaar* [New York], no. 2842, p. 200, October 1948

'Poetry of Miss Bowes-Lyon,' *New Statesman and Nation*, v. 36, p. 306, 9 October 1948

'Song: Now that fate is dead and gone,' *Orpheus I*, pp. 27–28, 1948

'Some Notes on the Making of a Poem,' *Orpheus I*, pp. 69–75, 1948

'The Canticle of the Rose,' *Wake*, no. 7, pp. 23–25, 1948

'Dirge for the New Sunrise,' 'The Bee-Keeper,' 'Early Spring,' *Quarterly Review of Literature*, v. 4, no. 3, pp. 231–237, 1948

'The Song of Dido,' *Botteghe Oscure*, quaderno II, p. 268, 1948

'Villa's Poetry,' *The Literary Apprentice* [Manila], pp. 64–66, 1948–1949

'Out of School,' *Atlantic Monthly*, v. 183, no. 6, pp. 37–38, June 1949

'Out of School,' *Horizon*, v. 20, no. 116, pp. 77–80, August 1949

'On My Poetry,' *Orpheus II*, pp. 103–119, 1949

'Medusa's Love Song,' *Penguin New Writing* 38, pp. 9–11, 1949

'A Vindication of Pope,' *Sunday Times*, 2 October 1949. [Review of *New Light on Pope* by Norman Ault]

'Street Acrobat,' *Arena*, no. 1, pp. 4–6, [Autumn 1949]

'Macbeth,' *Atlantic Monthly*, v. 185, no. 4, pp. 43–48, April 1950

'King Lear,' *Atlantic Monthly*, v. 185, no. 5, pp. 57–62, May 1950

'A Song of the Dust,' *Penguin New Writing* 40, pp. 9–12, 1950

'Whitman and Blake,' *Proceedings of the American Academy of Arts and*

Letters and the National Institute of Arts and Letters, 2nd series, no. 1, pp. 52–58, 1951

'Gardeners and Astronomers,' *Times Literary Supplement*, special supplement: The mind of 1951, p. iii, 24 August 1951

'Prometheus' Love Song,' *The Listener*, v. 47, no. 1216, 19 June 1952

'Bagatelle,' *The Listener*, v. 48, no. 1232, p. 586, 9 October 1952

'Two Songs,' *Atlantic Monthly*, v. 191, no. 2, p. 46, February 1953

'The April Rain,' *Atlantic Monthly*, v. 191, no. 4, p. 53, April 1953

'The April Rain,' *Times Literary Supplement*, no. 2672, p. 246, 17 April 1953

'From "The Road to Thebes": II: Interlude; III: The Night Wind,' *New World Writing* 3, pp. 170–173, May 1953

'The Love of Man, the Praise of God,' *New York Herald-Tribune Book Review*, section 6, pp. 1, 14, 10 May 1953. [Review of *Collected Poems* of Dylan Thomas]

'Sailor, What of the Isles?,' *The Listener*, v. 49, no. 1258, p. 607, 9 April 1953

'Sailor, What of the Isles?,' *Atlantic Monthly*, v. 191, no. 6, p. 53, June 1953

'The Queen of Scotland's Reply to a Reproof from John Knox,' *New Statesman and Nation*, v. 45, no. 1163, p. 738, 20 June 1953

'The Road to Thebes [I],' *Atlantic Monthly*, v. 192, no. 1, pp. 48–50, July 1953

'Two Songs: A Mi-Voix; An Old Song Re-sung,' *Encounter*, v. 1, no. 1, pp. 34–35, October 1953

[A Telegram], *Adam*, year XXI, no. 238, p. ii, 1953

'Dylan Thomas,' *Atlantic Monthly*, v. 193, no. 2, pp. 42–45, February 1954

'Down among the Glamour Girls,' *Sunday Graphic*, no. 2037, p. 4, 25 April 1954

'A Young Girl's Song,' *London Magazine*, v. 1, no. 4, pp. 13–14, May 1954

'The Rising Generation,' *Times Literary Supplement*, special supplement: American Writing To-Day, p. i, 17 September 1954

'Fruits and Flowers on a Poet's Vine,' *The Saturday Review*, v. 38, no. 25, p. 19, 18 June 1955. [Review of *Selected Poems* of Roy Campbell]

'A Tidy, Natural Taste,' *The Saturday Review*, v. 38, no. 28, p. 14, 9 July 1955. [Review of *Birthdays from the Ocean* by Isabella Gardner]

'Of what Use is Poetry?,' *The Reader's Digest* [New York], pp. 101–104, August 1955. [Re-published in the following editions of the journal: English–Canadian (August 1955), Australian, British (both September 1955), German, Portuguese (both October 1955), Spanish (November 1955), Finnish, French–Canadian (both March 1956)]

'Elegy for Dylan Thomas,' *Poetry*, v. 87, no. 2, pp. 63–67, November 1955

'Why I Look the Way I Do,' *Sunday Graphic*, no. 2117, p. 6, 4 December 1955

'The Last Days of Queen Mary the First,' *Vogue* [London], v. 112, no. 2, pp. 82–83, 145, February 1956

'In Praise of Jean Cocteau,' *London Magazine*, v. 3, no. 2, pp. 13–15, February 1956

311

'Dylan Thomas: tragic American visits,' *Sunday Times*, 22 April 1956. [Review of *Dylan Thomas in America* by John Malcolm Brinnin]

'Sweet-Brier Leaves,' *Sunday Times*, 3 February 1957. [Review of *The Player's Boy* by Bryher]

'What is Genius?,' *Everybody's*, p. 31, 2 March 1957

'Coming to London,' *London Magazine*, v. 4, no. 4, pp. 39–44, April 1957. [No. 14 of a series by various writers]

'Poets of Delight: Gordon Bottomley and Ralph Hodgson,' *Sunday Times*, pp. 4–5, 5 May 1957. [Great Writers Rediscovered Series, 5]

'The Priest and the Plague,' *Sunday Times*, no. 6996, p. 6, 16 June 1957. [Review of *Henry Morse* by Philip Caraman]

'The Progress of a Poet,' *Sunday Times*, p. 8, 8 September 1957. [A recorded interview]

'The War Orphans,' *Atlantic Monthly*, v. 200, no. 5, p. 78, November 1957

'Roy Campbell,' *Poetry*, v. 92, no. 1, pp. 42–48, April 1958

'His Blood colours my cheek,' *The Month*, new series, v. 19, no. 5, pp. 261–262, May 1958

'Better Bye and Bye,' *Sunday Times*, no. 7050, p. 7, 29 June 1958. [Review of *The Shaping Spirit* by A. Alvarez]

'The Death of a Giant,' *London Magazine*, v. 5, no. 11, pp. 11–12, November 1958

'Preface to Ezra Pound,' *The Yale Literary Magazine*, v. 126, no. 5, pp. 42–44, December 1958. [Partly from *Atlantic Book of British and American Poetry*, 1958]

'La Bella Bona Roba,' *The Listener*, v. 61, no. 1553, p. 14, 1 January 1959. [Reprinted in *The Guinness Book of Poetry 1958–59* (Putnam, 1960) and in *New Poems 1960* (Hutchinson, 1960)]

'The Yellow Girl,' *The Listener*, v. 61, no. 1557, p. 207, 29 January 1959. [Reprinted in *New Poems 1960*]

'At the Cross-Roads,' *London Magazine*, v. 6, no. 3, pp. 11–12, March 1959

'Of Wrath and Writers,' *Lilliput*, v. 45, no. 5, pp. 41–42, November 1959

'Praise We Great Men,' *The Listener*, v. 61, no. 1577, p. 1058, 18 June 1959; and *Atlantic Monthly*, v. 204, no. 5, p. 97, November 1959

'Choric Song,' *The Listener*, v. 63, no. 1618, p. 576, 31 March 1960

'A Visit to Lawrence. (Personal Encounters, 1),' *The Observer*, p. 25, 13 November 1960

'Dylan the Impeccable. (Personal Encounters, 2),' *The Observer*, p. 24, 20 November 1960

'Hazards of Sitting for my Portrait. (Personal Encounters, 3),' *The Observer*, p. 24, 27 November 1960

'Pride. (The Seven Deadly Sins, no. 2),' *Sunday Times*, no. 7231, p. 19, 17 December 1961. [Reprinted in 'The Seven Deadly Sins', *Sunday Times*, 1962]

'A Girl's Song in Winter,' *Encounter*, v. 18, no. 1, p. 41, January 1962

'The Two Cultures,' *Spectator*, no. 6977, p. 331, 16 March 1962. [A note]

'Young William Walton comes to Town,' *Sunday Times*, no. 7244, p. 40, 18 March 1962
'The Young Ones?,' *Daily Express*, no. 19352, p. 5, 17 August 1962

BOOKS ANNOUNCED BUT NOT PUBLISHED

'Sitwells' Omnibus.' Announced: '. . . begins running early in October' in *At the House of Mrs. Kinfoot*, September 1921, and as appearing 'shortly' in *Dr. Donne and Gargantua, Canto the First*, October 1921
'Le Canard à Chaud.' Announced as 'in preparation' in *Troy Park*, 1925
'William Blake, a selection, edited by Edith Sitwell.' Announced as a forthcoming volume in the series, on wrappers of *The Chiltern Library*, published by Messrs. John Lehmann, ca. 1950

TRANSLATIONS

Poème: an Interview with Mars. With a translation by Valéry Larbaud. Paris. *Commerce*, cahier VII, pp. 113–123, Printemps 1926
Victoria, Drottning av England, Kejsarinna av India. Translated by Hans Langlet. Stockholm: Hökerberg, 1936
Victoria von England. Translated by C. F. W. Behl. Berlin: Wolfg. Krüger, 1937
La Reine Victoria. Translated by Jean Talva. Paris: Gallimard, 1938
Le Cœur et l'Esprit; Chanson; Toujours tombe la Pluie. (Anonymous translations). Paris (Algiers): *Fontaine*, nos. 37–40, pp. 417–420 (561–564), 1944
Chanson Verte. Translated by Marie Laure. Paris: Confluences, 1946
Las Mujeres Inglesas. (Anonymous translation.) Buenos Aires: Espasa-Calpe, [1946]
Fanfare für Elisabeth. Translated by Margaret Rauchenberger. Köln: Schaffrath, 1947
Corazion y Pensamiento [Heart and Mind]. Translated by Charles David Ley. *Acanto*, v. 3, pp. [10–11], Marzo 1947
El Coronel Fantock. Translated by Silvina Ocampo. *Sur*, año XV, pp. 401–409, Julio–Octubre 1947
Canción Callejera [Street Song]. Translated by Ricardo Baeza. *Sur*, año XV, pp. 411–413, Julio–Octubre 1947
Il Canto di Didone [Dido's Song]. Translated by A. G. Roma. *Botteghe Oscure*, quaderno II, supplement, 'Poeti Inglesi e Americani,' p. 28, 1948
Fanfare for Elisabeth. Translated by Per Lange. København: Gyldendal, 1949
La Regina Vittoria. Translated by Margherita Santi Farina. Milano: Longanesi, 1949

Ich lebe unter einer schwarze Sonne. Translated by Hilda Mentzel and Paulheinz Quack. Düsseldorf: Schwann, 1950

Fanfare pour Elizabeth. Translated by Denise Van Moppès. Paris: Albin Michel, 1953

Sotto il Sole Nero. Translated by Ferdinanda Invrea. Milano, Roma: Bompiani, 1954

Genshi Jidai No Sambusaku [Three Poems of the Atomic Age]. Translated by Yônosuke Suzuki. Tokyo: Kokobun-sha, 1955

Fanfare za Elizabeta. Translated by Dr. Josip Ritig. Zagreb: Kultura, 1955

Cae la Lluvia Aún [Still Falls the Rain]. Translated by Esteban Pujals. *Nuestro Tiempo* (3rd year, no. 20), February 1956

Mroczny Spiew [Dark Song]. In: *Antologia Liryki Angielskiej 1300–1950.* London: Veritas Foundation Publication Centre, 1958

MUSICAL SETTINGS

Façade, by William Walton (1922)

Daphne, Through Gilded Trellises, Old Sir Faulk, by William Walton, being his 'Three Songs' (1932)

The Sleeping Beauty, a masque, by Leighton Lucas (1936)

The King of China's Daughter, by Arthur Duff, in 'A Broadside,' new series, no. 4 (1937)

The King of China's Daughter, by Michael Head, in his 'Five Songs' (1938)

The Weeping Babe, for soprano and unaccompanied chorus, by Michael Tippett (1944)

O Yet Forgive, a song, by Elisabeth Lutyens

Gold Coast Customs, for speakers, men's chorus and orchestra, by Humphrey Searle (1949)

The Shadow of Cain, for speakers, men's chorus and orchestra, by Humphrey Searle (1952)

Still Falls the Rain, by Benjamin Britten, being his 'Canticle III' (1956)

INDEX

INDEX

INDEX